CREATING
Cottage Gardens

MARY DAVIS

Angus&Robertson
An imprint of HarperCollinsPublishers

RIGHT: *Tall bearded iris and* Viola cornuta
at Kennerton Green, Mittagong, Australia,
where owner Marylyn Abbot orchestrates
colour beautifully.

AN ANGUS & ROBERTSON BOOK
An imprint of HarperCollinsPublishers

First published in Australia in 1993

CollinsAngus&Robertson Publishers Pty Limited
A division of HarperCollinsPublishers (Australia) Pty Limited
25 Ryde Road, Pymble NSW 2073, Australia
HarperCollinsPublishers (New Zealand) Limited
31 View Road, Glenfield, Auckland 10, New Zealand
HarperCollinsPublishers Limited
77– 85 Fulham Palace Road, London W6 8JB, United Kingdom
Distributed in the United States of America by
HarperCollinsPublishers
10 East 53rd Street, New York NY 10022, USA

Copyright © Mary Davis 1993

National Library of Australia
Cataloguing-in-Publication data:

Davis, Mary (Mary Elizabeth).
   Creating cottage gardens.
   Bibligraphy
   Includes index.
   ISBN 0 207 17779 1.
   1. Cottage gardens, English — Australia. 2. Gardening — Australia.
   I. Title.
635.9670994

Front cover photograph shows the garden of Elizabeth and
Graeme Robertson, Crosshills, Kao-kao, New Zealand
Cover background photograph by André Martin
Printed in Hong Kong

5 4 3 2 1
96 95 94 93

To my daughter Anne and all who are on the brink of discovering creative cottage gardening for themselves.

Acknowledgements

No author can write a book of this kind without the assistance and co-operation of many people and I am no exception in this regard.

In New Zealand firstly I owe a debt of gratitude to Maryan Bishop of The Roseaire, Auckland, for giving me every possible assistance in my quest for true cottage gardens, and for introducing me to many cottage garden owners. On the same note, my thanks to Adrianne Moore of Christchurch who unexpectedly met us at the airport with a list of gardens not to be missed, and to Alison McRae, who wrote *Gardens to Visit in New Zealand*, which proved invaluable. Alison's personal recommendations were gratefully pursued.

To the garden owners of New Zealand also my warmest thanks for allowing their creations to be photographed and answering my numerous questions. They are Mr and Mrs B. Allison, Mr and Mrs A. Bishop, Dr and Mrs H. Bashford, Mr and Mrs G. Collier, Dr and Mrs P. Doyle, Mrs Ethel Doyle, Mr and Mrs K. Innes, Mr and Mrs B. Jacobs, Mr and Mrs A. Laity, Mr and Mrs R. Lee, Mr and Mrs P. Masfen, Mr and Mrs G. Matheson, Mr and Mrs W. Maunsell, Mr and Mrs M. McConnell, Mrs M. Morris, Mrs Liz Morrow, Mr and Mrs S. Maling, Mr and Mrs H. Russell, Mr and Mrs B. Schneideman, Mr and Mrs W. Scott, Mr and Mrs J. Sturtevant, Mrs Jacqui Sutherland, Mrs Toni Sylvester, Mrs Pauline Trengrove, Ms Suzanne Turley and Mr and Mrs H. Whitehead.

In England, my sincere thanks to Beth Chatto of Essex, whose garden and writings I find inspirational; Mrs Walter Wigham of Cobham Court, Kent; Mrs Gerald Coke of Jenkyn Place, Hampshire; Captain and Mrs David Armytage of Sharcott Manor, Wiltshire; Anne and Alan Stevens of Ivy Cottage, Dorset; Mrs Anne Dexter of Oxford; and to The National Trust of England whose gardens Mottisfont and Sissinghurst are a joy to visit.

In Australia, firstly I must thank Gilbert Teague for encouraging me to write and Barbara Barnes for permission to quote from Edna Walling's *A Gardener's Log*. Thanks also to Mrs Mary Baker for permission to reproduce the plan of her garden; Beulah Grewcoe, who unselfishly shares her vast horticultural knowledge; and the members of the Creative Gardeners Club, whose gates were opened to photographers Roger Hanlon and Densey Clyne, both of whom have shown the utmost patience in meeting my requests. I am indebted to my friend Edith Toyer, who used 35 mm film for the first time to give me photographs of Rockleigh. To Rosemary Thodey, Cheryl Maddocks, David Wallace and Phil Aynsley, whose contributions were most gratefully received, my sincere thanks. Also to John Franken for his photographs of 'Windrush' and 'The Reeve'; and to the following gardeners who were so encouraging and co-operative, my humble thanks: Marylyn Abbot, Mr and Mrs E. Adam, Mrs M. Baker, Mr and Mrs R. Cant, Mr and Mrs H. Fowell, Mrs Christina Leal, Mr and

Mrs J. Mussett, Mr and Mrs C. Ng, Mr and Mrs D. Neall, Hilda and Neal Rahn, Kevin Rigby, Mr and Mrs P. Taylor, Mrs E. Toyer, the owners of Tintagel in the Southern Highlands of New South Wales, and Densey's friend, Mrs Barbara Cottee of Orange.

To Managing Editor Sally Harper and her team at CollinsAngus and Robertson who guided me along the way, my grateful thanks; and to my staff, who have been most understanding, I say thank you. Last, but not least, to my husband George, who has always supported and encouraged me in all my endeavours, and who cares for our garden during my frequent busy periods, my gratitude always.

Photographic Credits

Photography for this book was provided by:
Densey Clyne
Mary Davis
Roger Hanlon

With special contributions by:
Cheryl Maddocks

Rosemary Thodey
Edith Toyer
David Wallace

The work of Phil Aynsley appears courtesy of *Lifestyle and Gardening Australia*.

CONTENTS

Preface ix

Creative Gardening 1

What is a Cottage Garden? 11

Renovating and Remodelling 23

Designing Cottage Gardens 29

Inspiration 47

Colour and Harmony 55

Trees and Basic Structure 73

*Old-Fashioned Roses and
Their New Companions* 109

*Perennials, Groundcovers and
Free-seeding Annuals* 129

Bulbs 167

Maintaining the Garden 177

Further Reading 186

Index 187

*Tall cream mignonette, nigella, Queen
Anne's lace, old-fashioned roses and a* Lavandula
dentata *have been combined by Suzanne Thurley
of Auckland, New Zealand.*

Preface

As the title *Creating Cottage Gardens* suggests, the object of this book is not to dwell on the history of our cottage gardens, fascinating though that history may be, but rather to awaken an appreciation for this style of gardening.

The adaptation of its principles can serve in the creation of suitable gardens for those fortunate enough to acquire a cottage of significance or for those wishing to enhance a residence of simple architectural style.

Cottage gardening is not intended for the ultra-modern garden exponent nor for the no-maintenance gardener; but for the vast majority of gardeners wishing to be creative within their own scope and boundaries, it can be adapted for their ultimate enjoyment and satisfaction.

With my husband, I run Colonial Cottage nursery, which specialises in plants for cottage gardens. On an almost daily basis I meet people making their first garden. Young and old alike need guidance and correct information, and I therefore make no apology to the more experienced gardeners reading this book for presenting what some may consider common-sense garden lore.

LEFT: *Kevin Rigby of Mt Pleasant, south of Sydney, enjoys experimenting with colour and texture in his mainly shaded garden.*

CHAPTER 1

Creative Gardening

Few of us are 'born' gardeners and fewer still consider gardening an art form, but the creative gardener will find pleasure and fulfilment when creating a satisfying garden composition. The basic skills of gardening are usually learnt by example, and the urge to improve the external environment—the garden—comes to most people as they move into their first home. Even earlier, as children, we learnt of nature's miracles—from the germination of a tiny seed to perpetuate a species, to the marvel that something resembling an onion could grow to produce a beautiful daffodil. Today's children are more exposed to the environmental problems of our planet than were their parents: they know that the rainforests of the world are shrinking daily and that trees are the lungs of cities. While clean air and clean water were taken for granted in the past, we are now conscious of what is needed and how, as gardeners, we can contribute to a better environment.

Home making, too, is a creative art, and there is no shortage of printed matter on how to decorate, renovate and titivate your residence. Decorating magazines have long emphasised the indoor–outdoor relationship, especially in countries that are blessed with a climate that allows for use of the garden for so many leisure activities: alfresco meals, relaxation, quiet meditation. Often the simple pleasures are the sweetest—enjoying a cup of tea in warm winter sunshine, or a long cool drink in summer under the shade of a vine-covered pergola or favourite shade tree; taking the hand of a young child to watch a honeybee ruffle the pollen-laden stamens of a flower; admiring a butterfly flitting through the garden, alighting perhaps on a fragrant *Buddleia* flower, or listening to the musical tinkling call of blackbirds or a crimson rosella parrot. These simple pleasures are part of living and working with nature. As many gardeners will testify, these delights are therapeutic in a world that is too full of stress.

Many garden authors extol the virtues of getting your hands into the earth: I won't argue with this, but most gardeners are sensible enough to wear gardening gloves, except perhaps when handling tiny seedlings. As to getting your hands dirty, gardening appeals to people from all walks of life, but rarely do 'armchair gardeners' gain the satisfaction that comes with a job well done.

In my professional work as a garden designer I meet and work with clients from many different backgrounds. One who stays in my memory is a woman who was full of enthusiasm for the garden she wanted designed for her lovely home. The plans were drawn and her gardener carried out the planting while she walked around admiring his handiwork: she confessed to hating to get dirt under her fingernails, so she had never really gardened in her life. I came to realise that she had many health problems exacerbated by loneliness. I felt sad that she had not known the joy of creating beauty with her own hands or the therapeutic value of such activity. Many people seek professional help with their gardens, sometimes because they are too busy to construct a garden, but even so they need the relaxing physical activity of gardening. Others research garden making thoroughly, reading every book they can on the subject, and then undo earlier mistakes—we all make them—to create their own special world.

When I first walked into Beth Chatto's garden at East Elmstead, Essex, in Britain, I was enthralled with what was before me. This is one of the finest landscape gardens created in England in the last 30 years, but I could not understand how Beth Chatto had achieved this with no formal landscape design training. Later, as I read her life story in her *Garden Notebook*, I realised that it was her expertise in flower arranging that gave her her basic skills (she has won 11 gold medals for her nursery plant display stands at the Chelsea Flower Show). As a flower arranger she understands colour, scale, form and texture. She also stresses the importance of researching the origins of plants, understanding their climatic range and soil requirements, and reproducing it in your own garden.

Creating a beautiful garden can be a short- or long-term goal. A late aunt of mine, for example, became very professional in her property investment activities. She would buy a cottage that needed minimal renovation in what she saw as a good location, and would then establish a pretty garden to set it off. Within three to five years she would be looking carefully for her next investment. She used to say that 'you are never lonely if you are a gardener because you are always looking forward to the buds opening of the flowers you love'. I have met other gardeners who have worked on their masterpieces for most of their mature years, and who gain great pleasure in sharing the beauty they have created by opening their gardens for public viewing.

A difficult site, poor soil, a harsh climate or limited funding are just some of the challenges that dedicated gardeners face and overcome. Gardeners tend to develop a calm acceptance of the vagaries of the weather, while reserving gratitude for times when gentle rain is interspersed with warm sunny days, promoting healthy growth. Each season has its own special effects, be they delicate spring blossoms, vivid flowers of summer, brilliant colours of autumn leaves or the tracery of bare branches

LEFT: *Ox-eye daisies and red Flanders poppies welcome the visitor to this cottage garden, which complements a thatched cottage in rural England.*

against a winter sky. Every true gardener will strive to incorporate seasonal highlights into an overall garden composition. The component parts of such a composition can be planned over short or long periods. The success or failure of any scheme is governed by such factors as the suitability of the chosen plants to the location, soil conditions, planning for plant growth and colour harmonies. Keeping a balance between open spaces and planted areas is also important: the smaller the site the greater the need to keep open areas uncluttered. In colder climates winter sunshine is crucial, and so very few small cottages sport much more than a cherry or crabapple tree close to the house. Both are deciduous, thus letting in the winter sun.

Many architectural styles beg for the softness of a cottage garden—including Victorian, Edwardian, Georgian, Queen Anne, Australian Federation and Californian bungalow styles—although of course it is not obligatory. The architecture of many small cottages, terraces and town houses in inner city areas are reminders of their heritage. That does not mean, however, that the current owner must slavishly reconstruct gardens of the past. Many of the plants that were popular in the past are decidedly unpopular today. Yuccas, for example, with their barb-pointed leaves, were popular in the early 1900s but are now rarely used, and for good reason. They are unfriendly, very spreading in habit and difficult to eradicate. Similarly, cordyline and pampas were 'in' plants early in the nineteenth century; plumbago hedges have fallen from favour because of their suckering habit and the need for regular root pruning with a sharp spade each winter, and frequent top pruning. Grown informally in a dryish corner, however, plumbago can be a great asset. Many postwar homes also need softening, particularly those made from red textured brick: a scheme of blue and white flowers with silver foliage accents, for example, is an appealing one whose colour does not clash with the red bricks.

LEFT: *Cream, white, yellow, grey and blue are the main colours used to soften the red textured brick in this Sydney cottage garden.*

FASHIONS AND TRENDS

Garden history has witnessed many changes of style. Only a century ago garden makers followed the simple design concepts of William Robinson and Gertrude Jekyll. Two world wars and the Great Depression saw cottagers once again concentrating on vegetables to sustain both the family and, ultimately, the nation. I have the greatest respect for those who still produce home grown vegetables as a matter of course.

In England the upsurge of interest in the 'cottage garden' style is evident. No longer are they the meagre plots of the poor, but the gardens of the middle and upper classes are being embellished with flowers and furnishings in a 'cottage' style that would astound the humble cottagers of yesteryear. Town and farm gardens alike are adapting the cottage style of soft colours, soft silhouettes and softly curving outlines to produce an abundance that can be very charming. Those who hanker after little formality can use low clipped box hedges as dividers between lawn and a billowing mass of perennials, roses and background shrubs. The idea of creating rooms within a garden, or better still on even a slightly larger than average suburban block, can be most successful.

VALUES AND INFLUENCES

The excesses of Victorian bedding displays directly influenced the gardens created around Federation cottages built in Australia between 1890 and 1910, where central rose beds carpeted with annuals took pride of place. Californian bungalows were also built in this period, as this American architectural style was eminently suited to both the climate and the lifestyle, with the deep verandahs or porches providing coolness in summer and a place for informal dining. Once again the curving path to the front door was planted with roses and annuals.

A garden called Eryldene, planted in Sydney in 1913 by the late Professor Eben Gowrie Waterhouse, was first planned and planted as a cottage garden, which would surprise many who know

LEFT: *Nepeta 'Six Hills' and old-fashioned roses provide a foreground to low shrubs in this farm garden at Amberley, New Zealand.*

RIGHT: *A froth of white alyssum softens the edges of the stone path leading to Eryldene's front verandah.*

it today. Professor Waterhouse became world famous for his research into camellia nomenclature. He was the founding president of the International Camellia Society and in later life his garden reflected the passion he felt for that genus. The plan of Eryldene evolved by Professor Waterhouse and his architect William Hardy Wilson was probably a marriage of the design concepts of William Robinson with Hardy Wilson's desire to emulate the plantings in cottages along the Cowpastures Road leading from Sydney to Camden. Certainly blue plumbago featured in both. The only remnants of the cottage garden include an aging persimmon tree on the east side of what was the fruit garden, and the rectilinear beds that lead from the pedestrian gate to the front steps. The deep red China Roses 'Lady Brisbane' still bloom abundantly almost the whole year round and are enhanced by a froth of white alyssum, or sweet Alice. *Iris germanica*, the purple flag iris and *Iris florentine*, the white flowered, orris root iris, are grouped beneath a beautifully shaped *Jacaranda mimosifolia*. The garden contains dwarf pomegranates and blue and white agapanthus for summer colour, while in early autumn 'James Belton' azaleas unfold single mauve blooms, flowering almost continually from early autumn until late spring when the single pink azalea 'Ruth Kirk' takes over. Finally, like lace on a

handkerchief, the white sweet Alice unifies the overall composition.

Another and major influence on today's cottage garden is Edna Margaret Walling who was born in Yorkshire in 1896. Her formative years were spent in Devon, where the climate allows for the soft growth of bluebells and foxgloves under silver birches, a combination she never forgot. Her father, who was disappointed that she was not a boy, taught her woodwork, which proved useful to her later in her working life. The family left England for New Zealand in 1911, but eventually settled in Melbourne, Australia. Edna enrolled at Burnley Horticultural College at the

age of nineteen. She designed her first 'client' garden in 1919 for the brother of one of her gardening colleagues. Thus began a career that spanned some forty years of designing, creating and writing and inspired others. Many of her commissions were for the wealthy and the famous—including singer Dame Nellie Melba—but her own simple tastes, vitality and enthusiasm were the hallmarks of her style. In 1943 she wrote *Gardens in Australia—Their Design and Care*, followed by *Cottage and Garden in Australia* in 1947. Both books demonstrate her depth of feeling for cottage simplicity, the second going in to great detail. Her writings began in the

LEFT: *A tiny guest cottage around which Helen Russell has created a pretty garden—just part of the farm garden at Amberley, New Zealand.*

RIGHT: *A deep border at Sharcott Manor in Wiltshire, garden of Captain and Mrs David Armytage, features the yellow evening primrose (*Oenothera biennis*).*

1920s with articles published in *Australian Home Beautiful*. The building of her single room cabin, for example, appear in print in 1928 under the heading 'How We Put Up Our Little Stone Cabin—Another Adventure in Amateur Building'. Over the years she penned many articles and letters about her work, ideas, favourite plants, garden design, detailing and country road landscapes, all of which were intended to stimulate the interest of the reader. Her third book, *A Gardener's Log*, written in 1948, was one of the very first gardening books that I purchased and I still treasure it today.

Edna Walling built her first simple stone cottage with help from her nephew and friends in 1921, at Mooroolbark near the base of Mount Dandenong. It was on 1.2 hectares (three acres) of undulating pasture, and named Sonning, after a small English hamlet Walling had seen from a rowboat on the Thames as a child. Unfortunately the house was destroyed by fire in 1936, and Sonning II was built to replace it. This is the first cottage featured in her

second book, a work devoted to simple architectural detailing in cottages, construction advice for the owner-builder, specification notes for plans, and comments on pise and adobe houses.

Soon after building Sonning I Edna purchased a nearby parcel of seven hectares (eighteen acres) and conceived the idea of a rural subdivision of half or one hectare (one or two acre) lots which would be known as Bickleigh Vale. There, cottages built for other people would be integrated into the landscape, preferably using local materials.

The little country village was named Bickleigh Vale after a village in Devon, and over the years 16 houses were completed, among them Lynton Lee (built for her friend Lorna Fielden) and

Downderry. Both still today show Edna's keen eye for detail, always softened by planting.

Stone walling, paving, pergolas, simple fences, gates and garden steps are all given equal emphasis by this indefatigable woman who appreciated the importance of integrating all the component parts into an unpretentious, harmonious composition.

Deep in the garden at Sonning, Edna and an unnamed female friend entirely built a stone-walled cabin, only its corrugated iron roof needing to be completed by a local carpenter. A stone fireplace provided warmth and it was a cool and airy place for summer meals as it had ten casement windows on three sides and a large pergola with a

ABOVE: *Beth Chatto's valley garden is a symphony of colour, form and texture. The grey foliaged* Salix lanata *(at left) and* Salix repens '*Argentea*' *contrast with the other bog-loving plants.*

deciduous vine on the northerly aspect. The stone pillars supporting the pergola are half a metre (one and a half feet) square and on the east side a stone-paved verandah extends the usable space. A low stone wall at right angles to the building provides a useful resting spot beside the back door. This very simple building was not left unadorned. A chimney, a low stone wall beside the back door, a verandah and a pergola-

covered terrace all contributed to the overall plan, topped by a roof with two unusual little gables, front and back, in what would have been a plain hip roof.

The route from the house to the cabin was planted with a rich assortment of trees, flowering shrubs and soft groundcovers nestling between stepping stones, including the all-important Westmorland thymes that Edna Walling loved. Below the cabin verandah was a

sunny rock garden with rocks virtually hidden by massed plants; the corner nearest the pergola was softened by a flowering crabapple. The view from both the verandah and the terrace was of gently undulating lawn, well-screened boundaries and the path leading back to

the main house. This cabin was Edna's home after the disastrous fire that burnt Sonning I, and while Sonning II was being built.

Edna wrote that 'foundation planting is one of the most significant things about a country cottage. Turf rolling right up to the walls often gives the perfect setting when the cottage sits well down on the ground. At other times herbaceous perennials and some low growing shrubs give a touch of colour that may be desirable, and what is even more important, they help to link the cottage to the ground more pleasingly.'

Edna Walling acknowledges the help of her friend Lorna Fielden, owner of Lynton Lee, in selecting the material for *A Gardener's Log* from her 'letters' column in *Australian Home Beautiful*. The first chapter is entitled 'Mainly About Spring' and begins with a discussion of Australian plants, and it is true that in this period of her life she was enthusiastic about native plants, but they did not totally dominate her thinking. When she retired to Queensland she planted an exotic garden for herself. It is in spring that most of Australia's native flora is at its best. Walling knew this, and expertly blended them with exotics for her own designs.

The ability of Edna Walling to entice people to follow her example is shown in her discussion of a thyme lawn:

Luxuries of luxuries! I've been lying on my own thyme lawn, there was just enough room to turn over without landing on to the surrounding rock plants. You haven't lived if you have not lain flat on your middle on a thyme lawn. The bees do not seem to mind a bit either, but just go on busily exploring the possibilities of each thyme flower. How cool and fresh to the touch are these lovely little plants, how exquisitely dusky the colouring of the various varieties both in foliage and flower! From ground level the rock garden becomes the most enchanting place— it's like another world; Aquilegia longissima *almost towered above me, and the little flat faces of* Aquilegia clematifolia *looked down at me with surprised expressions.*

In this description her joy and enthusiasm reach out to us and we immediately want to know just as intimately the thymes of Edna's private world. In the hurly-burly of the postwar years her message was forgotten. Only now is the realisation dawning that Edna Walling, who died in 1973, influenced not only the clients whose gardens she designed but also the thousands of readers whose gardens she never saw.

CHAPTER 2

What is a Cottage Garden?

You may have recently moved house, or you may be planning to build a new house that would be enhanced by a cottage garden, or you may own a garden that is in need of renovation. The idea of planting a cottage garden may have come from an illustration in a magazine or book, or from the sight of a garden so pretty you felt compelled to stop and admire it while trying to absorb some of its detail. Whatever the source stimulating your desire to create a cottage garden, you cannot begin without a little understanding of what actually constitutes a cottage garden.

❧

LEFT: *On a large flat site create 'rooms' of particular interest with arches and focal points that entice the viewer.*

RIGHT: *The façade of this Auckland cottage is framed by trees. Lavenders and marguerite daisies spill out onto the pavement.*

Firstly, let's explode some of the myths. Cottage gardens do not have to be small or lawnless. Certainly where space is restricted, as in a townhouse, it is more sensible to replace lawn with pavers in an area for alfresco meals, but quite large gardens can and do have a cottage style. It is not uncommon in England, where the cottage style of gardening began and is carried on with great refinement, to find old rectories, manor houses, and farmhouses transformed by charming cottage gardens.

Sissinghurst in Kent, the creation of the famous author Vita Sackville-West, has been described as a glorified cottage garden. It is laid out as a series of visual delights, including the white garden, the rondel garden, the herb garden and the south cottage garden, which is planted in shades of yellow accented by white, orange, blue and red with no pink

colours in sight. Sissinghurst covers 2.2 hectares (5.4 acres) and is superbly maintained by two women head gardeners trained by Vita herself. They in turn control a staff of eight for the National Trust who welcome more than 166 000 visitors annually.

What is a cottage garden? It is best described as a profusion of flowers, particularly perennials, closely planted for a very soft effect. A cottage garden will usually include such delights as lavenders, daisies and old-fashioned roses. Its style is informal: a medley of soft shapes and harmonious colours. Plants that spill over walls, soften the edges of paving, clothe pergolas, hide fences and decorate verandahs definitely contribute to the soft 'it just happened that way' look. How to achieve this effect is what this book is about.

A bare block of ground can be just as

ABOVE: *Sissinghurst's white garden features a central bower canopied with* Rosa mulliganii. Buxus *hedges frame beds of white flowers and silver foliage.*

daunting as an overgrown jungle inherited from a previous owner. Each has its own particular problems: no shade or too much shade; exposure to adverse winds with no protecting trees or severe root opposition from trees that have reached maturity. The lucky ones are those who move house and find just a few gems, enabling them to remove unwanted vegetation with no qualms of conscience at all, ready to start afresh. If you are numbered among these, you might be tempted to skip a chapter or two and go straight to Chapter 3 (Renovating and Remodelling), but reading on you may learn more than you think.

NEW HOME, NEW GARDEN

It is rare to meet a client who is more excited about a future garden than a new house. For most the only consideration to the new garden is to put cardboard over the mud at moving time. Covering mud with turf to save ruining the newly laid carpet is often of paramount importance, as is rushing out to buy screening shrubs for privacy, for not everyone is inclined to 'love thy neighbour'. Neither of these, however, should take priority over attention to drainage. Roofs, paths, paved driveways and patios will have one hundred per cent run-off when rain falls. The builder will have piped the roof water to leave the property according to council requirements or, in the case of a farm, piped it into a holding tank with

overflow entering a dam, but for the garden in suburbia stormwater may be entering your property from a neighbour's land at a higher level. It is not neighbourly to concentrate stormwater runoff at one point on the common boundary unless that point leads into a drainage easement or stream.

It is imperative to collect stormwater at convenient points to prevent soil erosion through lawn areas and to prevent the scouring of soil from garden beds. Surface run-off can be diverted into channel drains or onto kerbed paths or driveways, but unless channel drains are regularly cleaned a blockage of leaves and debris can cause an overflow, resulting in the very damage such drains are meant to prevent.

People often wrongly assume that because there is a slope across or down their land it will drain easily. Factors affecting drainage include the presence of rock or shale below the surface topsoil, or clay close to the surface. On many new subdivisions clay is all that remains after earthmoving machinery has shaped the site, and it is a problem that will be addressed in this chapter.

Agricultural drains, laid to intercept water seeping below the surface from higher ground, can and do result in better growth of lawn grasses and other ornamental plants. Badly drained lawn areas stay wet for long periods, making mowing difficult. Patches of moss or algae can develop in areas with bad

drainage, particularly in areas of winter shade. Consequently soil becomes sour from lack of oxygen and the grass fails. Properly laid agricultural drains, however, will continue to move the subsoil water in a steady flow for several days after heavy rain.

If you ignore drainage problems you will join the band of nursery customers who complain of plant losses in very wet years or whose opening sentence is, 'What can I grow in a poorly drained soggy spot?' The choice is strictly limited. Even those with so-called heavy soil that drains well enough in normal seasons will testify to losing many plants in periods of prolonged wet weather.

THE SITE

Site Soil

Not all soils are heavy (that is, capable of holding large reserves of water and nutrients). Light sandy soils have excellent drainage but the soil structure means that it drains too freely and the moisture and nutrients needed by plants are quickly leached or lost from the soil. The remedy is to add humus in the form of animal manures, spent mushroom compost, shredded leaf litter or homemade compost to improve the crumb structure, fertility and water holding capacity of the soil.

RIGHT: *A white and silver garden planted by Gordon Collier of Taihape, New Zealand, is set on a steep knoll with only 15 cm (6 in) of topsoil.*

BELOW RIGHT: *The Japanese maple (Acer japonicum 'Aconitifolium') colours superbly in cool climates, turning a rich red in autumn.*

Not for nothing does the grower of asparagus take the time to thoroughly prepare the ground before planting, because it is a long-term crop that stays *in situ* for several years. Similarly, the rose grower adds manure that will decay and be broken down by the micro-organisms of the soil. When this has taken place and the whole area is forked over to an even tilth, it is safe to plant roses. Many a rose has had its roots burnt by the person who, trying to take a short cut, has added fertiliser into the planting hole—had there been homemade compost to hand, this would never have happened.

Composting occurs in nature on the forest floor below the closed canopy of foliage. The spent leaves fluttering to the ground begin to break down in an environment of warmth and moisture, aided by soil micro-organisms, fungi and bacteria. It takes nature half a century to make two centimetres (an inch) of topsoil: what we have in our gardens is precious and begs for a good custodian, not one who commits such sins as burning autumn leaves.

Where space permits, make compost in a service area in sunlight, in either a heap or a tumbler. A compost heap is made from layers of material such as shredded prunings, soft weeds (not bulbous weeds such as oxalis or onion weed), lawn clippings, animal manure, soft wood sawdust or buzzer chips (in small amounts) and a dusting of lime, all of which can be mixed by forking and then sprinkled with a little moisture and left to ferment. The heap will heat to a temperature of 62°C (176°F) within three days if there is sufficient green material and manure in the mix. After a week to ten days fork over, or turn, the material and leave it to break down further. Compost will not decay properly if it is too wet or too dry, so the balance of ingredients and moisture is important. It should not smell revolting: if it does it has become anaerobic (lacking in oxygen) and the best remedy is to work through as much shredded straw as needed to get it smelling pure and working properly again. Once this process is understood, it is possible to make compost of friable quality every three weeks, and when applied as a mulch or dug in to improve the soil, you will quickly see the result in the healthy growth of plants.

Compost can also be made in bins, which must have earth floors or be placed directly on the ground. If adding household scraps—which is quite in order—a covered bin discourages

vermin. Three bins side by side are useful as they enable continuous production: one's contents ready for distribution, one's half-decayed and one's newly prepared. If space does not permit such an operation, a tumbler in the sun will produce compost in two weeks if turned daily. For a tiny courtyard garden, spent mushroom compost is the answer, although it must be very old before it can safely be used around camellias, azaleas, daphne, rhododendrons and pieris, all of which are lime-haters.

When you apply compost as a mulch it is important not to build it up around the stems and trunks of plants and trees,

ABOVE: *This contemporary landscape on a steep site uses steps, low walls, a deck, seating and lattice panels, all softened with cottage plants.*

nor to bury the rhizomes of iris or bulbs that like their necks above ground level (eg belladonna lilies). Apart from being the best soil conditioner you can have, mulch helps suppress weed growth. Although it cannot suppress weeds entirely, weeding a mulched garden is a breeze compared to weeding an unmulched one. In times of drought mulch conserves water and in prolonged rain it prevents erosion by breaking the force of the raindrops hitting the soil.

ABOVE: *A tunnel of clipped hornbeam inside this entry gate leads the eye to a statue framed in an arch, a lovely focal point.*

The Scraped Site

Those trying to make gardens in a new subdivision fashioned by a bulldozer are often faced with raw clay in the front garden, particularly where levels have been changed by the construction of roads over hilly terrain. It is not possible to buy really good topsoil, only what I call brown sand, which is really silt from river flats. It is often very difficult to wet because of the presence of a soil

fungus, and only by progressively adding humus will the silt be changed into soil. Growing annuals or vegetables between additions of humus is the best solution. Before this so-called topsoil is spread over clay for lawn areas it is advisable to break up the clay with an application of gypsum and to feed the lawn first with lawn starter fertiliser. Each year apply lawn food in spring and ammonium nitrate in late spring and at the end of summer, being careful to water before and after the application with sufficient water to dissolve the fertiliser and carry it down to the roots or you risk burning the grass.

Working with the Site

The topography of your site can vary from flat to a gentle slope to steep. It is challenging to make a flat site interesting, and expensive to construct a garden on a steep site where steps and retaining walls are prerequisites. Both require attention to detailed planning, particularly the flat site where breaking or dividing it into small, medium and large areas (as space permits) with features such as a pergola, small ornamental pool, fountain, garden seat or tastefully chosen statuary can stimulate and carry the eye. In a tiny corner it can be as simple as adding a water bowl to float flowers in or placing a suitably planted urn on a pedestal.

ABOVE: *A long border tiered with railway sleepers gives deeper soil and adds interest on a flat site.*

RIGHT: *Tintagel, in the Southern Highlands of New South Wales, Australia.*

One of the smallest and flattest sites I have ever seen was behind a Victorian terrace house in Oxford, UK. It was transformed by a very knowledgeable gardener who conceived the idea of creating a focal point at the far end of a very narrow yard via a false gate. A gently curved path led to the gate but the journey along its length was made fascinating by the very clever use of plants carefully selected for colour, form

and texture. As you reached the gate it was perfectly natural to turn and retrace your steps, drinking in the detail of the other side. This is the garden of Anne Dexter, whose story appears in *The Englishwoman's Garden Book*.

Drainage was an issue at this site; drainage on any flat site can be difficult if absorption trenches for a roof water and septic system exist. A rubble pit in the lowest corner is one resolution, but in times of prolonged rain it will fill to capacity. Raised garden beds are important in such circumstances, and Anne Dexter's beds were retained with weathered stone. Brick or timber, treated pine or railway sleepers can be used for a neat appearance, or, if a softer look is required, groundcover edging

BELOW: *Rockleigh, a farm garden in New South Wales, Australia, was designed by the author for friends to complement their 1840 cottage.*

plants such as white alyssum and catmint (*Nepeta*) will hold a slope on a raised bed by binding it with their roots.

The gradient of a site can be the key to good and interesting design, but other factors also have to be considered. These include the macro and micro climates, the existence of site features (such as existing mature trees, outcrops of natural rock, a creek or stream), and the shadow patterns created by your dwelling and perhaps neighbouring houses or structures. Most important when designing your garden, however, is the usage requirements of your space. Children who want to kick a ball or play cricket cannot always be expected to do it in the local park for the sake of mum's vulnerable cottage plants or dad's tomatoes. The lawn in front of my home is dual purpose, as it provides open space to balance the planted areas and also serves as a practice green for putting and chipping golf balls. What could be fairer than the one who cuts, trims and fertilises the grass getting to utilise it for his favourite sport? The upper lawn has a two-directional slope and the lower has a gentle little hump that makes an otherwise flat area more interesting.

❧

BELOW: *Granite outcrops at Rockleigh dictated where plantings of silver birch (*Betula pendula*), shore juniper (*Juniperus conferta*) and daffodils were most appropriate.*

CLIMATIC RANGE AND PLANT GROWTH

Australia has great variations between its climatic zones, ranging from tropical rainforest and desert to the fertile plains which are often bordered by mountains, some of which receive snow. The native plants which evolved over millions of years have adapted to the soils and climates in their areas of specific origin. The spread of settlement has meant that Australia's new inhabitants have brought in exotic plants from their homelands or from other parts. Indeed, because China has comparable climatic zones, many of Australia's most loved plants originated in, and were brought from China, sometimes via the United Kingdom.

The United States of America has the same climatic variations and so it is not at all surprising for American gardeners to find themselves growing and loving the same cottage flowers, shrubs and trees as Australian gardeners do.

Parts of Australia and New Zealand have a Mediterranean climate. If travelling from Sydney to Hobart or from Auckland to Christchurch, one can see a large range of the plants which are popular in southern Europe and England, testimony to the universal pleasure of gardening.

MACRO AND MICRO CLIMATES

You may be unfamiliar with the terms 'macro' and 'micro' in relation to climate. Macro is the climate of a broad region, as shown each day on your television screen, and micro is that which occurs on your own site, the two most important influences being sun and wind. The sunny side of a house, for example, will suit a range of plants that would be totally miserable on the shady side. The macro climate of your region will determine your highest and lowest temperatures in summer and winter, whether you get light frosts, heavy frosts, snow or no frost at all.

ABOVE: *The rapid growth of the claret ash planted next door to my house has, in less than a decade, changed the micro climate of this garden, which is now shaded for longer on summer afternoons. The branches in winter, although leafless, do help to lessen the severity of heavy frosts.*

Minimum night temperatures vary within different climatic regions. The list below shows the lowest average winter minimum temperature for each climatic region.

- Hot climate: 15 degrees Celsius (59°F)
- Warm climate: 10 degrees Celsius (50°F)
- Temperate climate: 5 degrees Celsius (41°F)
- Cool climate: 1 degree Celsius (33.8°F) or lower depending on its altitude or distance from the equator.

In cool climate areas, frosts occur much earlier in autumn and continue later into spring than in temperate regions. However, some lower mountain slopes are free of frost because of cold air drainage patterns. In a micro sense, cold air drainage patterns across or down a site will dictate where you place a frost-sensitive plant, and the direction of the most adverse winds—cold winter, hot summer or salt laden—will also have to be considered.

Siting of the entertainment area, the swimming pool and the clothes-drying area are all influenced by your particular micro climate and available space. The more restricted the space the greater the need for privacy screening—be it shrubs or lattice and climbers—that can double as a windbreak or wind barrier.

VIEWS

Limitations for gardeners may be financial, physical or insurmountable. A serious limitation would be, say, a tall apartment building that casts too much shade on your outdoor living area for a large part of the day and robs you of privacy. Privacy is something that we all value and aim to achieve, particularly in the rear garden, though sometimes a small front garden becomes a walled courtyard, particularly on a busy road.

If the frontage of your site is too large to warrant the use of a high masonry wall, noise can be cut with thick evergreen shrubs such as *Camellia sasanqua* (choosing the upright hedging cultivars), or orange jasmine (*Murraya paniculata*). In colder climates *Escallonia macrantha* cultivars or *Raphiolepis* x *delacourii* would serve equally well. A row of narrow, upright *Camellia sasanqua* 'Marie Young' in the narrow space between a driveway and a side fence is much more reliable than a row of conifers such as golden *Cupressus macrocarpa* 'Brunniana'. These can look very appealing when young but may succumb to borer or storm damage later, causing a gap in the screen planting, or they may simply grow too large for the available space. If you must have something like that, *Cupressus sempervirens* 'Swane's Golden' is a better choice. Personally, I enjoy the plain rich shiny green backgrounds of *C. sasanqua* or orange jasmine that easily reach three metres (10 ft) and can be maintained with pruning. *Camellia sasanqua* 'Marie Young' is capable of five to six metres (16–20 ft), making it useful between two-storey residences.

Many views are unwanted, such as next door's toolshed or windows, but there are also very desirable views. You may enjoy 'borrowed scenery' such as a neighbour's beautiful jacaranda at flowering time, which might entice you to plant to maintain the line of vision. Views from windows or glass doors leading into the garden are also important. A view of a park or reserve is usually worth many real estate dollars, as is a view of distant mountains, harbour, lake, beach or ocean. Such broader views inevitably mean contending with exposure to strong winds blowing from open country or over open water—the two go hand in hand. In such circumstances, preserving the view is paramount and only low windbreak plantings should be used to shelter vulnerable plants. Alternatively, place 'soft' plants on the most sheltered side of the building.

The creative gardener aims to make the scene as beautiful and as soul sat-isfying as possible in the available space and in their macro and micro climate.

CHAPTER 3

Renovating and Remodelling

Not everyone makes their first garden on a bare block of ground. Many buy a house with an established garden because it is convenient, working first on renovating the house to reflect their own tastes and suit their lifestyle before addressing the problems of the garden. It is rare to purchase a cottage totally lacking in vegetation of some kind unless it is within an inner-city suburb where open spaces have been totally paved for vehicular or trade purposes. Even these situations, although daunting, can become small green oases with careful planning and planting and the removal of some concrete.

❋

LEFT: *Lucky indeed is a home buyer who moves in to find an* Acer palmatum *'Osakazuki' with such beautiful autumn colour.*

RIGHT: *When Henry and Francis Whitehead of Auckland moved into this 1940s cottage, they transformed its garden with roses and perennials. A magnificent silver birch was retained.*

Previously established suburban or country town gardens usually contain a few haphazardly planted shrubs and trees, often poorly chosen and almost certainly planted in spaces too small for their ultimate size. The lazy person's garden contains the 'volunteer plants' that arise from seed scattered abroad by the birds: privet, both large- and small-leafed forms, is common, but it is not unusual to find olive (*Olea africana*), *Ochna serrulata* and in Australian suburbs close to bushland areas, the native daphne *Pittosporum undulatum*, wild tobacco bush, and pest plants such as *Lantana camara* and blackberry vines. Not all unwanted greenery is of shrub and tree proportions—at ground level wandering jew, crofton weed, and kapok vine can also add to the enormity of the initial cleanup.

Before any work is begun it is important to look critically at all existing trees and shrubs. Decide which

are bonuses and which must go. The shape of a tree you like might have been spoilt by the close planting of a second, making you hesitate to remove the intruder for fear of displaying the misshapen form of the desired plant. Do not worry: except in the case of conifers, nature will compensate in due course, and the tree will fill out again to its natural shape when provided with uncluttered air space in which to spread. If in doubt, consult a qualified tree-surgeon whose experience will benefit the tree as well as the ultimate resale value of the property.

In my present garden there is an English oak (*Quercus robur*), which had three lilli-pilli trees (*Acmena smithii*) spoiling its shape on the south side and a large coral tree (*Erythrina* x *sykesii*) (syn. *E. indica*), blocking its spread to the north. Those four trees were removed and the tree-surgeon skilfully removed crossing and dead branches. What was once a hemmed-in tree has now become a beautiful tree in its own right, the crown filling out on the south side, and an asset to the property, lending maturity to a young garden.

The trees and shrubs inherited with your property may not be what you would have chosen but in some instances they need to stay because they provide privacy or screen an unwanted view. Even so, if it is a species you absolutely cannot abide—such as a privet if you are an asthmatic—then it

has to go. To adjust to this, the temptation is to plant something like *Virgilia oroboides*, the 'tree in a hurry', but at best it provides a short-term solution not in keeping with your cottage garden image. Pretty though the pink pea-shaped flowers are, the tree grows so rapidly it exhausts itself and quickly dies.

The angle of vision from your yard to any unwanted view will ultimately determine your choice of solution, which must take into consideration the mature height and width of the desired

ABOVE: *A selection of* Camellia sasanqua *cultivars of upright habit provides an informal privacy screen planting.*

tree or shrub. Small trees or tall shrubs, for example, are the answer in a situation where the angle of the winter sun outweighs the need to screen out the neighbouring property. Plants such as *Camellia sasanqua* and *Gordonia axillaris* have the advantage of being evergreens that are both capable of growing into dense shrubs and, with thinning and shaping from an early age, can become small trees with very pretty bark and pleasant softly rounded shapes. Both are capable of reasonably rapid growth in good growing conditions. Good conditions for these two species include an open sunny aspect with a minimum of half a day of sunlight, a reasonable depth of soil (not just a few centimetres on top of a rock ledge), and regular feeding and watering. Given such attention, and spraying *Camellia sasanqua* to prevent aphid attack on tip growth in spring, you can expect a minimum of 0.5 m (1.5 ft) of growth per year. If this is not fast enough, resort to trickery: use a temporary screen of evergreen climbers on lattice while permanent greenery is developing. If local council ordinances do not permit lattice above 1.8 m (6 ft) use a screen of tubbed bamboo, but never, *ever* plant either golden or black-stemmed bamboo in the ground. It is only permissible to use bamboo in the ground as a screen if it can't escape its confines. Using 0.5 m (1.5 ft) diameter plastic tubs is the most sensible solution, and they should be elevated on bricks to prevent roots taking hold through drainage holes. The tubs require daily watering, especially in summer. Regular watering and fertilising ensures rapid growth. Be wary of grey aphids, which can sometimes be troublesome in spring. If the infestation is severe and goes undetected, major defoliation can occur, as it will with lack of water.

Use plastic tubs rather than concrete for bamboo, as it is necessary to retub every second year. Use an old carpenter's saw to cut the root ball in half, and return half to the tub, allowing space for fresh soil. Plastic tubs are lighter, and do not crack as readily as concrete if the bamboo is blown over in strong winds, which can sometimes happen. If strong winds are a problem, inconspicuous green nylon cord strung between steel posts in front of the tub will prevent the bamboo from toppling. When using heavy decorative tubs in your cottage garden, bear in mind that tall plants—be it bamboo, weeping fig (*Ficus benjamina*) or a large *Camellia japonica*—can blow over in strong wind.

If you have a tree that draws admiration then plan the associated plantings to complement it, and if it is centrally located it may become the feature tree of your whole scheme. The smoothness of green lawn meeting the basal trunk of a small, medium or large tree can be more beautiful in its simplicity than fussy little collar beds of busy annuals or garishly coloured perennials. A tastefully chosen, well designed garden seat placed in the shade of such a tree is again preferable to a circle of flowers or greenery such as ivy. In fact, uncontrolled ivy can menace the life of your lovely tree.

The shadow pattern cast by a splendid tree across the lawn in summer moves with the hour of the day and can influence the placement of an outdoor entertainment area, particularly if the tree is deciduous, letting the winter sun into your summer shade area. Shade cast by dense evergreen trees growing in your neighbour's property can also influence your planting scheme.

Too many evergreen trees close to a house will keep the house colder and darker in winter, but it is often very difficult to persuade the local authorities

ABOVE: *Lattice panels have been employed to gain privacy in this narrow side garden, which features Queen Anne's lace and daisies.*

that you should be allowed to remove some trees for the sake of heat and light in winter. In most areas it is permissible to remove certain trees—such as rubber trees (*Ficus elastica*), poplars and willows—that are known to block drains and sewers. Consult with your local officer and a tree-surgeon. Often a letter from the tree-surgeon, landscape architect or landscape consultant with an accompanying plan of the proposed new garden will be viewed more favourably because you are demonstrating that you are concerned with improving not destroying the local environment.

Nature seems to have divided her plants into one-third shade-lovers and two-thirds demanding sun to grow properly. Among the shade-lovers are some real gems that will not be happy in full sun, such as daphnes, most *Camellia japonica* with delicately coloured

BELOW: *Our English oak lends maturity to a young garden. Rose 'Ballerina' adds her contribution in late spring.*

flowers, the majority of azaleas, rhododendrons, fuchsias, ferns and double impatiens. I stress double because the singles behave like weeds, though they are very pretty. Either you accept the challenge of making a garden in the shade or you move house.

In trying to establish new plantings, root opposition from mature and even semi-mature trees can be a frustrating problem. In our own garden the very act of making a garden beneath the oak tree's canopy has been made difficult by the mat of feeder roots enjoying the compost mulch. Each time a plant is planted we must dig a hole of greater proportions than would normally suffice, using a drainer's spade which has a marvellous cutting edge. The desired plant is given an enriched planting mix around its root ball and regularly watered to encourage quick root growth before the oak roots move in on it. The

oak, enjoying the extra food and water, has doubled its size in six years. Fortunately oak roots do not sucker but if I accidentally damage the roots of nearby crepe myrtle or robinia both quickly respond with suckers.

One of the best ways to get results under a tree that is already big enough is to liquid feed those plants you wish to keep healthy by spraying fertiliser onto their leaves. There are several good brands of soluble fertiliser to which azaleas and camellias respond, as will many other plants, but be careful to get the formulation right because if it is too strong, leaf burn will result. Applied once a month it is a very useful method of feeding your chosen plants but not the big tree.

Results can also be achieved by creating a garden in tubs or pots under a hungry tree. With the advent of dripper irrigation, which is ideal for people who

travel frequently and have the system on automatic control, it is possible to make an interesting garden, particularly if the tubs are in graduated heights. By placing large tub subjects like camellias towards the rear and stepping down with azaleas, daphnes, dwarf rhododendrons and a foreground planting, the tubs can be largely hidden from view. A word of warning, though— place the tubs on bricks to prevent tree roots entering the drainage holes of your tubs. It can happen with species like camphor laurel.

New shrubs being planted in an established garden do need extra care to attain optimum growth and if something you planted is languishing or has just not gained in height for a long period, it is a safe bet that it is struggling with dryness caused by severe root opposition, for the bigger the tree, the more water it draws up.

CHAPTER 4

Designing Cottage Gardens

Unlike country gardens, suburban or town gardens do not have moveable fences but they can be shaped into public and private areas. Public areas are those visible from the street or used for public access, for example, to the front door.

On an initial inspection, professional designers look at existing paving and vegetation, especially any existing trees and shrubs, and whether the style of the front fence is in keeping with the architecture of the house. The architectural style of the house, the site problems and the personal tastes of the client govern how the garden will be designed.

As the cost of land increases the size of the average building block seems to decrease. The paving required for

❧

LEFT: Many special treasures have been planted in this narrow but sunny side garden by owners Pam and Harry Fowell of Sydney.

vehicular access for a double garage covers a significant percentage of the front garden. With the building alignment or set-back being reduced, the drive has to be short and direct, usually without even the gentlest of curves. The larger the area occupied by the drive, the more important the choice of paving material becomes. For a cottage garden brick paving or bonded gravel has a softer appearance then newly laid concrete, which can be very glary until it ages to grey.

The very large area of paving needed to access a triple-fronted garage can be softened by the careful placement of two or three trees, remembering that their height, shape and canopy spread must suit the dwelling. A small cottage may be offset by a crabapple (*Malus floribunda*) or two, whereas a two-storey residence can, with its increased height, be enhanced by trees capable of reaching six metres (20 feet) or a little more. Such trees should not be planted too

close to the paving as strong root development can lift the drive. Possible choices are the Chinese tallow tree (*Sapium sebiferum*) or *Pistacia chinensis*, both renowned for their beautiful autumn colour. *Pistacia chinensis* is a particularly graceful tree. Such trees can be underpruned, leaving trunks free of low branches to well above head height before being allowed to spread over the drive so that service vehicles can be driven right up to the house.

There are many suitable species but it is important to know the mature dimensions of your chosen tree. I have seen a Chinese elm (*Ulmus parvifolia*) planted in the front garden of a 1904 cottage grow so large and spread so widely that eight cars could be parked in its shade. Chinese tallow and pistachio trees are of course deciduous and you may protest that you do not want to be sweeping leaves up in the late autumn. It is worth remembering that every leaf is valuable when turned into compost and that, contrary to popular belief, planting evergreen trees does not do away with leaf litter. The life of a leaf for most evergreen species is about three years and the owners of mature eucalyptus trees will testify to constantly cleaning up gum leaves, bark, gumnuts, twigs and dead wood, particularly after strong winds.

There is no such thing as the perfectly tidy tree. They will all at some time drop flowers, leaves, fruits, nuts,

seed, bark, twigs or dead branches. If you think about it, the much loved jacaranda drops its beautiful blue bells in early summer then, in late winter, its tiny golden leaflets followed by the leaf stalk or midrib and also its seed follicles. Owners of swimming pools curse the tiny leaflets which elude the pool sweep, but our whole world would be so much the poorer without trees. Those who stubbornly refuse to plant a tree will also never know the pleasure of watching beautiful birds as they visit the garden. Parrots love the coral coloured bunches of fruit produced by the lilli pilli (*Syzygium leuhmanni*); however, it is unwise to plant its purple fruited cousin *Acmena smithii* where it may drop its fruit on paving.

In a small front garden the same paving material chosen for the drive should be used for the path to the front door except, perhaps, where black bitumen or bonded gravel have been used. The gravel will be tracked in on footwear. Why would anyone choose bitumen, you may ask. It can be a very practical choice for a long drive on a steep slope affected by high rainfall, and in a very leafy setting it blends in quite well.

The old central pedestrian path often seen in the tessellated tile patterns of

🌿

LEFT: *Lamb's ears, lavenders and foxgloves combined attractively by Jill Maunsell at Rahui, New Zealand.*

houses built early this century has been superseded by a path joining the drive at a point convenient to visitors alighting from a car. Whether this path is softened by planting along part of its length, or by lawn, it is the starting point of your planting plan.

Another important factor is the view, wanted or unwanted, from the front

🌿

LEFT: *Federation cottages built in Australia early this century often had a central path of tessellated tiles ending in slate steps.*

BELOW: *The same garden seen from the front verandah features honeysuckles,* Felicia *daisies, lavenders and old roses, planted by Mr and Mrs Ng of Sydney.*

door and front windows. Some
immovable objects such as power poles
may be made to disappear with suitable
plantings, but if overhead wires exist,
beware of planting trees beneath them
or the electricity authority will demand
that they be kept pruned. The position
of underground services such as power,
gas, phone, water and sewerage pipes is
crucial in planning a garden and should

❧

ABOVE: *Visitors always appreciate the care and
attention that both plants and cottage receive
from owners Dr and Mrs Doyle of Auckland.*

RIGHT: *This garden features bearded iris, roses
and perennials. Shading the terrace is a* Magnolia
x soulangiana, *the pride of Dagmar and Dennis
Neall of Sydney.*

be recorded by the owner for future reference.

The approach to the front door can be very illuminating in that it will signal to the visitor the personality, tastes and habits of the owner. Remember when planning that your garden can be a mirror image of your tastes. So often people will be extraordinarily fussy about colour schemes and the arrangement of furniture and ornaments indoors, but forget the rules when it comes to their gardens. They wouldn't dream of putting a heavy piece of furniture in the middle of the lounge room, but they will plant a deodar (*Cedrus deodara*) in the middle of the front lawn, completely destroying the available open space.

A sweep of lawn sets off plants in a sunny garden and in small or shady gardens, paving or gravel will provide alternatives for maintaining open space. One might argue that groundcovers and stepping stones could also be employed. Try photographing such a scene and you'll find it can look messy. It can work well in odd corners but not in main areas such as the front garden or front door approach. You also need to remember that visitors at night need safe passage over firm surfaces, and when two or more people are arriving or leaving, the area of paving needs to be adequate, otherwise you'll have them falling into the flowers. It is also important to remember that both

paving bricks and split sandstone paving will become dangerously slippery where moss grows in winter shade, but there are finishes that can be applied to combat this problem.

Suitable lighting along the drive and front path is necessary for night visitors and security. Lights which turn on automatically as the visitor approaches are useful security aids. Crime prevention plans cannot be effective if the front garden is heavily planted. Those who need such plantings to reduce traffic noise should consider

ABOVE: *Heather Cant's free seeding cottage plants (such as cosmos,* Gaura *and* Cynoglossom)*, roses, delphiniums and perennials delighted thousands when the garden was opened for charity.*

installing a security system to guard against burglary.

Plants positioned against the house walls are often referred to as foundation plantings. The height of the windowsill above ground level is a determining factor in selecting what to use, as are the background wall colour and the aspect.

Some low-growing frost-tender subjects that revel in the heat of summer will respond well if planted against a sunny wall; *Otacanthus* 'Little Boy Blue', for instance, is definitely a warmer climate plant. It is worthy of correct placement as it flowers from mid summer to early winter—growing to 80 cm (2 ft 8 in)—and looks great with hybrid penstemons such as 'Garnet' and 'Swan Lake'.

The aspect of some of the windows may be cool and shaded and the choice for adjacent plantings is just as wide as for the hot and sunny positions. A garden bed receiving full sun beside a verandah will not be as dry as one against the house walls with an overhanging eave which shelters it from rain, but the latter will be hotter in summer because of heat reflected off the walls, particularly if they are painted white.

Planting unsuitable shrubs between windows or at the corners of the house walls can result in constant cutting back to let in light or keeping the side path access free of impeding foliage. Preference should be given to plants with a slender upright habit of growth, such as sweet olive (*Osmanthus fragrans*) or *Camellia sasanqua* 'Yuletide', but you should also be prepared to prune the chosen plant to the desired shape and height without making a box or rectangular shape. Both of these look so unnatural.

There are two schools of thought regarding dressing the cottage walls. One is that good architecture should have its clean lines left uncluttered; the other, of English origin, is to use the house walls for climbing roses, honeysuckle or whatever climber appeals to you. I personally feel that it depends on how pretty the cottage is and what the owner's personal tastes are, but there are a few 'don'ts'.

Wisteria can do enormous damage to verandahs, as can creeping fig (*Ficus pumila* 'Minima') and ivy to masonry. The best way to enjoy wisteria is to use it on a pergola and learn the art of pruning it to keep it under control, or else have a standard wisteria, but it, too, must be pruned. The idea of using the ornamental grape along the verandah in a hot climate is good, again provided it is properly pruned in winter. It will keep the house cooler, though somewhat darker, in summer.

I often shudder when a very determined customer wants to train the Climbing Rose 'New Dawn' up a verandah post, for I know it will be an uphill battle to control it. Sometimes, having suggested various roses with more disciplined growth and finding that the advice is falling on deaf ears, I let the customer find out the hard way.

A plant which I refuse to stock but which is often used on verandah posts is *Jasminum polyanthum*. Not only does it affect asthmatics, but it behaves like a weed given half a chance—it can runner while your back is turned and suddenly pop up in the middle of one of your

ABOVE: *Roses 'Heritage' and 'Leander', delphiniums and many other favoured perennials delight visitors to The Roseaire in Auckland.*

treasures. I do grow and love four other jasmines with more controllable growth habits. *Jasminum azoricum* on my front fence in the yellow garden is bountiful of flower and tough in a dry situation. *Jasminum sambac* is a shrub jasmine, highly fragrant and in flower from mid summer to early winter, its white flowers making it a good harmoniser amongst old-fashioned shrub roses. *Jasminum nitidum* from New Guinea is my favourite and though it is a climber

I keep mine as a bun-shaped shrub of 1.5 × 1.5 m (5 × 5 ft) in a very hot, sunny position beside the front verandah. Its sweetly fragrant white blooms are produced for ten months of the year. Finally there is poet's jasmine (*Jasminum officinale*) which is much easier to control on a column or lattice and will flower for six months. Its delicately perfumed white flowers and ferny foliage are so superior to *J. polyanthum*, which only flowers in the spring.

The message is that whatever you choose, be it roses, jasmine, clematis or honeysuckle, be prepared to prune. Those who own timber cottages should try not to cover their walls with roses or climbers because the life of the timber will be significantly reduced. You need to repaint timber regularly, so avoid making problems for the painter. A well-turned and smartly painted verandah post is beautiful in its own right and if you must grow a climber, the open growth of poet's jasmine (*J. officinale*) will allow the timber to dry out after rain.

If your cottage has those lovely iron lace columns supporting the roof of the verandah, choose a very light climber or pillar rose and do not thread it through the lace. Instead, use ties to hold it to the outside so that when the column is due for repainting, the rose can be untied and laid back out of the way. Likewise, keep roses on arches attached by tying them to the outside of the arch. Wayward thorny growth on the inside is a pedestrian hazard and pruning is easier if the growth is all on the outside.

It is wise to be wary of the romantic cottage gardens so often portrayed in decorator magazines. They can be misleading for the gardening beginner in that someone else's mistakes, flowering profusely at the time the photograph was taken, are presented as being worthy of imitation, be it the front verandah festooned with wisteria at its flowering peak, or an 'Albertine' rose racing up to chimney pot level and literally dislodging the roof tiles as it seeks anchorage. What upsets me even more is to see a hanging basket of delicate maidenhair fern, imported just for the day, hanging off the verandah eave exposed to the sun and the wind when it should be hanging in the bathroom or fernery. Inexperienced gardeners may be tempted to try for the same effect, with disastrous results.

SIDE AND REAR GARDENS

Designers of cottages built in the past two decades have in the main avoided side wall windows, except perhaps for the bathroom and laundry, and concentrated on the most important rooms having views to the front or rear gardens. The owners of cottages from the 1930s and earlier frequently have the problem of windows overlooking neighbours' windows. It is usually necessary for one side of the house to be paved to allow passage of items such as lawn mower and wheelbarrow. The side not in use for these purposes frequently becomes a dumping ground for things that are unaffected by weather but need to be hidden from view. Such an area will usually have closed access at the front corner of the house.

Where the shape of the building block is long and narrow, side windows are unavoidable and neighbours will find bedroom or kitchen outlooks screened only by the side fence. The determined gardener will not be content to just live with this problem but will seek solutions to gain privacy.

On page 25 I referred to the use of lattice screen panels above fence height which can, with the consent of your neighbour, support an evergreen climber such as *Solanum jasminoides*, the white-flowered potato vine, or *Trachelospermum jasminoides*, the sweetly fragrant star jasmine. The former flowers for ten months of the year and the latter throughout summer. Pruning will require a joint effort so that wayward growth, of the potato vine in particular, does not get out of hand. If the garden area has been paved right up to the fence, you have two options. One is to jackhammer some of the concrete at the base of the fence to allow for the

that at some stage the painter has to have access to paint the underside of the eaves and, if not pre-coated, the guttering as well.

Sometimes the urge to garden is so strong and the available area is so small that the narrow side garden has to play a vital role, especially in duplex or semi-detached cottages in inner city suburbs. For the vast majority of people, however, it is the rear garden that serves as their private retreat. Many cottages built at the beginning of this century in sought-after locations have undergone internal and external transformations, particularly at the rear. Where formerly there was little or no view of the garden, kitchen-family rooms have been rebuilt with sliding glass or French doors, and the garden is permanently on view. If the new glass openings have a sunny aspect, it is vital to have a pergola with deciduous vine cover or timber slating designed to admit winter sun while reducing summer sun. Part of it may be covered with a translucent material and there are many products now on offer which are aesthetically pleasing.

Paving of the area under the pergola, and perhaps beyond, is necessary as a solid base for outdoor furniture, but if the land slopes steeply at the back of the house, a timber deck or retained terrace

planting of a vine, and the other is to plant the vine in a tub. The second option may have the disadvantage of taking up too much space, and the risk of failure due to haphazard watering and feeding is a consideration.

Without a gate at one end, the side passage is invariably a draughty wind tunnel, particularly on the shady side. If the shady side is paved for access it may be possible to use the house walls on the sunnier side for climbing roses, stephanotis, petrea or mandevilla with stepping stones and groundcovers for maintenance access.

ABOVE: *A garden like this needs to look right in both directions (see photo on page 28).*

Planting to block a view is more difficult in that the choice for narrow spaces is very limited. *Camellia sasanqua, Cotoneaster pannosus* and *Osmanthus fragrans* can be used successfully, but skilled pruning is required to take them up on a single trunk before allowing a small canopy to develop. This same canopy will significantly reduce the amount of light entering the window. Remember, too,

RIGHT: *Ivy Cottage at Anstey in Dorset, garden of Anne and Alan Stevens, features a softly curving double border close to a little brook.*

becomes the favoured spot for alfresco meals. If the back of the house does not receive much winter sun, such an area could be used only in summer, so the owners might also want paving in a part of the garden bathed in winter sunlight. To ensure privacy for outdoor eating areas, screen planting along the side and rear boundary fences becomes a priority. It needs to be evergreen in the main, otherwise privacy is lost each winter. It is still possible to plant some deciduous trees and shrubs, and in fact they will be better offset amongst, or in front of, evergreens.

No other single item makes such an impact on the planning of the rear garden as does the swimming pool—unless it is a tennis court in a very large garden. Tennis courts should have a north–south axis whenever possible and the family pool also needs to be in full sun. Shade on the area means the volume of water takes longer to warm up in spring and cools down more quickly in autumn.

On a flat site a pool will blend in without requiring a change in levels but for the majority of sites the natural slope of the land will involve what is known as cut and fill where on one side of the pool a cut has to be retained and on the other a retaining wall has to be built and then backfilled to ensure a level area around the pool. It is important that the fill be consolidated, or the paving will invariably settle or sink, which is most unsatisfactory. It is probably better to backfill with sand or to pave over reinforced concrete which

will have steel rods tied into the pool bond beam by prior arrangement with the pool builder. In many instances part of the catwalk around the pool can be cantilevered and constructed by the pool builder at the time of pouring the concrete for the pool.

There are many variations of this simplified example of cut and fill, and the way in which a change of levels is handled can greatly improve the usage of an area. On a steep site part of the extended pool surround could be a timber deck beneath which it may be

ABOVE: *Climbing Roses 'Wedding Day' and 'Alberic Barbier' have been used effectively on tennis court walls by Elizabeth Morrow of Auckland.*

LEFT: *Thorny rose bushes and swimmers do not usually mix, but Toni Sylvester, a New Zealand rose expert, has managed it.*

possible to have a fern garden or some brightly coloured semi-tropical plantings, depending on the aspect. (Knowing just where north is seems to be a problem for a large number of people. If you stand facing the sun at noon, east will be on your right and west on your left in the southern hemisphere, and vice versa in the northern hemisphere.)

One area in which the glossy magazines have been a tremendous help is in providing information for the intending pool owner. Looking at examples in photographs makes it easier to decide in advance on such things as the preferred shape, the degree of formality or informality, the choice of paving material, or at least the colour, tiles for the waterline, and safety fencing. Both the pool builder and a landscape designer can also help with these important decisions.

Finding general design answers in gardening magazines is not quite so easy. There is far greater scope for individuality and rarely does a plan or photograph match up with your intentions or aspect. No two sites are ever the same unless they are the back gardens of identical project homes facing in the same direction, and developers are generally too smart to fall into that trap.

One very enlightened developer to whom I am a consultant has created a mini village on a large site by building homes of compatible but varied styles,

without front fences, on curving streets. The gutters are rolled brick, whick looks so much better than the engineer-designed concrete kerbs. The residents are encouraged to preserve the uniform character of the streetscape gardens by using approved plants, although there are occasional plantings which are not in tune but reflect the householders' personal tastes. The rear gardens are all 'do as you please' schemes and the high resale value of these houses is proof in itself that proper planning really pays.

In small rear gardens and courtyards, function often dictates the amount of space left for planting. Owners may wish to have a spa with or without a swimming pool, although in restricted space the spa alone is easier to accommodate. Other more mundane

items such as a clothes-drying area, toolshed and service area must be taken into consideration. Folding clotheslines that can be removed for a party, or pull-out lines that can be retracted, both have the same capacity to cope with the family wash. In very tight spaces, fold-down lines secured to a wall are also useful.

If you wish to make compost in bins or in a tumbler, the area must be located in the sun. Trying to make compost in deep shade is a waste of time and energy as the heat of the sun is needed for the compost to begin its breakdown cycle.

❧

BELOW: *Climber 'Sparrieshoop' has soft pink single blooms; here it is trained over an arbour backed by lattice panels.*

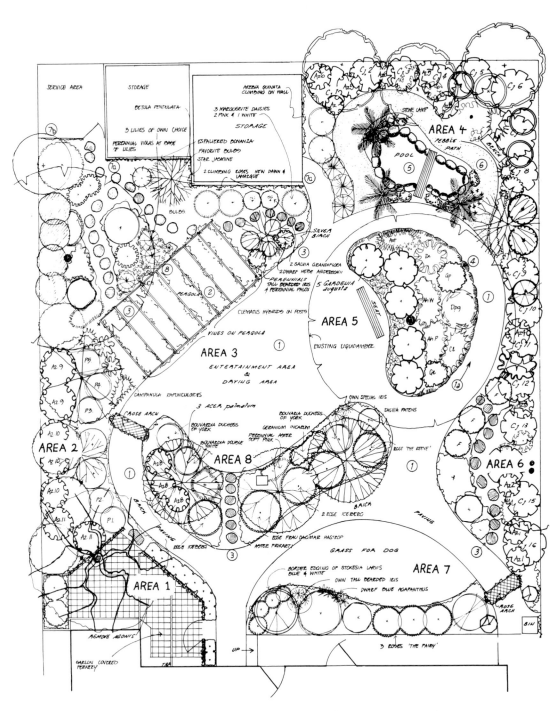

PLANTING DETAILS OF MARY BAKER'S PLAN.

This is the landscaping plan for Mary Baker's garden, described on page 42.

AREA 1. This small paved area is screened from the main garden by a brush fence softened with star jasmine (*Trachelospermum jasminoides*). A clipped *Buxus* hedge follows the line of the path and an existing jacaranda casts shade over shelving for potted plants. *Osmanthus fragrans*, underplanted with violets, was chosen for perfume and privacy. Shade cloth partly covers the area to protect ferns and fuchsias from hot afternoon sun.

AREA 2. A mature mulberry tree on this side of the garden has been underpruned to allow fence-screening evergreen blue and white plumbago, and *Camellia sasanqua* 'Bonanza' and 'Little Pearl' to be planted. The Irish strawberry tree (*Arbutus unedo*) will within a short time provide privacy for the pergola area, as will upright *Camellia sasanqua* 'Jane Morgan' 'Setsugekka' and 'Jennifer Susan' along the fence line. Azaleas, including the sun hardy 'Kalimna Pearl', serve as underplanting. A *Betula pendula* near the path completes the tree cover; at its feet are two *Lavandula dentata*. Perennials found here include *Campanula rapunculoides*, *Sidalcea* and *Felicia*.

AREA 3. A rose arch festooned with 'Sombreuil' and 'Altissimo' leads into the paved entertainment area. Two additional silver birches will soften the outlines of the storage sheds, as will Climbing Roses 'Lamarque' and 'New Dawn'. Marguerite daisies, tall bearded iris, daffodils and perennials such as pale pink *Achillea*, shasta 'Chiffon' and *Salvia involucrata* 'Bethellii' are grouped near *Philadelphus* 'Minnesota Snowflake'. The pergola supports hybrid *Clematis* 'Nelly Moser' and 'William Kennett', *Mandevilla laxa* and *Pandorea jasminoides* 'Rosea'.

AREA 4. Three *Elaeocarpus reticulatus* have been placed along the rear boundary to shade this corner on summer afternoons and protect the *Camellia japonica* and azaleas beneath them. Mary asked for a small ornamental pool in this corner which was to feature tall *Cyathea cooperi* tree ferns, but later she chose weeping maples *Acer dissectum* 'Ever Red' and 'Washimoo' instead. Mondo grass, *Iris kaempferi* and *Gardenia radicans* are a few of the species chosen for edge planting close to the pool. Beneath an existing rhododendron was planted a groundcover mat of *Campanula poscharskyana* in blue, pink and white.

AREA 5. The young liquidambar originally planted on a slope was enhanced by a low stone retaining wall on the lower side, which was then

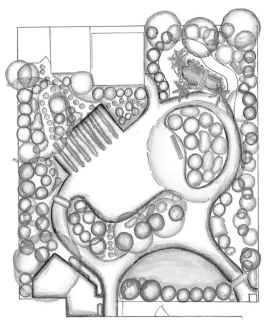

ABOVE: *Green shows evergreen plants and yellow indicates deciduous plants.*

backfilled with enriched planting mix. A spine planting of *Gardenia augusta* provides an evergreen backdrop for a seat, while on the other side a collection of perennials encircles a mass planting of pink and white wind anemones. The perennials include *Astilbe, Rehmannia, Geranium pratense* and *Geranium Macrrohizzam*. Forget-me-nots, heartsease and delphiniums add seasonal colour while pink and blue wood violet (*Viola sylvestris*) occupy space under the gardenias.

AREA 6. A neighbour's invading bamboo is a constant problem on this side. Mary has learnt to pounce using herbicide painted onto the cut stem. An existing *Prunus* and the bamboo provide

shade for her favourite camellias, and in the partial shade cast by the *Prunus* she grows fuchsias and azaleas. Under a newly planted *Malus spectabilis* are fragrant dwarf rhododendrons 'Suave' and 'Princess Alice' and the blue may *Caryopteris* x *clandonensis*.

AREA 7. From a side path one enters here through an arch covered by climbing roses 'Carabella'. *Salvia regia* and *Gaura* are to the right, both blooming for months. To the left *Philadelphus* 'Virginal' is beside the arch and three low-growing roses 'The Fairy' allow an overview of the garden from the kitchen. *Jasminum nitidum, Lonicera periclymenum* and *Salvia leucantha* complete this long flowering, fragrant group.

AREA 8. Mary chose three *Acer palmatum*, including 'Senkaki' and 'Atropurpureum', because she loves their form and foliage. On the sunny side of this group roses 'Chaucer' 'Iceberg' and 'Graham Thomas' give repeat displays together with *Aster frikartii* (which she loves as much as I do), *Geranium incanum, Salvia patens* and *Scabiosa*. The double white and pink *Bouvardia* 'Duchesse of York' have been planted behind the maples and Mary adds her favourite annuals to cover bare spots while her plants are filling out. Mary now wants to transform her front garden into a miniature glade and will have great pleasure in doing it.

In large gardens there will be a constant source of compostable material available for recycling. It therefore pays to think about a location for the service area that can be screened with shrubs or lattice and climbers, without intruding upon your recreational use of the garden.

Rear gardens for young families will centre on the neeeds of growing children. Ideally, there will be lawn space for playing ball games or for a trampoline, and space for the swing and the sand pit, which should have a cover to stop it being fouled by cats. The activities of the children and their pets may or may not prevent the beginnings of your first cottage garden. If cricket and football are played in the rear garden, the starting point for planting could be the front garden. As the children outgrow the various play activities, and the area remains unused, it will become another corner for conversion, and you can begin to make the changes which will suit your own desires.

The plan presented on page 40 was designed for a woman who, while still having responsibilities to grown-up children and holding down a full-time job, adores plants and her hobby of gardening. Her brief was for a rear garden with no lawn, although we compromised on that for the sake of her dog. Her daughter has a horse on agistment and so the tack room at the bottom of the garden and the toolshed

were to remain, as was the young liquidambar that she planted to shade the kitchen windows from the hot afternoon summer sun. There were also a number of newly acquired camellias that needed to be accommodated.

One landscape contractor quoting for the construction only told her it was much too grand for her address. He did not get the job and, as intended, she did all the planting herself. Every time we meet she expresses her delight in what has been achieved in her formerly very ordinary backyard. The pergola has become the pivotal area for outdoor relaxation. In all such schemes, it is the detailing that counts.

ARCHES, PERGOLAS AND GAZEBOS

Pergolas can be used to support a leafy shade cover in a hot aspect, but there are also decorative pergolas that can enhance an access gate, or be used as a support for climbers along paths and driveways. Pergolas attached to the

❧

BELOW: *Mary Baker's newly planted rear garden. See plan page 40.*

a shorter life. Chemically treated timber is readily available. Untreated poles need to be soaked or painted with creosote before being set into the ground in concrete. The risk of termite damage is also ever present.

house or garage are easier to brace than freestanding structures, which must be cross-braced for stability. A centrally located pergola on an otherwise flat site draws the eye and invites inspection of the area beyond as side plantings also guide your steps towards the pergola.

An arch over a path can have a similar effect, drawing you through to explore further. In a sunny location the choice of climbers is much greater than for an arch or pergola in semi-shade. Make sure that you select a vine or climbing rose that is not rampant in its growth. Roses like 'Albertine', 'New Dawn' and 'Mme Alfred Carrière' are far too vigorous for slim arches.

Rustic arches constructed with bark-covered poles will support climbers but if the timber is untreated they will have

ABOVE LEFT: *This pergola is set off-centre in both directions, inviting the visitor to explore Del and Eric Adams' Sydney garden.*

ABOVE RIGHT: *Hybrid* Clematis *'William Kennett' was chosen by Mary Baker and gives her great pleasure.*

cupboards and sink constructed inside a gazebo or cabana will save on the tracking back and forth. There are so many mobile barbecues available that can be wheeled out of sight when not in use.

LEFT: *Climbing Rose 'Mme Grégoire Straechlin' syn. 'Spanish Beauty' flowers only in spring but is featured in the New Zealand garden of Elizabeth and Warren Scott.*

BELOW: *The backdrop for this garden seat contains lime green* Euphorbia palustris, *'Iceberg' roses and white and soft apricot foxgloves.*

The placement of a garden seat also requires forethought. If it is heavy in construction, it may suit you to leave it permanently under a shade tree. When positioning the seat remember that although it may become a focal point itself, it should also enable the occupant to enjoy a particular view within your garden. Fortunate indeed is the gardener who can place a seat or setting to enjoy a wide landscape view.

Outdoor dining furniture is best located close to the kitchen. I am always critical of the heavy masonry built-in barbecue being constructed at the bottom of the garden, or otherwise at the furthest possible distance from the source of food. If the bottom of the garden has some special delight, then

The siting of a gazebo is affected by three factors: its intended use, the direction of the worst winds, and its decorative effect as a focal point in the landscape. The smaller the structure, the fewer people it will accommodate, but remember that in a small garden a large gazebo will be out of scale. If it is to serve as a shelter near a swimming pool or tennis court, the number of people it can hold is critical. Alternatively, if it is to be a haven to go to with a cup of tea and the newspaper, or a picnic lunch for two, its smallness does not matter. What will be important for year-round usage is that it turns its back on cold winds.

ABOVE LEFT: *An unusual half beehive shaped gazebo with lattice wing walls for climbers averts cool breezes, as well as terminating a vista.*

ABOVE RIGHT: *Kay and Brian Jacobs' gazebo is reminiscent of a Maori meeting hut. Kay has chosen white 'Sparrieshoop' roses to adorn it.*

CHAPTER 5

Inspiration

Although children may show no desire to have a garden plot of their own, they will subconsciously absorb their garden surroundings. At the age of three and a half I spent some eight weeks with my grandmother in the summer–autumn period. Though not knowing the names of her flowers then, years later I came to realise that she grew plants like Shasta daisies, gaillardias and Michaelmas daisies (also called perennial asters). Outside the breakfast room windows was a large frangipani bush with coralbells (*Heuchera sanguinia*) at its feet. I loved the fragrance of the white blooms with their yellow-gold throats, and I was allowed to gather the fallen flowers and place them in a green glazed float bowl. As a bride, many years later, I carried a bouquet of frangipani.

The first cottage garden that fascinated me as a child belonged to an elderly couple whose front garden I enjoyed on my route to and from school. The drive was straight and direct on the right side of the block and led past the entry door, located at the side of the house, to a garage at the rear. The rectangular space in front of the small cottage was perimeter planted and also contained a central circular bed which featured roses and tall delphiniums. There were small diamond-shaped beds in the four corners and the lawn had

LEFT: *A tubbed cumquat sits on the manhole cover of the well which is under the herb garden made colourful by nasturtiums.*

BELOW: *Colonial Cottage as purchased in February 1983.*

been reduced to grass paths giving access to the flowerbeds.

The display of pansies, primulas, love-in-a-mist (*Nigella damascena*), forget-me-nots, stocks, poppies and sweet william (*Dianthus barbatus*) in spring gave way to roses, lilies and larkspurs and there was always something to enjoy looking at over the low front fence. The winter–spring annuals carried the bare roses; this gem of a garden was the highlight of a long dusty journey between school and our farm gate.

The farm garden was a mixed bag. Down the drive there was Christmas bush (*Ceratopetalum gummiferum*), which was sold as a cut flower in early summer. Probably the part I liked best was the fernery covered with the fragrant white vine *Mandevilla laxa*, and, in the small home orchard the heady perfume of citrus blossom was always a joy in spring.

As young postwar marrieds my husband and I were fortunate in having a landlady who allowed us a small plot at the bottom of her garden to try our luck with flowers and salad vegetables— and for a bit of fun we grew loofahs on the back fence. Thirteen years were to pass before we built our first home and I drove my young husband mad by buying trees and shrubs the minute we had purchased the land. For 23 years we lived in a suburb not renowned for its trees, but we left it the richer when we moved to Dural (an outer suburb of Sydney) in

1983. Dural is a semi-rural district on the north-western outskirts of Sydney's ever-spreading metropolis. I had left the district as a bride and was happy to be back, although many of its orchards and paddocks have disappeared under housing.

The old stone and timber farmhouse was in a very poor state of repair. In front of it was a buffalo grass lawn, to its right a small sheep paddock and on its left a jungle of horticultural rubbish within which we found a few bonuses. Nine months passed before we could move in, but work proceeded—starting with a new roof. A new kitchen, bathroom and laundry were high on the priority list: I reasoned that if we could cook and wash while the house was being gutted, we could cope. True to form I had trees and shrubs begging to be planted, for this time it was to be a cottage garden with a purpose.

Soon after moving into our first home, my husband and I had discussed what we might do in retirement and we opted for a small nursery. I enrolled at the Ryde School of Horticulture in 1970 and there followed seven years of part-time study, as I had a young family to care for as well.

RIGHT: *A very pleasing combination is the iris 'Mandolin' against a froth of* Euphorbia palustris—*carrying as many as ten spikes, it is a strong focal point in the overall scene.*

On our first visit to England in 1977 we visited the garden of the late Margery Fish, whose cottage garden was legendary, and in 1979 we spent a month looking at the great gardens of England and Scotland. We later made a return visit to Margery Fish's East Lambrook Manor, this time finding that there was a small nursery at the rear selling plants which were characteristic of her garden. We decided this was the concept that we should try to emulate. Finding the cottage to fit the image of the business in a suitable location took a while and, when we did, it was in such a terrible state that there was nearly a divorce.

ABOVE: *The gates of Colonial Cottage opened in August 1986 to a young garden softening the remodelled cottage.*

LEFT: *East Lambrook Manor, Somerset, as planted by the late Margery Fish.*

When our development application went to the local council for approval, the young engineer inspecting our proposal complimented me on the landscape plan but clearly the officer in the Health and Building Department had no such appreciation, nor did he connect the applicant's name with the name and qualifications on the plan's title block. It came back with a 'How To Plant A Tree' diagram attached and, among other requests, we were asked to use 75 mm (3 in) of pine bark mulch on all garden beds. That would have been death to many of the perennials and groundcovers that I desired to plant, because pine bark is acidic. It releases its resinous chemicals over a long break-down period and groundcover plants which make roots on the surface of the soil cannot make those roots when pine bark separates them from the soil.

At first I worked only in those areas where I knew there would be no tradesmen's trucks or activities, for I had seen first-hand for many years how careless many of them are of the value of existing plants and trees. The two safer areas were what is now the yellow garden, formerly in the sheep paddock, and the top or eastern section.

The kikuyu grass existing in the paddock was poisoned and I began to hand dig the soil. This astonished my Italian vegetable growing neighbour, who wanted to help me by using his cultivator on it. I declined his generous offer as I wanted to get all of the roots and not have them chopped up into small starter pieces which I might have missed with the herbicide, as it was winter and chemicals are not so effective then. I did a small area at a time and changed my occupation when I felt tired, which is a good rule to follow for all active and would-be gardeners.

A local rose grower driving past thought I had planted tropical fruits

when I put hessian shade covers over the *Camellia japonica* that went into the ground from containers in that spring of 1983. He assumed I was covering them against the possibility of a late frost, but in truth I knew there was not enough shade and that, having come from a shade house, their foliage would burn. *Hymenosporum flavem*, the native frangipani, is a tree of the Australian rainforests and is a fast grower with a naturally upright habit. These were planted for quick shade. One that forked at around 1.2 m (4 ft) has proved to be the best in shape and appearance. In hindsight, I now wish I had used *Elaeocarpus reticulatus*, the native blueberry ash, instead. The blueberry ash has a better shape in maturity than the beanpole-like *Hymenosporum*.

The bones of all good gardens are the trees and shrubs, for they provide the structure to carry the garden, especially in winter. Because trees in particular take some years to establish, they take priority in the first plantings.

I had been a member of the Foundation Branch of the Australian Camellia Research Society for over 20 years and knew the value both of *Camellia sasanqua* and *Camellia japonica*, the latter carrying interest in

BELOW: *Pink and blue* Aquilegia vulgaris *and* Geranium canariensis *beside steps leading to the camellia plantings.*

RIGHT: *The smooth sculptured trunks of the crepe myrtle are nature's poetry.*

the garden in winter when cottage garden flowers are not so plentiful. I had some favourites that I brought with me, but these days I am drawn to the small-flowered fragrant species like *C. lutchuensis* and hybrids like 'Scentuous', 'Scented Gem' and the non-fragrant 'Tiny Princess', because they best suit cottage gardens.

Camellia vernalis 'Star Above Star', a species similar to *C. sasanqua*, is another that I have planted for its unusual hose-in-hose type flowers. The flowers, produced from mid autumn to early spring, can also be informal and are white shading to lavender pink. This species' upright habit of growth makes it a good boundary screening shrub.

Among the bonuses we found, apart from an oak tree, was a mature deep rosy red crepe myrtle, a macadamia nut tree—these three comprise a triangular arrangement or group planting—an old rose bush that was later identified as 'Old Blush' or 'Parsons Pink China', and some interesting bulbs. The three trees form the basis of the shady garden and although I may not have chosen the crepe myrtle's colour, the tree itself is handsome indeed. Fortunately, it had only been pruned once in its life, at a height of 1.2 m (4 ft). Although some people prune to achieve bigger and better blooms, we love this small tree for its sculptural shape—its beautiful smooth-barked multi-trunks arising from a common base have arranged

themselves so artistically as to ensure admiration in all seasons.

Close to the rear of the house in the eastern side garden was an old well, cut out of shale, which leaked at the half-full mark. We decided to make it into an underground water tank but first it had to be emptied. After pumping it out we were greeted with the depressing sight of years of accumulated junk. It took my husband George three days of trekking up and down the ladder to clean it out. A pool engineer friend took over and it was steeled up and gunned like a swimming pool. It measures 3 m (10 ft) × 3 m (10 ft) × 3 m (10 ft) and later George and his good mate Frank poured the

concrete lid. The well receives roof water via a pipe hidden in a vine-covered arch as well as recycled nursery water which is pumped into it; this water is used to irrigate the display garden. The well lid is covered with 23 cm (9 in) of soil and is part of the herb garden.

The first old-fashioned roses to be planted in the garden were 'Duchesse de Brabant', 'Autumn Delight', 'Penelope', 'Ballerina', 'Crepuscule' and 'Old Blush', which was given pride of place because

❧

BELOW: *'The Yeoman' is a floriferous small Bush Rose with a wonderful myrrh fragrance.*

it was a survivor. When we extracted it from the roots of a now-removed coral tree, it broke in two, with very little root on each piece. Both halves grew and are now planted side by side. 'Old Blush' flowers non-stop from mid spring to mid winter. It has to be pruned while still flowering.

When I planted it in front of the front verandah, I did not know that 'Crepuscule' could also be trained as a climber. Its coppery yellow blooms are much admired, but because of its very vigorous growth, it requires heavy pruning in winter. Most grow it as a climber.

Also among the roses we brought with us in containers in 1983 were David Austin's 'The Prioress' and 'The Yeoman', and these two were enough to make me fall in love with his newly bred, old-fashioned looking English shrub roses. Of the 120 different old-fashioned roses our nursery offers for sale, a quarter are now Austin roses, so lovely and diverse are they both in bloom and growth habit.

I did not set out to have a rose-filled garden, originally planning to have fragrant shrubs mixed with perennials and some roses. Now I am struggling to keep the balance of the original concept, which was to demonstrate by example how to place and grow cottage garden plants, because I must also accommodate new roses or phase out some of the earlier plantings. The

regular customers who stroll in the garden are quick to ask why I took out a particular rose. In the case of 'The Knight' I truthfully answer that it was too prone to black spot.

Work on the restoration of the house took up most of 1984, and stone that

ABOVE: *Sun loving spillover perennials above a newly planted scree garden.*

was removed from the internal walls of the house because of rising damp was recycled to form retaining walls in the garden. We know that the middle two rooms were built of field stone, possibly in the 1880s for a tenant farmer. The two front rooms were added in 1903 in block stone quarried on the farm, which then covered 12.5 hectares (31 acres). The stone used for the garden walls was thus a mixture of field and block stone. I showed the stonemason a photograph of the chimney of Edna Walling's Lynton Lee, saying that was how I wanted the walls to look, and he did his best with the stones he had to hand.

Development of the site continued through 1985 until August 1986, George having retired at the end of 1985, when we opened the gates of our nursery. In the years since, we have continued a planting program that emphasises colour harmony.

Each part of the garden plays its part in the seasonal displays. I was asked by Cheryl Maddocks, well-known garden author, as she was photographing 'The Yeoman', 'Do you have a favourite part of the garden?' I love it all but I particularly enjoy certain scenes at different times of the year.

The area made shady by the oak, crepe myrtle and macadamia nut has its rewards with fragrant white azaleas 'Morti', white helleborus and 'Green Goddess' lilies that look great as the oak unfurls its soft apple green leaves, and in autumn the massed white wind anemones draw admiration. In spring the area is carpeted with blue and white

forget-me-nots above which many old-fashioned granny's bonnets (*Aquilegia vulgaris*) in pretty colours display their charm. In summer the 'Lacecap' and species hydrangeas make their contribution, and in winter white camellias 'Nuccio's Gem' and 'Margarete Hertrich' bloom profusely. The soft spring growth of dissectum maples takes

ABOVE: *A spring scene of blue forget-me-nots and purple* Campanula rapunculoides *silhouetted against white feverfew.*

the eye as the camellias, now quite tall on the east boundary, finish blooming. This area has become a little glade with an ambience that is very pleasing.

CHAPTER 6

Colour and Harmony

The artist selects his or her subject and the medium with which to express it. Skill with the brush or palette knife comes only with training and practice. There are few 'naturals' in the art world. The buyer of a painting will be happy to hang it and continue to enjoy its special qualities year after year. No matter what the subject, the artist's ability to use colour in its many hues, tones and tints, its light and shade, all contribute to the viewer's pleasure.

Like the painter, the embroiderer and the patchwork quilter select coloured silks or fabrics with the common goal of creating a petit point tapestry or quilt that will not only be artistically pleasing but perhaps become a family heirloom. Once completed, the picture, the tapestry and the quilt all have fixed qualities and measurements, but the creative gardener must work with plants which grow and change their dimensions seasonally and/or year by year.

Many young gardeners starting with a bare block bemoan the lack of shade and are quick to plant wide-spreading or tall trees. However, such trees will alter the growing conditions in the garden by reducing the amount and duration of sunlight reaching the plants under the trees' canopies. A full sun situation can change to half-day shade in less than five years, depending on the species of trees chosen. Part of the challenge of gardening is to create compositions which are pleasing to the eye, with elements relating harmoniously to one another, and suitable for the purpose for which they have been chosen.

Colour appreciation is individually expressed in the clothes we choose and the schemes devised for each room within our homes. Some like flamboyance, others are subdued in their taste. A gardener who has had to endure hot dry summers and frosty winters, and who then moves to a climate where lush green foliage is abundant, may create a purely green garden that is appreciated and enjoyed to the full. On the other hand, such a garden may be enlivened with the rich colour of bougainvilleas, jacaranda blossom or Hawaiian hibiscus.

The use of strong or subtle colours and their effect upon us can be explored by visiting a public rose garden. You will automatically be drawn to the colours you are comfortable with and turn away from those you find unappealing. Some of the breeders of modern hybrid tea roses seem to delight in gaudiness and would do well to emulate the skills of David Austin, whose roses are, in most instances, so

ABOVE: *A scene in our yellow garden.*

easy to blend into desired colour schemes.

As with interior design, there has to be a starting point for the plan you have in mind. In the home it may be a carpet colour that cannot be changed and therefore has to be complemented, subdued or enhanced. In an established garden, a yellow flowering background shrub that cannot easily be removed may look best with a blue and white middle ground and foreground pattern of planting, or perhaps a lemon, cream and white scheme with a touch of orange as an accent.

The month or months in which that yellow shrub blooms will also influence your complementary seasonal show and by careful choice the effect can be sustained for longer, perhaps by the addition of *Hemerocallis* species. The new hybrid daylilies flower in late spring, summer, and repeat in autumn and come in a very wide range of colours from very soft pastels through creamy lemon, yellow, deep golds, apricot, peach, melon, orange with brown tones and very deep red. There is not a pure white yet. White is, of course, a colour that is so effective as a harmoniser, which perhaps explains why the 'Iceberg' rose is so popular as a shrub, whether standard or climber. White flowers are a must in the shady garden to lighten up otherwise dark areas. Roses will not grow in shade but plants such as white azaleas, foxgloves, and

ABOVE: *Gordon Collier planted this white and silver garden bounded by a hedge of wall germander, to be in perfect harmony with the view of snow-capped Mt Ruapehu, often hidden by cloud.*

LEFT: *The view from Gordon Collier's white and silver garden.*

❧

wind anemones (*Anemone hupehensis*) enjoy semi-shade.

Such schemes benefit from the addition of pale pink, cream, pale blue and soft mauve. *Plectranthus argentatus*, with its silver grey foliage, adds another dimension in the semi-shaded garden, but the vast majority of silver foliaged

plants require full sun and they are great harmonisers.

In the garden of Mr and Mrs Gordon Collier of Taihape, New Zealand, a silver grey and white garden has been planted in front of their cottage, which is sited on a knoll facing north-east. A clipped hedge of wall germander (*Teucrium fruticans*) encloses the little garden but gives no hint of the sharply sloping hillside below. Gordon Collier, who has a Diploma of Horticulture, says the soil depth here is little more than

15 cm (6 in), but the silver pear (*Pyrus salicifolia*) that stands in the small lawn has obviously sent its roots down amongst the hidden rocks. It is underpruned so that when one sits on the verandah the view is only slightly interrupted. A curtain valance of white wisteria drips from the eave of the front verandah and Gordon understands well how to control its vigorous growth with regular pruning. This garden is in perfect harmony with the distant snow-capped Mt Ruapehu.

ABOVE: *At Cobham Court, Kent, Lois Wigham has perfected her colour schemes using white, blue and grey between pink and yellow.*

The colour of your house walls, be they brick, stone, timber or painted masonry, must be taken into account in choosing plants for foundation plantings. The hardest colour I have ever had to work with for a client was a mustard gold, which immediately ruled out pink flowers.

The yellow garden at our home, Colonial Cottage, was planted to encourage gardeners to use yellow flowers, which to my eyes are always so cheerful, particularly in late autumn. The yellow garden is a blend of white, cream, lemon, gold, blue and silver, with some unusual colour contrasts provided by daylily hybrids. My one basic rule is that there should be no pink-flowering plants in the yellow garden and no yellow flowers in the pink sections, but there are many who can and do happily mix pink and yellow in their borders, though rarely side by side.

Pink covers an enormous range of hues, tones and tints, as one soon discovers when looking at massed azaleas. The easiest way to divide pink azalea colours is to look for blue or orange tints in the flowers. Blue will give rise to lavender pink while the orange content is responsible for the many shades of salmon pink. These two groups are best separated by white, which is termed neutral. Some very vibrant azaleas and rhododendrons need softening with white or pale colours used nearby. In any chosen scheme you can interrupt a theme with white flowers to progress into a different colour combination, as Dallis Sturtivant of Palmerston North, New Zealand, has demonstrated (in her garden shown below), changing from pink at one end to yellow at the far end. In the foreground grey garden, the cardoon or globe artichoke (*Cynara scolymus*) makes a wonderful textural contrast.

The colour preferences of our nursery customers making colour coordinated gardens are as follows: pink in its many shades, white, blue, cream, apricot, mauve, lavender, silver grey, purple, lemon, yellow and gold, with red and

LEFT: *Dallis Sturtevant of New Zealand demonstrates how to use colour effectively with the placement of this globe artichoke.*

ABOVE: *Here, a purple leafed* Leptospermum × coppersheen *matches the wall colour. Kay Jacobs has used white extensively in her garden.*

RIGHT: *The blue flowering* Isotoma fluviatilis *grows as lawn in front of the teak garden seat.*

ABOVE: Erigeron, *violas and dianthus are used beside steps leading to the main lawn in Kay Jacobs' garden.*

orange being the least popular colours. Many young women begin with a pink and white theme with which they feel comfortable, whether or not it is the current fashion.

That is how Kay Jacobs of Auckland, New Zealand, began, but she now happily mixes blues, mauves and soft lemon with the basic pink and white. However, Kay still avoids very strong colours in the many delightful areas of her very interesting split-level garden. She retained the foundation plantings and, with a cut and fill operation, gained enough level space on a steep site to lay a long narrow lawn, the focal point of which is a gazebo in the style of a Maori meeting hut.

Her use of brick paving, timber decking, planters, steps and retaining walls of treated logs may be modern in concept but the flowers Kay Jacobs prefers are the old-fashioned cottage garden types such as clove pinks, properly called dianthus. In a damp area she has used a blue flowering *Isotoma fluviatilis* as a substitute for lawn near stepping stones.

Kay had the help of Mike Fife, a landscape designer, with the construction of the four sections of her garden which comprise the front entry; the kwila wood deck and blue lawn; the main lawn and wooded area below it; and the area behind the gazebo. However, Kay has done all the planting herself. The wooded area is a backdrop of closely planted trees, mostly native, for quick screening.

Kay has been very selective for the background encircling the blue lawn, planting white *Camellia sasanqua* 'Moonlight', white Judas tree (*Cercis siliquastrum*), white crepe myrtle (*Lagerstroemia indica*), and *Malus* 'Rosea Plena' with its rosebud-like pale pink flowers, among others. Her colour schemes are always soft with just a touch of cyclamen in the penstemons

ABOVE: *Cyclamen penstemons are in harmony with neighbouring perennials. The background rose is 'Pearl Drift'.*

LEFT: *The touch of red comes from Miniature Rose 'Born Free' with* Heliopsis *'Light of Lodden' beyond.*

❧

used to accent the pinks and blues, and her flowers are also selected for use in decorative arrangements. Roses such as 'Tiffany' and 'Royal Highness' are grown for this purpose but it was her rose 'Pearl Drift' that had me enchanted, profuse in its pearl pink blooms and with such healthy foliage.

Always thoughtful in the placement of small treasures and ardent in the use of spillover plants to soften retaining walls, Kay has become expert at orchestrating her 'pictures', particularly for open days in spring.

Red flowers, like the azaleas, can be divided into two basic groups: those with a hint of blue are often described as cyclamen or magenta, and those with an orange tint give us scarlet. Cyclamen red flowers highlight beautifully lavender pink, blue and white schemes. The less popular orange–red found in daylilies and nasturtiums lifts a yellow garden.

Male gardeners are more likely to use vivid red and seem to prefer roses such as Mr Lincoln or Altissimo. In Alistair

boundary shrubs but it has become a leafy protected environment in which many alfresco meals are served, and in which beauty abounds.

Dell loves subtle schemes and perfumed flowers and enjoys trying new introductions. The garden is shaded both by neighbouring trees and by those planted in the past 15 years, most of which are deciduous. A *Metasequoia glyptostroboides* beside Eric's garden studio is now 13 m (43 ft) tall and a *Magnolia* × *soulangiana* 'Lennei' has become a lovely spreading small tree. White flowers are very desirable in a shaded garden and Dell has planted *Viburnum macrocephelum, V. juddii, V. plicatum* 'Lanarth' and *V.* × *burkwoodii* along with white cherries, white datura

Neill's garden near Christchurch, New Zealand, a deep red pillar rose was sharing its pole with the pure white large-flowered hybrid *Clematis* 'Marie Boisselot' (syn. 'Mme le Coultre') and both look wonderful in each other's company. In my garden the snowball bush (*Viburnum opulus* 'Sterile') and the Austin rose 'Redcoat' are a happy combination.

Occasionally a true deep red will be produced as demonstrated by the poppies in the garden of Dell Adam of Sydney. They were sown in the belief that they would flower pink, and what a tremendous contrast they have created in this otherwise softly blended scene.

ABOVE: *These red poppies were meant to be pink; however, they have created a strong accent in a softly blended scene.*

RIGHT: Viburnum opulus *'Sterile' and rose* 'Redcoat' *with* Euphorbia palustris *provides a pleasing effect.*

❧

Dell and Eric Adam have made five gardens over the years and have perfected their skills to the point where gardening is pure pleasure. Eric assists with any heavy tasks; he enjoys spreading home-made compost as mulch and generally cleaning up, particularly in autumn. At the time of purchase the rear garden consisted of lawn and a few

and a pendulous *Leptospurmum flavescens* 'Cardwell'. However, it is the multitude of small plants, generously planted, which completely hide the compost mulch. Actively involved in a number of garden clubs and groups, Del seeks both information and new ideas. Eric is accustomed to the many changes as Dell plays horticultural draughts; he enjoys the benefits as he passes under the pergola to the studio.

A collection of abutilons grows happily in part shade and is augmented by begonias, helleborus and hostas. Sunny areas are not abundant in this garden and are therefore prized. Tall bearded iris coincide with the spring

❦

RIGHT: *The rose 'Tamora' is complemented here by a tall bearded iris called 'Coral Beads'.*

BELOW: *Yellow nasturtium 'Alaska' below a white arum lily, chosen by Dell Adam for its long flowering period.*

flowering of roses and I have been delighted with the combination of the rose 'Tamora' and the iris 'Coral Beads'. Another iris which is perfect with 'Tamora' is a pale apricot called 'Peach Tree'. Dell is not afraid of using yellow either, as seen in the composition of foliage and flowers close to the house. Beside the patio a white arum lily (*Zantedeschia aetheopica*) holds court above lemon and gold nasturtiums, and beyond them a lemon Louisiana iris thrusts its sword-like leaves upwards, as do the hemerocallis which will open in early summer. Such close plantings discourage weeds. The photo on page 3 shows this scene from the opposite direction.

Beauty is said to be in the eye of the beholder, and what charms and delights one gardener may not please another. For example, all-white gardens are seen as a challenge, or boring, according to individual taste. One of the most delightful suburban gardens I have ever visited has been created by Joan Innes of Christchurch, New Zealand, on a very flat site, although this is not apparent because of the compartmentalising of the various 'rooms' by clever divisional planting. Roses are her passion and they have been employed in a gentle blending of formal and informal treatments in the overall layout, either on arches, or as shrubs with complementary plantings.

New vistas open with every corner turned. A small central rectangular lawn below the steps leading down from the small rear verandah features a matching pair of white hybrid musk roses ('Prosperity') in each of the far corners that are connected by white waisted balustrading. Four clipped box (*Buxus*) domes add a formal touch. A path to the left leads into the white garden, which is reminiscent of the central arbour at Sissinghurst, but here the white rose is 'Lamarque', which repeats very generously. A neat low hedge cum edging of clipped box again pre-empts

☘

LEFT: Laburnum *'vossii' covers an arch in a country garden. Close by are lamb's ears and white and red valerian.*

formality. A path running parallel to the balustrading at the rear leads the visitor across the site to another series of vistas punctuated by three rose arches. Every plant has been chosen with the utmost care to blend with its neighbour and to contribute to the overall beauty.

Herbaceous borders in Australia are a rarity and are only occasionally encountered in New Zealand because of the maintenance required in climates

RIGHT: *A grass path leads the visitor to the white garden where rose 'Lamarque' covers an arbour.*

BELOW: *A rose arch frames part of this formal lawn area designed by Joan Innes.* Allium christophii *and pink delphiniums are at left.*

warmer than England. The most famous herbaceous border in England is located at Jenkyn Place where the use of blooming periods is impeccable. With 40 years of experience behind her, it is little wonder that Mrs Gerald Coke has its content and presentation down to a fine art. However, you do not have to have such a large space or a high clipped yew hedge as background as is used at Jenkyn Place. Such perfection can be emulated with your own garden in an informal manner and in limited areas of space. Many gardeners are mixing shrub roses and perennials informally and gaining great pleasure from the results.

Probably the most important rule for

because the lavender pink rose has a definite blue tint in its petals.

While the herbaceous border is but one part of a very large garden, her meticulous attention to detail led Marion Morris of Auckland to create beauty on a much smaller scale. Picture a free-standing two storey house with but 4–6 m (13–20 ft) of space from house walls to fences on three sides.

LEFT: *China Rose 'Old Blush' with the tall bearded iris 'Flair'.*

BELOW: *Jill Mussett of Sydney has surrounded rose 'The Reeve' with grey* Helichrysum petiolatum, Verbena *'Candy stripe', and* Chrysanthemum pallidosum.

RIGHT: *The beautifully orchestrated herbaceous border composed by Patricia Coke.*

those who seriously wish to have a colour coordinated garden is to resist the temptation of finding a spot for all the gift plants and impulse buys. The placement of bits and pieces, as I call them, can result in a garden which has no cohesion, and this is most evident in the garden of the person who has to have one of everything.

In my own garden the greatest satisfaction comes from placing contrasting and complementary colours together, always keeping in mind the timing of the blooming period. The soft blue iris 'Flair' complements the rose 'Old Blush'

Each of these areas has been cleverly designed by Marion Morris to lead from the hornbeam tunnel entry pictured on page 16, to flow on to the next ending with the charming gazebo pictured on page 45.

Marion, a part-time physiotherapist, also designs gardens and knew exactly what to do with her tiny garden. She began by keeping an old persimmon tree through which she allows the Climbing Rose 'Wedding Day' to partly ramble; the rose is firmly controlled on the wall above the french doors opening into a mainly green and white garden.

Marion Morris' colour co-ordination skills are very evident as one enters

ABOVE: *A rose arch designed to support two Climbing Roses 'Kathleen Harrop' in the former garden of Marion Morris.*

LEFT: *Steps lead from a sunny garden to the lawn below. Rose 'Golden Showers' forms a backdrop to the metal seat.*

through the clipped hornbeam tunnel into the sunny and predominantly yellow, white, blue and grey garden. Roses featured here are 'Graham Thomas', 'Buff Beauty' and 'Alchemist'. 'Crepuscule' is trained over an arch in which a small statue is featured.

Stone steps lead down to a small scrap of immaculate lawn. A low clipped box hedge edges a free-flowing curved bed

under the persimmon, containing shade
loving perennials. Beyond, one steps on
to a small timber deck which in turn
steps down to the third garden, shaded
by a silver birch and an *Acer palmatum*
'Atropurpureum'. In their shade is a fine
collection of handsome hostas and in the
sunnier areas many roses beg attention,
including 'Sparrieshoop', 'Balmain

Rambler' and 'Penelope', trained against
a grey wall under the windows. The hoop
arch was specially made and will support
two 'Kathleen Harrop' roses. As this arch
is approached the gazebo comes into full
view; it has been back planted with a
Michelia doltsopa and a white *Magnolia
campbellii*. 'Lucetta', an Austin rose of
soft apricot pink, has been planted

ABOVE: *Yellow snapdragons, blue* Cynoglossom,
*lamb's ears, white alyssum and violas make a
pretty picture beside this path.*

against the left lattice wing leading into
the gazebo. This charming little town
garden excels in its reverse direction
views, a tribute to Marion's skills. But

LEFT: *Suzanne Turley of Auckland used cream mignonette and Queen Anne's lace to soften the rose 'Monsieur Tillier'.*

realise that ten years ago there was no tree or shrub to be seen, except privet. After transforming the house internally and adding the verandahs, Suzanne began by planting trees which included *Prunus* species, *Magnolia denudata* (now renamed *M. heptapeta*) and a golden elm pictured on page 76. She has very firm ideas on the importance of permanent background plantings because, as she says, 'it's easy to change internal schemes, but not the trees.' Experience in handling fabrics has provided the basis for her unerring judgement in the use of colour. One of the most breathtaking sights is the rose 'Albertine' in full bloom, a mantle of salmon pink covering the carport roof. 'Albertine' flowers only in spring and must be hard pruned to achieve such a floriferous display. Nearby are 'Mutabilis' and 'Penelope', both harmonising well with 'Albertine'. Another strongly coloured rose is 'Monsieur Tillier', best described as a salmon-strawberry blend. Suzanne placed it to the right of the front steps but has softened it with tall cream mignonette and Queen Anne's lace. Lining both sides of the pedestrian path to the front steps is a hedge of *Lavandula dentata*, valued for its nine

like many a gardener, Marion hankers for a garden with a stream, and she is looking for such a garden in Christchurch.

Suzanne Turley of Auckland, a clothing designer, is also a passionate gardener and deserving of the accolades accorded to a master gardener. Her garden, located close to the harbour, is a masterpiece of colour co-ordination.

Panels of white painted wooden pickets set between tall brick pillars are festooned with the blue-purple flowering rose 'Veilchenblau', a spectacular sight greeting visitors and passersby alike. Once inside the high gates one is faced with one visual delight after another. The garden extends into a triangular area beyond the drive which adds spaciousness to the layout. It is hard to

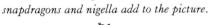

beautifully with the rich dark green background of camellia foliage.

Perfume comes from *Philadelphus* and the numerous Austin roses which are Suzanne Turley's favourites: 'Abraham Darby', 'Chaucer' and 'Mary Rose', to name a few. Full plantings of cottage garden annuals and perennials surround the roses, with spikes of foxgloves and delphiniums accenting the softly rounded shapes.

Of course this kind of growth is not achieved in poor soil. A programme of liquid feeding is necessary, but for new gardens the preparation involves the addition of compost, sheep pellets, pumice and coarse sand to provide a rich tilth for planting into.

Suzanne makes no secret of the fact that she keeps a garden diary entered from a finger-marked scrapbook muddied by her labours. The diary is invaluable because busy people do not always remember just what they did last year, and such information is so important in the timing of 'pictures'.

What matters most is the basic framework or background with which you are working, be it evergreen shrubs or a dividing fence covered with a vine or climbing rose. Working with layers of foliage is the subject of the next chapter.

month flowering period. It is a better choice than English lavender for Auckland's humid summers.

Space is restricted behind the cottage by a steeply rising hill which necessitated a log retaining wall of 1.2 m (4 ft) being built to obtain a small paved area close to the kitchen. Here we see terracotta pots of herbs, tubbed citrus and a bay tree, all enlivened with yellow violas. Variegated hostas, lady's mantle (*Alchemilla mollis*), and feverfew daisies add their contribution, later to be augmented by tubbed white hydrangeas, making this a cool retreat on a summer's afternoon. The cream and lime green theme is repeated under the golden elm with the help of *Euphorbia palustris* and white and yellow aquilegias.

The verandah posts are festooned with old-fashioned roses and wisteria. These frame views into the garden, which takes on a magical luminosity in the twilight because there are so many white flowers included in the plantings around the side lawn, contrasting

CHAPTER 7

Trees and Basic Structure

It takes less than two decades for a treeless new suburb to become a leafy one with the co-operation of the residents. In individual gardens, harsh sunshine can quickly change to dappled or deep shade depending on the concentration of dense canopies of foliage.

Every good garden is composed of six layers of foliage. The trees form the uppermost layer, followed by tall, medium and small shrubs. The fifth layer is for perennials and bulbs and the sixth the groundcovers and/or grass. When all six are used with an artist's eye for colour as well as an appreciation of scale, form and texture, the result will be a garden which is challenging for its owners and a pleasure to sit or stroll in.

SCALE

Scale may be a term not fully understood by many who choose to make a garden and who also fall victim to impulse buying. It is senseless to plant the tree of your choice or a giveaway tree if it is going to grow so rapidly and broadly as to dwarf the house or take up half the available space. Plane trees (*Platanus* × *hybrida*), liquidambars and camphor laurels can and do become too large for medium and small suburban gardens, but planted in areas where they have space to spread as they grow, they will truly be in scale with the wider landscape.

The requirements of local authorities can sometimes lead to problems. For example, one particular council I have had to deal with is exasperating. In a misguided attempt to ensure a leafy future for the suburbs over which it has jurisdiction, it insists, when presented with ratepayers' plans for a new house or redevelopment on an ordinary sized suburban block, that ten trees be

❧

FACING PAGE: *White arabis with violas and existing granite outcrops beneath a weeping cherry 'Shimidsu Sakura' at Rockleigh, planted by Edith Toyer.*

LEFT: *This eucalypt and conifer windbreak protects Jill and Bill Maunsell's garden and is in scale with surrounding farmland.*

planted to reach a mature height of 13 m (43 ft). The shade cast by such trees, which will grow to be three times taller than a single-storey dwelling, is very widespreading in summer, and if the trees are evergreen, they make the site colder and damper for longer after rain in winter. The light values within the dwelling in mid winter will be lower and the heating bills higher.

Medium to small trees will be greater assets and less expensive to have removed if damaged in a violent storm. The English hurricane of October 1987 and the disastrous Sydney storm of January 1991, with winds gusting up to 120 km (75 miles) per hour, resulted in costly damage to houses, particularly where there was a greater concentration of very tall trees. People who delight in living amongst such trees need to have a tree-surgeon regularly check the limbs of *Eucalyptus* species, especially for damage caused by the longicorn beetle or termites—although even this precaution will not stop damage caused in a hurricane.

BELOW: *Aged* Cupressus macrocarpa *have been back-planted to provide a replacement windbreak for the garden at Rockleigh.*

CHOICE AND PLACEMENT

Most people who delight in planting a tree do so in the hope that they are planting for posterity. There are a number of factors to be considered in choosing trees that will suit both the climate and the purpose for which they are being planted. Privacy and shade are high on the list, but you may also wish to attract birds into the garden. Seasonal blossom, autumn colour or placing trees to act as a windbreak may be the object.

The mature height and spread of any tree will be governed by its genotype, the fertility of the soil it occupies, the availability of water and additional nutrients in the form of applied manures, fertilisers, or mulch. Information on both the mature height and spread can be obtained from many sources such as your local nursery or forestry protection authority. What they cannot tell you is how quickly your chosen tree will reach its mature height, because of the variables listed above. A jacaranda can grow to 10 m (33 ft) in 20 years, while *Elaeocarpus* species will do it in half the time; the former makes a spreading crown and the latter has fast, narrow, vertical growth. It is important to know all the data before purchasing and planting the tree of your choice.

FORM

This term is applied to the shape of plants and there is great variation in the outlines of trees. Some are narrow and upright, others have broad spreading crowns and yet others, such as the Japanese maple (*Acer palmatum*) and some of the *Malus* and *Prunus* species, are vase- or V-shaped. Some trees, like *Nyssa sylvatica*, have a pyramidal shape, where the lower branches stretch out almost horizontally. If a tree with a conical appearance is desired, many of the conifer species from the northern hemisphere can be used. Finally, there are trees described as columnar, such as the Lombardy poplar (*Populus nigra* 'Italica') or the Australian conifer *Callitris columellaris*, which is very deep green in colour. When this conifer produces its new spring growth, the lighter coloured foliage resembles puffs of green smoke. Conifers in the main are better suited to cooler climates and are definitely not happy in polluted city environments.

When bare of leaves, the shapes of deciduous trees outlined against the sky

can be a source of delight. The branch framework is often referred to as tracery, and this casts shadow patterns across lawns and paving, or can be dramatic outlined on a white wall.

Tree lovers will testify to enjoying the misty green halo of unfurling leaf buds on willow or oak in early spring, or the pronounced bark colours of the coral barked maple (*Acer senkaki*) or the golden ash in winter.

Few think to look up through the branches at white clouds moving in a blue sky, or the moon as it silhouettes a tree with its silvery light. Fragrant and white flowers in a moonlit garden are a special delight.

The following list of small to medium trees, both evergreen and deciduous, may be helpful. Note that in giving dimensions, the height is given first, followed by the spread.

EVERGREEN TREES

ARBUTUS unedo (strawberry tree) is one of the most desirable small evergreen trees. With a domed crown and deep green foliage, it is tolerant of both frost and mild drought. It is grown for its interesting bark, flowers and unusual strawberry fruit, from which it draws its common name. The flowers resemble pendulous lily-of-the-valley and are borne at the same time as the orange red fruit from the previous year's flowers. 6 m (20 ft) × 6 m (20 ft).

BANKSIA marginata (silver banksia) is native to Australian coastal areas from Queensland to Tasmania and across to Adelaide. It can also be found inland. The common name arises because of the grey white underside of the leaf which is visible when leaves are moved by the wind. The pale yellow flowers are carried from autumn into winter and in good soils it can reach 5–8 m (16–26 ft), less where wind is a problem.

CALLISTEMON viminalis (weeping scarlet bottlebrush) is much acclaimed worldwide but taken for granted in Australia. It is one of Australia's most useful natives. It can be tall—up to 10 m (33 ft) with a 5 m (16 ft) spread. The attractive scarlet red brushes are abundantly produced in spring, with repeat flowering in autumn, and are visited by honeyeaters.

CALODENDRUM capense (Cape chestnut) is evergreen in warm climates but almost bare of foliage in cool areas in winter. It is a broad domed tree and much admired for its beautiful pink flowers, produced in panicles from late spring to mid summer. It can reach 10 m (33 ft) with an equal spread but in cooler sheltered sites it will slowly reach 6 m (20 ft) × 5 m (16 ft).

CERATOPETALUM gummiferum (New South Wales Christmas bush) is a small tree native to Australia's coastal gullies. In the domestic garden it can be used very successfully as a boundary screening subject. The red calyx develops in early summer, having dropped its small creamy white flower in spring. It is frost-sensitive when young and benefits from regular pruning immediately after flowering to promote density. Grows to 5 m (16 ft) × 4 m (13 ft).

CITHAREXYLUM spinosum (fiddlewood) is also frost-sensitive while young. It is a fast-growing tree, particularly in warm climates with a high rainfall. It is a medium domed tree of 8 m (26 ft) × 5 m (16 ft) and has a quick leaf drop in mid to late spring when the leaves turn apricot. It retains about one-third and quickly puts out new dark green leaves. The small white fragrant flowers are produced in a pendulous raceme from mid summer to early winter. May require frost protection while young.

ELAEOCARPUS reticulatus is commonly called the native blueberry ash because of its pretty blue berries which attract birds to the garden. A slender tree with attractive fringed bell flowers in white or pink in mid spring to early summer. Its quick growth and light canopy make it doubly useful as a background subject. 10 m (33 ft) × 5 m (16 ft).

GORDONIA axillaris is native to southern China and is a very desirable small tree, either as a specimen or as a background screening subject. The glossy deep green leaves accentuate the white single camellia-like flowers, which are produced from mid autumn to mid winter. It grows 3–5 m (10–16 ft) tall with an equal spread. For those who appreciate beautiful bark, the smoothness of its trunks is a delight.

MAGNOLIA grandiflora (Bull bay magnolia) is native to the south-eastern United States of America (USA) where the humid climate makes for majestic growth, but I have also seen it snow-covered in Washington. In a warm climate it is capable of growing to 10 m (33 ft) × 6 m (20 ft) but needs adequate water to achieve such dimensions. The very large creamy chalice-like flowers open to display purplish stamens and have a lemon perfume. A noble evergreen if you have the space. In England it is often espaliered on the south facing stone walls of two-storey residences.

MELALEUCA linariifolia (snow in summer) is one of the most attractive members of this genus of Australian native paperbark trees. It occurs in the northern coastal areas of New South Wales and into Queensland, on heavy soils close to river systems. When the crown is covered with snowy white flowers in mid summer, it is not hard to see how it came by its common name. 8 m (26 ft) × 4 m (13 ft).

METROSIDEROS excelsa is called pohutukawa by the Maoris and also New Zealand Christmas tree. It is an

ABOVE: *This pohutukawa* (Metrosideros excelsa) *has been thinned so its trunks are silhouetted against sea and sky.*

evergreen with a tall spreading habit capable of withstanding direct, salt-laden winds, which makes it a popular choice in coastal situations. Away from the sea it can be a very handsome broad domed subject carrying its vivid scarlet red staminate flowers, like gum blossoms, in early to mid summer. 10 m (33 ft) × 6 m (20 ft).

MICHELIA doltsopa is native to the lower slopes of the eastern Himalayas, entering China, and does particularly well in Hong Kong. In cold winters its large leaves will droop but in warm weather its growth is rapid and habit very upright. The flowers, which resemble those of *Magnolia stellata*, are white with an unusual sweet fragrance. They open in late winter 10 m (33 ft) tall and spreading with age.

PITTOSPORUM rhombifolium is native to the rainforests of the coastal areas of northern New South Wales and southern Queensland in Australia. It is evergreen, slender and upright, later spreading to a medium domed tree if in an open situation. It has glossy, deep green, diamond-shaped leaves which contrast well with the creamy white flowers in spring, and the heavy crop of orange yellow berries which are displayed from mid summer to winter. They are a source of food for visiting birds. 10 m (33 ft) × 5 m (16 ft).

SYZYGIUM leuhmannii (small-leafed lilli-pilli) is found in the same regions as *Pittosporum rhombifolium*. This very handsome Australian native tree attains 6 m (20 ft) and is medium domed. Its beauty lies in its foliage, which emerges cream at the tips ageing to bright pink before turning deep green, and its coral red berries follow the creamy white gum blossom type flowers. A great screening tree that prefers warm, frost-free sites.

SMALL TO MEDIUM DECIDUOUS TREES

ACER buergeranum (trident maple) is a small erect tree of 6–8 m (20–26 ft), spreading 3–4 m (10–13 ft). Sometimes, as does *Acer palmatum*, it assumes a vase shape. The three-pointed leaf gave rise to its common name and in autumn it is capable of colouring to vivid scarlet, orange and yellow. Dark red spring growth is a good colour indicator, and it is an ideal shade tree.

ACER palmatum is native to Japan and Korea but is commonly known as the Japanese maple. It is always a delight but more so in autumn when the range

ABOVE: Acer palmatum *colours well in cool climates.*

of foliage colours can be superb. Growing 4–5 m (13–16 ft) tall with approximately the same spread, the ascending branches are produced from a short trunk. A well-grown specimen can be equally beautiful when displaying a tracery of bare branches against the winter sky. There are many cultivars of great appeal, such as: 'Atropurpureum', with deep claret red foliage; 'Aureum', with lime green leaves turning deep yellow in autumn; 'Nigrum', with black red foliage; and 'Senkaki', whose leaves turn yellow before dropping to display bright red barked stems which add so much interest to a winter garden scene.

'Aureum' needs a semi-shaded position and, in general, the more delicate the foliage, the greater the need to avoid moisture stress during heat waves.

***BETULA* pendula** (silver birch) is known as The Lady of the Woods in Europe, and it is at its best in cooler climates. A graceful tree whose beauty makes all gardeners want to plant it for the joy of its smooth, white barked trunk and branches and its pendulous foliage. In warm, humid climates a fungal leaf spot causes defoliation in late summer, thus robbing the grower of the wonderful yellow gold autumn display. It has a narrow upright habit up to 10–12 m (33–40 ft).

ABOVE: *A silver birch (*Betula pendula)
underplanted with Rugosa roses in the garden of
Sally and Bay Allison, Rangiora, New Zealand.

ABOVE: *The golden* Robinia pseudoacacia
'Frisia' is a good choice for this Auckland cottage.

***FRAXINUS* excelsior 'Aurea'** (golden ash) is a handsome small shade tree reaching 8 m (26 ft) × 6 m (20 ft). It is a good companion for *Fraxinus raywoodi*, both colouring manificently in autumn.

***JACARANDA* mimosifolia** It is human nature to want to try to grow plants out of their climatic range and those who can grow good birches do not dare plant jacarandas in areas of heavy frost. A native of Brazil, it loves both heat and moisture. A broad domed spreading tree in open situations reaching 10 m (33 ft) × 10 m (33 ft) and deciduous from late winter until it covers itself with mauve blue bells in November. Protection from strong south winds is desirable.

***KOELREUTERIA* paniculata** (golden rain tree or varnish tree) is from China as is *K. bipinnata*, or Pride of China, depicted on willow patterned china. Both turn deep gold in autumn, but *K. bipinnata* has unusual inflated seed pods like miniature Chinese lanterns, carmine pink in early autumn, followed by bright yellow flowers in summer. 8–10 m (26–33 ft) × 5 m (16 ft).

***LAGERSTROEMIA* indica** (crepe myrtle) comes from India, Myanmar (formerly Burma) and southern China. It grows in both temperate and tropical areas. It is a small spreading tree if left unpruned, and it has beautifully smooth bark. There are a number of cultivars: 'Eavesii' flowers soft mauve and 'Newmanii' produces soft, shell pink flowers. It also comes in white, deep pink, carmine red and heliotrope colours and makes an ideal small shade tree. 6 m (20 ft) × 5 m (16 ft).

MAGNOLIA hepterpeta (syn. *denudata*) (yulan) is a great favourite. It is upright to 7 m (23 ft) with a spread of 5 m (16 ft) in old age, but it is more usual to see it at 4–5 m (13–16 ft). Its beauty lies in its wonderful pure white, chalice-like, large blooms carried on bare branches in mid to late winter.

MAGNOLIA × soulangiana hybrids are usually the result of crossing *M. hepterpeta* (syn. *denudata*) and *M. liliiflora* and numbered among them are some extremely beautiful varieties. Top favourite is 'Lennei', which is white inside and deep mauve pink outside. I like 'Brozzonii', which has large white flowers with a pink zone running down the midrib on the outside of each petal. Both grow to 5 m (16 ft) × 4 m (13 ft) and, as does *M. hepterpeta* (syn.

denudata), appreciate being heavily fed in spring immediately after flowering. This ensures a good flowering the following year.

MALUS floribunda is one of the quickest growers amongst the crabapples and outstanding when covered in blooms in early to mid spring. The ruby red buds open to single palest pink blossoms fading to white. It develops a spreading crown, making a useful shade tree in less than a decade. 6 m (20 ft) × 6 m (20 ft), but it can be pruned to remain smaller.

MALUS ioensis 'Plena' (Bechtel's crabapple) has a lovely soft pink, sweetly perfumed double blossom which comes later than any other *Malus*

variety and occurs on short spur growth amongst the new apple green leaves. A tree of dense branching beginning as a vase shape but later spreading to a small dome shape. 5–6 m (16–20 ft).

MALUS spectabilis has a cherry blossom type double flower. The pale pink blossoms come from rose red buds and fade to near white, making it one of the prettiest spring trees, particularly for those whose climate does not suit Japanese cherries. The growth is erect and vase-shaped, making it easier to accommodate. 5 m (16 ft) × 4 m (13 ft).

NYSSA sylvatica is called the tupelo in its native North America. It is one of the best autumn foliage trees to grow, as long as it receives a reasonable rainfall.

RIGHT: *Flowering cherries (*Prunus serrulata*) are better suited to cool climates. A seat and unjointed paving are added here.*

It has a pyramidal shape with the lower branches being almost horizontal. If planting it in a lawn area, it is advisable to remove sufficient of the lower limbs to enable the grass to be cut without decapitating yourself. It is one of the earliest to colour gold, scarlet and claret red in mid autumn, remaining bare of foliage until mid spring. 10–12 m (33–40 ft) × 6 m (20 ft).

PISTACIA chinensis originates from central western China and is a medium domed tree that is grown for its autumn foliage of yellow and orange, which can change to scarlet and crimson before falling. It has ferny leaflets which give the tree a very soft appearance in spring and summer, and it makes a good shade tree. 8 m (26 ft) × 8 m (26 ft).

PRUNUS campanulata (Taiwan cherry) flowers in mid to late winter, displaying its rosy carmine bell-like flowers along bare branches. A vase-shaped, tall, medium domed tree. 6 m (20 ft) × 4–5 m (13–16 ft).

PRUNUS 'Elvins' is one of the spring blossom small trees which becomes a show stopper when it covers itself with white flowers that are tinged very pale pink. Growth is rapid to 4 m (13 ft) with a similar spread.

PRUNUS serrulata (Japanese cherry) is at its best in cool climates where it can

age to 4 m (13 ft) × 4 m (13 ft) and more in the case of 'Shirotae' (syn. 'Mount Fuji'), which is pure white and double. 'Kwanzan' is a strong mid pink and 'Shimidsu Sakura', late to flower, has a pink bud opening to a double white flower. Both of these are strong upright to vase-shaped growers. In warm summer climates they benefit from the shade cast by taller neighbouring trees, and are not happy as weeping standard lawn specimens in exposed positions.

ROBINIA pseudoacacia 'Frisia' from northern Holland has adapted very well to warmer climates elsewhere and is deservedly popular. Its foliage ranges from butter yellow in spring to lime green in summer and golden yellow in autumn, rendering it outstanding in a mixed group or as a focal point. It grows to approximately 8 m (26 ft) × 6 m (20 ft) and is best served by removing the lowest branches to above head height. It is grafted onto *R. pseudoacacia* understock which suckers plain green if the roots are damaged, an important point to bear in mind when digging.

SAPIUM sebiferum (Chinese tallow tree) is one of the most reliable autumn foliaged ornamental shade trees, even in warmer areas. The heart-shaped leaves turn gold, crimson, scarlet and purple before falling in late autumn. It is a

small domed tree reaching 8 m (26 ft) × 6 m (20 ft) and can perform well in all but the coldest climates.

The above list is restricted by mature height and spread and not by climate, though obviously those trees not suited to cool climates should not be contemplated by gardeners living in areas of heavy frost or the occasional snowfall.

It may be helpful to take a large sheet of paper and, using a scale ruler, draw the outline of your house in its correct position in relation to the boundaries, and then to make cut-out paper circles representing the mature diameter of the crowns, again to scale, of your chosen trees. When you move them about within the boundaries on the paper plan, it quickly becomes obvious that the average-sized garden cannot support a forest of trees.

If, for instance, you plant a tree close to your fenceline in a corner position, almost three-quarters of the crown will use the air space of your neighbour's property and so you must ask yourself, 'am I going to be considerate and consult with my neighbour, or am I just going to do it anyway?'. The result could be that your neighbour will be entitled to cut off the offending overhanging branches and throw them back over the fence (depending on your local laws).

The grouping of, say, three Japanese maples in close proximity to one another in a triangle, but not an equilateral triangle, can be very pleasing. It is a species that lends itself to creating a mini forest without taking up the whole garden, and this can also be a very effective way of using silver birches in a cool climate garden.

The blueberry ash (*Elaeocarpus reticulatus*), with its slender upright habit of growth, is perfect for screening out overlooking windows and provides light-dappled shade which is so necessary for *Camellia japonica* and azaleas, the majority of which need some protection from direct sun.

ABOVE: *Though it is next door the weeping willow (*Salix babylonica) *adds maturity to the young garden of Margot and Brett Schneideman of Auckland.*

LEFT: *The mauve-blue bells of* Jacaranda mimosifolia *open on bare branches in late spring in the Sydney garden of Jill and Ted Mussett.*

A blend of evergreen and deciduous trees—with space for the chosen summer-shade lawn specimen, such as *Jacaranda* or *Pistacia* species, to spread its branches widely—is desirable. Trees planted too closely, except for the deliberate triangular placement of maples or birches, will be forced upwards to fight for light, with the slower growing ones leaning out from under the stronger growers as they struggle to expose leaf surfaces to the sun.

This is only one consequence of overplanting. Others are too much shade; concentrated root opposition to the desired shrubs, perennials and groundcovers; dryness caused by the moisture uptake of the trees; and in showery humid weather, a haven for mosquitoes—somehow they find enough water, maybe in leaf-filled gutters, to breed with great rapidity.

SELECTING AND PLANTING TREES

Having made your choice, what do you look for at the nursery? And when you get ready to plant, what is the correct procedure? At the nursery, look for a well-developed shape with a clean main stem which has not forked to become twin leaders in trees which have a naturally upright habit. Low branching is acceptable in *Malus* and *Prunus* species and *Acer palmatum* but for trees overhanging a drive, low branches must be removed while the tree is young.

Because you are going to plant your tree with no thought of moving it at any stage, the preparation of the soil is very important. If the soil is poor and you have some compost to hand, forking it in for, say, one square metre (3 sq ft) is

desirable. You need to dig a hole at least 10 cm (4 in) wider and deeper than the size of the root ball, but not if it means making a well in clay. Such a hole will hold water in rainy periods and because the water cannot drain away, the plant will be lost due to root rot. If there is only a shallow depth of topsoil, it is advisable to mound plant, that is, plant on top of a little hill of soil so that the roots will spread out before sending down anchorage roots.

When you remove the tree from the nursery pot or bag, chances are it will be potbound, meaning that the roots have formed a thick mass on the outside of the root ball. Tease them out so that they can be spread in the hole. Trees which are planted in a potbound

ABOVE: Part of Ethel Doyle's 40-year-old garden shown here demonstrates the six layers of foliage referred to earlier.

condition do not get their anchorage roots established properly and are frequently uprooted by strong winds following prolonged rain. Always water immediately after planting to settle the soil around the roots. This firms it evenly. A heavy boot stamping the ground down can damage tender roots.

If you have had to untangle the roots to spread them evenly, then your young tree will need to be double staked until it stabilises itself. Use two hardwood stakes and some soft webbing ties or old nylon stocking looped to cross over in front and behind the stem. This prevents pressure from the tie being exerted on the young bark. Too often labels and string ties are left on the plant, eventually causing strangulation of a branch or main trunk.

Some gardeners with no compost on hand might be tempted to use manure instead, but be warned that fresh manure can burn the roots. Better to use it as a mulch on the surface after planting, but do not spread it right up against the bark. Blood and bone or slow release pelleted fertiliser can be used at planting time but feeding must not stop there. To ensure the growth rate of which the tree is capable, regular watering in dry weather and twice yearly feeding at a minimum will be necessary.

TEXTURE

This is not something that can be felt by touching the leaf with the fingers as you would a piece of fabric, but is determined by the light value deflected by or passing through the foliage. Thus trees like *Populus alba*, which has a grey or tomentose undersurface seen as the breeze ruffles the leaves, is said to be light in texture. Silver birches and the golden *Robinia pseudoacacia* 'Frisia' would also qualify, while a tree with

very deep green leaves and a dense crown, such as *Syzygium leuhmannii* or a well-grown *Magnolia grandiflora*, would be considered coarse in texture.

There are many gardeners who, having visited rainforest areas, are keen to simulate a little of the same effect in their own gardens. *Syzygium leuhmannii*, *Magnolia grandiflora*, *Arbutus unedo* and *Ceratopetalum gummiferum* all have deep green shiny leaves, reminding one of their origins. If they are planted in combination with *Gordonia axillaris*, *Camellia japonica*, *Camellia sasanqua*, *Osmanthus fragrans* and other shrubs like *Murraya*, *Abelia*, *Choisya* and *Gardenia* species, the deep green theme is reinforced, but it also needs to be relieved with, perhaps, tree ferns in semi-shade or the golden *Robinia pseudoacacia* 'Frisia' for contrast, otherwise the whole scene can become too sombre.

BACKGROUND SHRUBS AND WINTER FOLIAGE

Tall, medium and small shrubs were previously referred to respectively as the fifth, fourth and third layers of foliage in our gardens. They are also the fabric

ABOVE: *Always admired*, Liquidambar styraciflua *grows too large for small gardens.*

RIGHT: Malus floribunda *planted on the verge, plus azaleas and* Prunus *species were chosen by Chris Leal of Sydney for a spring show.*

upon which we build. It is true that in a suburban garden evergreen shrubs are a means to achieving privacy. They also serve as an integral part of the overall scheme and should be chosen not only for their scale, form and texture but also for their colour and season of blooming and possible fragrance, and perhaps as a source of food for birds.

Not only do evergreen shrubs function as the walls of the garden, but they can serve in other capacities, too.

For example, they can be used as soil binders against erosion on sloping ground, or as dividers between different areas. The gardener who is intent on making 'rooms' on a flat site knows full well that the element of surprise cannot be achieved without divisional screening. The growth habits of some are ideal for hedging effects, formal or informal, while others are so outstanding they can be used as highlights or focal points.

A combination of small evergreen trees and tall evergreen shrubs will

❦

BELOW: *A secret garden created by Elizabeth Scott features candelabra primulas, hostas, iris and a lovely dissectum maple.*

afford privacy between neighbours, screen dividing fences and provide a permanent foliage background against which deciduous subjects flowering on bare branches, such as magnolias, can be highlighted. Too many deciduous shrubs and trees planted means loss of privacy and exposure of fences in winter.

Throughout the remainder of this chapter, the list of shrubs is not intended to be encyclopaedic but to be used as a guide for the fifth, fourth and third layers of foliage in the garden, the governing criteria being their ultimate height. If I have omitted your favourite small tree or shrub, go ahead and plant it anyway, taking into account the factors mentioned on page 75, and

always providing that it is within its correct climatic range. As beginners we all want a botanical feast on an ordinary allotment, but we soon learn that we have to be discerning in our choices.

The following list, divided again into evergreen and deciduous, may help you to choose shrubs which are both functional and pleasing.

Evergreen Shrubs

ABELIA × *grandiflora* is evergreen in warm climates, hardy and free flowering from late spring to mid autumn and its

❦

ABOVE: *Shrubs, roses and perennials blended by Noreen and Ray Lee in a young farm garden south of Auckland.*

RIGHT: Ceanothus × edwardsii, *a hybrid raised in Victoria, Australia, blooming to perfection at Tintagel Australia.*

reddish calyces persist until mid winter. The pale pink bell flowers have a light honey fragrance. It makes a good informal hedge growing to 2 m (6.6 ft) and should be pruned each winter by removing one-third of the old canes and reducing the remainder by half their length. There are two golden variegated forms, 'Francis Mason' and 'Variegata'.

ABUTILON × ***hybridum*** (Chinese lantern) This popular evergreen shrub offers many cultivars in an outstanding colour range. The paler colours seem to revel in part shade situations, where they make rapid growth and generally have a rather loose habit. Pruning is essential in early spring, or whenever necessary, to keep them tidy. 2 m (6.6 ft) × 2 m (6.6 ft) is desirable but left unchecked they will be taller and wider. The pale pink and cream are top favourites, but white, deep pink, red, three shades of yellow and orange are also available.

AUCUBA *japonica* **'Variegata'** (gold dust shrub) is a lover of shade. The large leaves are mottled or spotted golden yellow and can burn if exposed to hot summer sun. It can reach 3 m

(10 ft) but responds to pruning and looks better as a compact shrub. A green foliaged male plant will ensure a good crop of red berries in winter.

BUDDLEIA davidii (butterfly bush) is a tall, fragrant, summer-flowering shrub of which there are a number of cultivars such as 'White Bouquet', 'White Profusion', 'Royal Red' (with a magenta flower spike), various lilac and mauve shades and a new variety called 'Lockinch', which has grey foliage and blue mauve flowers. Growth of 2–3 m (6.6–10 ft) is rapid and pruning to control both the height and width is very necessary in early spring and, lightly, in summer. *Buddleia salviifolia* has smoky lavender mauve blooms in August and a strong honey fragrance. It is an excellent screening shrub.

CALLIANDRA haematocephala (powder puff flower) can be watermelon pink or tomato red. It is a native of Bolivia and does best in warm climates. It can reach 3 m (10 ft), spreading even wider, and in a hot position is hardly ever without a flower. The greatest display occurs in autumn and winter. The spectacular blooms resemble a pompom and are 6 cm (2 in) across.

CALLISTEMON citrinus (scarlet bottlebrush) has lemon-scented foliage; it has been extensively hybridised to produce some lovely cultivars, such as 'Burgundy', 'Endeavour', 'Mauve Mist',

'Reeves Pink' and 'Harkness' but the prettiest is undoubtedly Candy Pink. It can grow 2–3 m (6–10 ft) in height and benefits from removal of the seed heads immediately after flowering.

CAMELLIA japonica This species of the genus usually has larger leaves and larger flowers than the *C. sasanqua* varieties and, except for a few sun-hardy cultivars and hybrids, it must be planted in semi-shade. There are early, mid-season and late-flowering varieties which makes it possible to enjoy their flowers from mid autumn to early spring. In old age they can become small trees, but with annual pruning in late winter their size can be controlled. Where the water supply is alkaline they can be grown in tubs and watered with tank water only. Colours are white, pink and red with many variations in between. The most reliable and beautiful are listed below with their flowering periods.

'Betty Ridley': blue toned pink, formal double, mid autumn–early spring.
'Blushing Beauty': white edged pink, formal double, late autumn–early spring.
'Bob Hope': large black red, semi-double, late autumn–early spring.
'Desire': white with a pink edge, formal double, mid autumn–early spring.
'Ecclefield': very large white, informal double, late autumn–early spring.
'Great Eastern': rose red, large semi-double, sun hardy, late autumn–early spring.

'Julia France': light silvery pink, large semi-double, early winter–early spring.
'Laurie Bray': light to deep pink, large semi-double, mid autumn–early spring.
'Lovelight': one of the best whites, semi-double, mid autumn–early spring.
'Pink Gold': soft pink with prominent gold stamens, semi-double, late autumn–early spring.
'Sally Fisher': palest pink, deeper at petal edges, semi-double, late autumn–early spring.
'Silver Chalice': whitest of white, large informal double, early winter–early spring.
'Wildfire': glowing scarlet red, medium semi-double, mid autumn–early spring.

Two sun-hardy hybrids worth considering are:

'Dr Louis Polizzi': pale pink two toned, semi-double, late autumn–early spring.
'Wynne Rayner': lavender pink, medium double centre, mid autumn–early spring.

CAMELLIA reticulata, like *C. japonica*, is native to China and much more open in its growth, eventually forming small

🦋

RIGHT: *Alfresco meals are enjoyed on a raised deck which overlooks this garden.* Camellia sasanqua *planted across the rear boundary gives privacy; in the foreground is a white nicotiana, which releases its perfume at night.*

trees. It produces very large and outstandingly beautiful blooms in mid to late winter and early spring and is more tolerant of sun than *japonica* species.

Visitors from every country where camellias grow come to Eryldene in Sydney, Australia, such is the fame of this garden where for over 60 years (until his death in 1977) Professor Waterhouse planted some 700 camellias. His collection can be divided into three groups: those representative of cultivars imported during Australia's early settlement; the sports and seedlings he raised and named; and those given to him by international friends.

In late summer sasanquas begin to

ABOVE: *A side view of the Eryldene teahouse.*

LEFT: *In Eryldene's meditation corner, Chinese roof tiles overlook a tiny pool in a rock sculptured by nature.*

flower and in very early autumn they are joined by some of the japonicas. Along with massed azaleas the whole garden reaches a crescendo of colour in late winter and early spring. However there are many other species adding their beauty, including some expertly pruned *Acer palmatums* plus a wonderful jacaranda by the front verandah and several more in the rear garden.

A Chinese teahouse designed by architect Hardy Wilson was built to overlook the grass tennis court.

White wind anemones are perfect in this semi-shaded garden, and so too are the columbines and helleborus. Blue plumbago and blue and white agapanthus add summer colour, but it is in the camellia season that visitors flock to the garden.

The following short list of *Camellia reticulata* varieties is given as a guide, with the recommendation that a specialist nursery catalogue be studied.

'Dr Clifford Parks': brilliant rich red, very large informal double, 13 cm (5 in).

'Howard Asper': soft salmon pink, huge loose informal double, 15 cm (6 in).

'Lasca Beauty': soft pink, very large semi-double, 15 cm (6 in), early winter–early spring.

'Valentine Day': salmon rose pink with rose bud centre, 12 cm (4¾ in), early winter–early spring.

'Valley Knudsen Orchid': pink, large semi double 12 cm (4¾ in), early winter–early spring.

CAMELLIA sasanqua, native to Japan, is one of the most versatile evergreen shrubs for all but the coldest climates where early frosts burn the flower buds. They flower in shades of white, pink and rosy red from late summer to mid winter, with many variations of flower form and growth habit. The upright hedging varieties are particularly useful as boundary screening subjects in full sun or part shade and some can be rapid in growth, the cultivar 'Jennifer Susan' reaching 4 m (13 ft) in seven years. Others have a pendulous growth habit which makes them ideal for espaliering on walls or fences. Following is a short list of the upright growers:

'Edna Butler': soft silvery pink, single to semi double, early autumn–early winter.

'Hiryu': bright rosy red, single to semi double, early autumn–early winter.

'Jane Morgan': white edged rose pink, single, early autumn–early winter.

'Jennifer Susan': clear pink with petaloid centre, early autumn–early winter.

'Plantation Pink': large cupped, soft pink single, early autumn–early winter.

'Pure Silk': pink buds open pure white, medium semi double, early autumn–early winter.

'Russhay': pale orchid pink, large semi double, mid autumn–late winter.

'Setsugekka': large white single, waved and fluted, early autumn–early winter.

'Star Above Star': white shading to lavender pink, semi double, mid autumn–early spring.

'Yuletide': glowing ember red, small single, compact growth, early autumn–mid winter.

Geneticists are working towards perfumed camellias but in the meantime the species *C. lutchuensis*, which has small, perfectly formed, single white fragrant flowers, has been used to cross with cultivar 'Tinsie' to give us 'Scented Gem', a miniature of deep pink with white petaloids which is fragrant. Another called 'Scentuous' is the most fragrant yet available.

CEANOTHUS species (Californian lilac), as the common name implies, comes from the western regions of the USA and Mexico, where they enjoy a dry climate with excellent drainage in light sandy soil. Their brilliant blue flowers make them popular as a spring subject but many are lost through over-watering in heavy soils. The cultivar 'Blue Pacific' can grow quickly to 2 m (6.6 ft) × 2 m (6.6 ft) and has intense deep blue flowers while 'Trewithin Blue', a soft powder blue, shows every indication of being a very tall back-ground shrub to 3 m (10 ft) or more.

CHOISYA ternata (Mexican orange blossom) is popular for its fragrant white flowers produced in spring on a rounded shrub which can reach 2 m (6.6 ft). Like *Ceanothus* species, it can be lost through overwatering or being planted in shade.

COTONEASTER species There are a great many species in this genus but for background screening *C. parneyi* from China is one of the best. It is shorter than *C. glaucophylla*, only reaching 3 m (10 ft), whereas the latter grows into a small tree that feeds hungrily. *C. parneyi* has the best berries, which ripen in autumn in full, deep red bunches that the birds adore.

ELAEAGNUS pungens 'Maculata' from Japan is a valuable shrub in that it will perform equally well in sun or semi-shade and is drought and wind tolerant. It produces sweetly perfumed creamy white flowers under the foliage from late summer to mid autumn. Though the flowers are not visible their scent can be pervasive in the garden. 'Maculata' has a golden yellow leaf with a green margin which is popular with flower arrangers. Growth is not fast and any green branches should be removed. 2 m (6.6 ft) × 2 m (6.6 ft).

ESCALLONIA *rubra* var. *macrantha* from southern China makes an excellent tall—3 m (10 ft)—clipped hedge for windbreak purposes. The flowers are red and bloom from mid spring to autumn. Among the Donard cultivars is one called 'Slieve Donard' which opens shell pink fading to white; although listed at 2 m (6.6 ft), it can certainly exceed this. Full sun positions and regular pruning.

FEIJOA *sellowiana* (fruit salad plant) does produce edible fruit in late autumn but it is also a very decorative shrub with grey green leaves which are silvery white and tomentose (hairy) beneath. The flower has greenish white petals curling back from prominent red stamens; it blooms in late spring and throughout summer. A native of Brazil, it can reach 4 m (13 ft) but is best kept lower by pruning lightly in early spring.

GARRYA *elliptica* (silk tassel bush), from North America, is another florist's delight, loved for the pendulous catkins which are silvery greyish yellow and carried in winter. Only the fertilised female plant will develop the catkins, so a male plant must be grown as well. 3 m (10 ft) × 2 m (6.6 ft).

HYPERICUM *leschenaultii* comes from the highlands of Indonesia and has a golden yellow poppy-like flower, which it bears in great profusion from late spring to late autumn. It can easily reach 2 m (6.6 ft).

ILEX *aquifolium* (holly) is grown most successfully in cooler regions. In warm climates infestations of aphids or scale can produce the disfiguring sooty mould growing on the sticky honeydew. The deep green shiny leaves and scarlet berries in winter are its chief attraction, and a number of variegated foliage forms are popular. *I. aquifolium* can grow to 5 m (16 ft) or more, spreading in old age, but the variegated forms are slower and should be pruned in late winter to preserve a good shape.

JASMINUM *nitidum* from New Guinea can be kept as a bun-shaped shrub by regular trimming. If left unpruned, it will revert to its climbing habit. The white flowers opening from a burgundy bud are highly fragrant and produced over ten months of the year. It needs the

warmest wall position in frost free areas. 1.5 m (5 ft) × 1.5 m (5 ft).

JASMINUM *sambac* (Arabian jasmine) is another climber which can be pruned to become a dome-shaped shrub of 2 m (6.6 ft) × 2 m (6.6 ft). The pure white, sweetly perfumed flowers open in clusters from summer to winter.

KALMIA *latifolia* (mountain laurel or calico bush) is native to eastern USA where it grows as an understorey to deciduous trees. The pale pink flowers open in spring and many new cultivars are available in most countries. It can reach 2–3 m (6.6–10 ft) in the right situation.

LEUCOTHE *fortanesiana*, from the same origin as *Kalmia latifolia* and with the same requirements, has pendulous branches along which it flowers with racemes of pendulous flowers like lily-of-the-valley, with as many as 30–40 flowers in a chain, the pink buds opening waxy white.

LOROPETALUM *chinense* (fringe flower), from eastern Asia, can easily reach 2.5 m (8 ft) in less than a decade, though people complain that it is slow initially. The cream flowers open in mid spring and it looks effective as a walling shrub.

MAHONIA *aquifolium* and **MAHONIA *beali*,** the former from the USA and the latter from the eastern Himalayas, are both handsome foliaged plants with bamboo-like canes growing 2–3 m (6.6–10 ft) tall for *M. beali* and less for *M. aquifolium*. The lemon yellow fragrant flowers are carried in late winter through spring and are followed by blue berries. Best in semi-shade.

MICHELIA figo (port wine magnolia) is a dense shrub capable of 3 m (10 ft) × 3 m (10 ft), so pruning after flowering is a must. The small brownish purple flowers which open amongst the foliage throughout spring are strongly fragrant and to some are reminiscent of ripe bananas.

MURRAYA paniculata (orange jessamine) has flowers which look and smell exactly like orange blossom. It has four flushes, the first in mid spring, then again in early summer, late summer and mid autumn. Once established, pruning should be carried out after the spring flowering. Suited to all warm districts, it needs frost protection in marginal areas when young, and is versatile as a hedge or background subject in full sun or part shade.

NERIUM oleander, although poisonous, is included in this list for its value in hot, dry climates or salt tolerance in coastal gardens. The much despised oleander is very long flowering in the warm months of late spring through

summer, but still produces some flowers until winter. It comes in single white, double white, dark red, cerise pink, double pale yellow, rose pink, salmon and a variegated foliaged deep rose pink. Grows to 3–5 m (10–16 ft) × 3 m (10 ft)—less if pruned regularly.

OSMANTHUS fragrans (sweet olive) is used in hot, humid New Orleans as a small street shrub where its narrow upright habit is ideal. Reaches 3–4 m (10–13 ft) but less if pruned regularly. Its chief attraction is the strong apricot perfume which comes from tiny lemon flowers from late winter to early summer.

PIERIS japonica (pearl flower) is native to the foothills of mountains in Japan and can grow 2–3 m (6.6–10 ft) tall, producing chains of white lily-of-the-valley flowers in spring. Many cultivars with brilliant foliage colours, produced as spring growth, are now on offer and thrive in cool climates in part shade.

PLUMBAGO auriculata (leadwort) Its common name is rarely used, as most gardeners know it by its correct name and admire the soft, sky blue flowers which occur continuously from late spring to late autumn. There is also a white form. If used as an informal hedge, pruning is necessary each winter and, as mentioned earlier in the text, root pruning with a spade is advantageous,

or, if you have the space, lay weedmat down and cover it with mulch—this cuts the light needed for photosynthesis. It is frost-sensitive while young. Grows to 2 m (6.6 ft) × 2 m (6.6 ft).

PYRACANTHA (firethorn), from eastern Asia, is another berried shrub which the birds appreciate during winter. The various cultivars produce scarlet, orange, deep red, and yellow fruits. *P. rogersiana* 'Flava' has deep butter yellow berries like little flattened pumpkins. This variety can grow 3–5 m (10–16 ft) tall, developing from a vase shape to a broad bun shape. Ideal in a country garden where space is not a problem.

RAPHIOLEPIS (Indian hawthorn) *R. x delacourii* is a rose pink, spring flowering subject capable of 2 m (6.6 ft) or more. Both its parents, *R. indica* and *R. umbellata*, can be 3–4 m (10–13 ft), with a similar spread; again, useful in country gardens or for coastal hedges. All are tolerant of frost and light drought.

RHODODENDRON and AZALEA belong to the same subgenera but for the purposes of this list the only azaleas to be considered as screening shrubs are those that are classified as *indica* hybrids. Among the best are 'Alba Magna', white; 'Alphonse Anderson' and its sport 'Kalimna Pearl', both fragrant and two tone orchid pink; 'Exquisite', lilac pink; 'Jean Alexandra', peach pink; and 'Lady Poltimore' and 'Morti', both white and fragrant. All can reach 2–2.5 m (6.6–8 ft) and—with the exception of 'Jean Alexandra', which likes some shade—they are sun hardy.

The large-leafed rhododendrons are the most dependable screening subjects in cool climates with cultivars such as 'Alice', 'Beauty of Littlemore', 'Broughtonii', 'Cornubia', 'Countess of Athlone', 'Cynthia', the *R.* x *loderi* hybrids, 'Mrs E. C. Stirling', 'Pink Pearl', 'Sappho' and 'White Pearl'. All are capable of exceeding 3 m (10 ft). After two to three decades of growth, they become small spreading trees unless regularly pruned. There are many very beautiful cultivars and specialist catalogues or advice should be sought.

RONDELETIA amoena from central America is a vigorous multi-branched shrub to 3 m (10 ft) × 3 m (10 ft) producing heads of soft pink tubular flowers with a slight fragrance. Prune lightly after flowering to shape the bush.

TIBOUCHINA granulosa is another warm climate subject that is finding favour with many gardeners who previously ignored the purple forms but find the recently introduced cultivars of 'Kathleen' and 'Noeline' more acceptable. 'Kathleen' flowers in mid autumn with soft lavender pink blooms and 'Noeline' opens mauve, fading to

lavender and near white in early summer. Both can reach 3 m (10 ft) or more.

VIBURNUM japonicum is globular in shape and useful as a fragrant background shrub, carrying white heads of flowers in early spring followed by red berries in late autumn. Prune to control dimensions after flowering. 2.5–3 m (8–10 ft).

Deciduous Shrubs

BERBERIS thunbergi 'Atropurpurea'

There are many species of *Berberis* and a number of cultivars of *B. thunbergi*, but the purple claret foliaged form is popular

in mixed borders for its strong accent colour. 'Keller's Surprise' is similar to 'Atropurpurea' and 'Nana' in growth habit but the leaves are splashed with maroon, pink and white, which also makes it an eye-catching accent.

CALLICARPA dichotoma (purple bead bush or Chinese beauty berry) reaches 2–2.5 m (6.6–8 ft) and has small purplish flowers in late spring followed by bunches of lilac violet shiny berries

BELOW: *Berberis, viburnum and cotoneaster species combine berry and leaf colour for an autumn effect at Mt Tomah Botanic Gardens, Australia.*

in late autumn and winter. When cut and stripped of leaves for decorative work it looks most attractive.

CHAENOMELES japonica (flowering quince) is seen in mid to late winter flowering bright scarlet on bare stems, but it is *C. speciosa* cultivars that are most sought after. 'Nivalis' is pure white, 'Moerloosei' is white with rose pink shadings. 'Simonii' is blood red, 'Rosea Pleana' is semi-double pale rose pink and 'Falconnet Charlet' is semi-double salmon pink. Branches are spiny but when cut in bud will open indoors. All *Chaenomeles* species have a suckering growth habit. 2 m (6.6 ft) × 2 m (6.6 ft).

***COTINUS coggygria* 'Purpureus'** (purple-leafed smoke bush) is a shrub with most unusual flowers resembling puffs of purple smoke. These rise above the foliage from late spring to early summer. The leaves turn ruby red in autumn and a full sun position is essential for good colour. 3 m (10 ft) × 3 m (10 ft), but controllable by heavy pruning in late winter if necessary.

DEUTZIA (wedding bells) The species *D.* × *rosea* and *D. scabra* seem to have produced some of the best cultivars in this genus, and there are new varieties, such as 'Magician' and 'Rosalind', both highly desirable. *D. scabra* 'Pride of Rochester', with double white flowers tinged carmine pink in the bud, is

possibly the best available to us now, along with 'Pink Pom Pom'. Grows to 2 m (6.6 ft) × 2 m (6.6 ft).

ENKIANTHUS campanulatus is a gem for cool climates and grows 2–3 m (6.6–10 ft) tall. The soft pink-tipped white bell flowers are borne in·

ABOVE: Lonicera periclymenum, *seen here with roses 'Heidisommer' and 'Roseromantic', is very fragrant and requires hard pruning as a shrub.*

pendulous clusters in mid to late spring, and in autumn the foliage has brilliant autumn tones.

EXOCHORDA **racemosa** (pearl bush) is well named as the inflated pure white buds swell along the bare stems from early to late spring, depending on the locality. It loves deep soils, adequate summer moisture and temperatures that do not exceed –8°C (17°F). 3 m (10 ft) × 3 m (10 ft). Prune after flowering.

FORSYTHIA × **intermedia** has produced three excellent cultivars, namely 'Spectabilis', 'Lynwood' and 'Karl Sax'. It is a popular shrub for cool climates and marks the end of winter with its brilliant rich yellow blooms carried on bare stems, but it must be planted in full sun. Without pruning it can grow 3–4 m (10–13 ft) but shaping is desirable.

HAMAMELIS **mollis** (witch-hazel) is prized in cool climate gardens for its sweetly fragrant, yellowish brown blooms which open in mid to late winter. Cutting basal stems for decorative work benefits the shape of the shrub, which can grow to 4 m (13 ft).

HYDRANGEA **species** *H. macrophylla* is the most widely grown, flowering in early summer in shades of blue, mauve (on acid soils), pink and red (on alkaline soils) and pure white. You can change

❧

the blues to pink with 250 gm (9 oz) of calcium carbonate per square metre (3 sq ft) once a year, or you can change pinks to blue using four parts of sulphate of aluminium to one part of sulphate of iron, dissolved in 20 litres (4.5 gallons) of water and watered into the root zone. The white cannot be changed, and all have large round heads of flower which, if left uncut, age to green and can be dried for decorative work.

There are, however, other varieties that have great appeal, such as 'Lacecap', with flat heads of flower composed of the inner, coloured, fertile flowers which are encircled with much larger sterile white flowers. There is a variegated foliaged 'Lacecap' which is very useful in the shaded garden. The fertile flowers can be pink, mauve or blue, depending on your soil.

HYDRANGEA **paniculata** 'Grandiflora' is pure white with a flat-backed conical flower head that is ideal for picking. *H. quercifolia*, the oak leaf hydrangea, so named because of its unusual shaped leaf, has similar large white heads of flower, and has the added advantage of good autumn colour in its foliage. All prefer semi-shade and a combination of these various species provides flowers for picking throughout summer. *H. macrophylla* and 'Lacecap' need hard pruning in mid winter. *H. villosa* needs thinning and shaping, remembering its

natural vertical habit, while 'Grandiflora' and *H. quercifolia* are pruned to develop a bun-shaped shrub.

HYDRANGEA **villosa** has similar mauve flowers surrounded by white sterile flowers but its leaves are totally dissimilar, being long and narrow. It is very tall, growing 3–4 m (10–13 ft), and a delight in mid summer.

KERRIA **japonica** 'Plena' When well-grown, the double form of this bright yellow, spring-flowering shrub is attractive, with its long, arching canes carrying a heavy crop of blossom throughout spring. Pruning to preserve its natural shape should be carried out immediately after flowering, with some old canes being removed entirely to encourage new basal growth.

KOLKWITZIA **amabilis** (Chinese beauty bush) is a gem in cooler climates, growing 2–3 m (6.6–10 ft) tall, with arching canes carring soft lavender pink tubular bell flowers in mid to late spring. Prune as for *Kerria japonica*.

LONICERA **fragrantissima** is the winter-flowering shrub honeysuckle, which in a cold winter will open its cream-coloured, highly perfumed flowers along bare branches. In a mild winter it will hold its leaves and the flowering takes place amongst them. It can grow 3 m (10 ft) × 3 m (10 ft) but is best pruned in late

fragrant varieties which combine so well with old-fashioned roses. *P. virginal* grows 2.5 m (8 ft) tall and has semi-double to fully double pure white flowers with pointed central petals and petaloids. Unfortunately, many other cultivars are offered under the same name. From *P.* x *leomoinee* comes 'Manteau d' Hermine', which has smaller, semi-double white perfumed flowers and has a smaller bun-shaped habit. *P.* x *purpureomaculatus* has given us 'Belle Etoile' and the pink-centred 'Etoile Rose'. A cultivar from the USA called 'Natchez' has the largest cupped semi-double fragrant white bloom yet seen, while the evergreen *P. mexicanus*, with cupped soft cream perfumed blooms, needs pruning after flowering to encourage an arching bun shape. It is late in flowering, giving flowers in early summer.

winter to control its dimensions. Suckers can be root-pruned with a spade.

Lonicera periclymenum (Dutch honeysuckle) is a climber which, with pruning, can be kept as a shrub. The fragrant pink and cream flowers are borne in spring and summer, with spasmodic flowering in autumn. Hard pruning in late winter to reduce it by two-thirds of its height is advisable, as is light pruning of its wayward canes in summer.

Magnolia stellata (star magnolia) flowers in late winter on bare branches to display its narrow petals, which number between 12 and 18 (depending on the cultivar) and are fragrant. Cultivars 'Rosea' (pale pink), 'Rubra' (cyclamen) and 'Water Lily' (pale pink) are all lovely. Pruning to shape after flowering is desirable as they can reach 3 m (10 ft) × 3 m (10 ft) if allowed.

Philadelphus **species** The range of species available is slowly increasing and there are some spectacular, sweetly

Ribes sanguinium (flowering currant) is seen mainly in cooler climate gardens where the cultivars flower in early to mid spring: 'Carneum' (deep pink), 'King Edward VII' (crimson), 'Plenum' (rosy red) and the rarer 'Album' (white). Several older canes should be removed after flowering to encourage new canes to grow. 2 m (6.6 ft) × 2 m (6.6 ft).

SPIRAEA cantoniensis 'Lanceata' No prizes for guessing its region of origin, it is known as white may. It has arching growth and, when well grown, becomes a cloud of double white blooms in mid spring, completely concealing the foliage. Prune after flowering, as for abelia. 2 m (6.6 ft) × 2 m (6.6 ft).

STACHYURUS praecox (early spiketail) is from the Himalayas and has an unusual pale yellow pendulous chain of flowers on open, long, arching branches in spring, making an eye-catching display in full sun or light shade. 2.5 m × 2.5 m (8 ft × 8 ft).

VIBURNUM species can be divided into fragrant and non-fragrant groups, both of which are highly desirable. *V.* x *burkwoodi* has pink buds opening to white salver-shaped flowers which are carried from winter until early to mid spring. *V.* x *carlcephalum* has similar flowers but they open later (in spring) and it has a broader leaf. It is very fragrant. *V. fragrans* (syn. *farreri*) produces pink-flushed, sweetly perfumed flowers on bare branches through winter. *V. juddii* is similar to *V. carlesii*, but is a stronger grower, flowering throughout spring. A new hybrid, *V.* x *bodnantense* 'Dawn', flowers almost continuously in winter, producing pink fragrant blooms in tight little bunches along the stems.

Most commonly grown of the non-fragrant types is the snowball or guelder rose *V. opulus* but the Japanese *V. macrocephalum* has the largest pure white hydrangea-like heads and can easily and quickly grow to 4 m (13 ft) in an upright manner. Among the lacecaps, *V. plicatum* var. *tomentosum*, with flat white heads of flower along horizontal branches, was the forerunner of hybrids like 'Lanarth' and 'Pink Beauty', the latter opening white and turning pink on the edges of the petals as it ages. All require shaping while young, with *V. opulus* needing heavy pruning after flowering. The lacecap varieties need space to spread for best effect.

WEIGELA cultivars The *Weigela* seems to be less popular than it was in the late 1940s when white, ruby red, shell pink, rosy salmon and crimson varieties were sold under their cultivar names, along with *W. florida* 'Argenteo marginata', *W. florida* 'Aureo variegata' (both with variegated foliage) and *W. florida* 'Mont Blanc' (pure white), 'Newport Red' and 'Styriaca' (pale rose pink). This is possibly because so many other spring flowering shrubs are now commanding attention. Reaching 2.5–3 m (8–10 ft), they need pruning after flowering as the flowers are produced on the previous summer's growth. Prune in the same manner as abelia.

❦

BELOW: *A rarely seen soft pink* Weigela florida *'Esperance' blooms well for Pam Fowell in her semi-shaded garden.*

Small Shrubs for Semi-Shade

The small shrubs of the third foliage layer are divided into two main groups, those for semi-shade and those for full sun. The reason for splitting them this way is to give a choice of small shrubs suitable for mixing with old-fashioned roses, which in turn must compete with other desired deciduous shrubs for the space available in individual gardens.

ABUTILON savitzii has a large amount of white variegation in its green leaves which is extremely useful in lighting up a dark corner, and with pruning to achieve a compact shape, it can be kept to 1 m (3 ft). Any plain green foliage should be completely removed or it will take over, and too much sunlight will change the white to yellow. It rarely flowers but can produce a small orange Chinese lantern bell.

ARDISIA crenulata is grown for its bright red holly-like berries which it produces in bunches. They hold from early winter to early summer if not taken by birds. It looks better for having old, tall canes cut out to near ground level. 1 m (3 ft).

AZALEA (evergreen compact hybrids) The range of low to medium height single, semi-double and double azaleas runs into hundreds, and they can, by

careful selection, be in flower from late summer to mid spring. The colour variations are such that you can use them either as accents or harmonisers.

BUXUS sempervirens (box) and its variegated form, Marginata, will tolerate light shade and this may prove useful in

❦

LEFT: *Clipped* Buxus sempervirens *gives a neat line to the exuberant plantings in Toni Sylvester's rose garden.*

BELOW: *Here* Buxus *flows with the curve of the gravel drive in a garden created by Lesley and Gordon Matheson of Christchurch, New Zealand.*

your design. A pair of clipped *Buxus* specimens may be used to introduce a formal note if placed on either side of short steps or in tubs at the beginning or end of a pathway.

CARYOPTERIS × *clandoniensis* is a small bun-shaped deciduous shrub which opens its sky blue flowers in early summer. If given a light prune, it will give a second flowering in autumn. 0.8 m (2.6 ft).

CERATOSTIGMA *griffithi* is deciduous and grows as a low spreading bun and carries sky blue flowers for many weeks in autumn. It can also be grown in sun in cooler regions. 0.5 m (1.5 ft) × 1 m (3 ft).

DAPHNE *odora* and its various cultivars, on the other hand, will not tolerate being in full sun. Light-dappled shade or a protected south-easterly aspect is preferred. In my view, they are better under trees, where they cannot be overwatered. The pink or lemon-scented creamy white flowers are one of winter's delights and persist for two months.

EUPHORBIA *wulfenii* can be in part shade or full sun but performs better in hot areas with a little shade. It produces huge heads of lime green flowers which are great in decorative arrangements. Developing slowly, they are best in mid winter to early spring. 1 m (3 ft) × 1 m (3 ft).

FUCHSIA × *hybrida*, while not as numerous as azalea cultivars, offer an extended and breathtaking range of beautiful varieties. They do very well in warm climates or micro climates that are relatively frost-free, given semi-shade and protection from strong winds as they have brittle stems. There are small, medium and large pendulous flowered forms to choose from, and they all benefit from pinch pruning to encourage compact growth. As some can grow to 2 m (6.6 ft), it is best to seek advice from a specialist grower as to the growth habit of your chosen fuchsia.

GARDENIA *augusta* (syn. *G. florida*), is ever popular because of its fragrant creamy white flowers which open in late spring and early summer in great numbers, followed by spasmodic flowering until late autumn. Although able to tolerate full sun, they are much happier in part shade and can be kept as a 1 m (3 ft) × 1 m (3 ft) bun shape with light pruning in late summer. They appreciate rich feeding, which is most necessary in early spring as the buds swell. Yellow leaves in spring mean the plant is taking food from the old leaves for its developing flower buds.

GARDENIA *radicans* is a low growing groundcover form with perfect little gardenia flowers opening at the same time as *G. augusta*. It looks equally pretty as a foreground subject or used to spill over a wall.

HYPERICUM × *moserianum* 'Tricolor' can be used in the same way as *Gardenia radicans* and has two attributes in its favour: it opens golden cupped yellow flowers from late spring to early summer, and has attractive leaves which are green with creamy variegation and a pink margin. Light shade only, and semi-deciduous in cooler climates.

JUSTICIA *carnea* (syn. *Jacobinia*) is a soft-wooded, large-leafed shrub with very large heads of bright pink flowers opening from late spring to late autumn. Removal of the spent flowers and early light pruning to encourage compact growth is desirable. There is a pure white form that lights up a deep shade area. 1.2 m (4 ft) × 1.2 m (4 ft).

PENTAS *lanceolata* is a soft-stemmed shrub to 1 m (3 ft) available in white, three shades of pink, mauve and 'Candy Star', which is a two-tone pink and red. The latter will take full sun. The flower head is composed of many tubular blooms which open out to a five-pointed star shape, and it is a good picking flower.

PLECTRANTHUS *argentatus* is a silver foliaged, soft-wooded sub-shrub which performs better in shade and benefits from pruning to keep it tidy. Its flower is a small spike of pale blue or near white, but it is really grown for its attractive felted broad grey leaves.

ABOVE: *The blue-grey felted leaves of* Plectranthus argentatus *are used effectively between lavender and rose 'Graham Thomas'.*

PLECTRANTHUS saccatus is very soft-wooded and very useful in dry shade under trees. The soft sky blue flowers are borne from mid summer to late autumn and it has a spreading habit which is controllable. 0.5 m (1.6 ft) × 1 m (3 ft).

RHODODENDRON cultivars There are many evergreen dwarf cultivars available from specialist nurseries and for cool climates the colour range is extended by blue and yellow. I grow 'Suave' and 'Princess Alice' for their fragrant white and white-edged pink bell flowers. In warmer climates the Vireya rhododendrons from the rainforests of New Guinea and Indonesia, and *R. loche* from northern Australia, are worth a place, particularly the fragrant 'Sweet Wendy'.

SALVIA involucrata 'Betheli' is a soft sub-shrub for a wind-sheltered semi-shaded position where it will flower from early autumn to mid winter on long stems, producing a rose pink flower with a curious closed bud at the tip. Useful as a cut flower. 1.5 m (5 ft) × 1 m (3 ft).

STROBILANTHES anisophyllus (syn. *Goldfussia*) can occasionally reach 1.5 m (5 ft) but 1 m (3 ft) is more usual. It is valued for its foliage which in late autumn turns deep purple, at which time it also flowers with small soft lavender tubular bell flowers giving a generous and pleasing show.

Small Shrubs for Full Sun

ABUTILON megapotamicum 'Variegatum' is a tough useful groundcover variety which flowers almost perpetually, displaying its tricoloured blooms, which are composed of a deep yellow bell with a brown clanger of stamens and backed by a bright red calyx. They develop pendulously along the stems of green speckled gold foliage. It is a valued soil binder on an embankment or can be used as a spillover.

AGRYRANTHEMUM frutescens (Marguerite daisies) are undergoing name changes. They are widely grown and loved for their many flower forms and long flowering habit—early winter to early summer, and beyond with the right care. Although considered a soft-wooded, short lived sub-shrub, their appeal has ensured them a place in all cottage gardens. It is advisable to keep them compact by regular picking of the flowers and regular light pruning. It is wise also to strike cuttings for replacement plants as they are easily lost in prolonged rainy and humid periods.

AZALEA cultivars which are sun hardy, such as 'Red Wing', 'Hexe', 'Pink Lace' and 'White Lace', can be placed to advantage but you should study a specialist catalogue and buy only when you can see the colour of the flower.

BOUVARDIA humboldtii is a low growing, long flowering little soft-wooded shrub prized for its fragrant four-petalled white flowers opening out from a 50 mm (2 in) narrow tube. 1 m (3 ft). Grow in warm sheltered micro climates as it does not like frost.

RIGHT: *Ever popular white marguerite daisies with heart's-ease (*Viola tricolor*) and forget-me-nots.*

BOUVARDIA leiantha hybrids are enjoying a revival with 'Duchesse of York', a soft pink single with flowers slightly larger than those of *Pentas lanceolata*, being the most popular. It is a soft-wooded, small shrub which flowers from late spring to early winter and needs cutting back each spring for new cane growth. Other flower forms include single white, single red, double salmon pink and double white. It is popular as a cut flower for posies.

CARYOPTERIS incana is similar to *C.* x *clandoniensis* except in its foliage. The leaf is slightly broader and sun-hardy, making it handy for use among old-fashioned roses where its soft blue flowers contrast beautifully.

CERATOSTIGMA willmottianum has intense deep blue flowers mid summer to late autumn, and is deciduous in cold climates where it will develop good autumn foliage colours. It grows into a 1 m (3 ft) bun shape, and it is very hardy.

COTONEASTER dammeri is a low growing evergreen species which is effective on an embankment, or it can be used as a wall spillover. The white

flowers appearing in spring are followed by coral red berries in mid autumn to early winter. *C. horizontalis* is similar but deciduous and has a smaller leaf. (0.5 m (1.5 ft) × 2 m (6.6 ft).

DEUTZIA gracilis flowers with a small single white bell flower on bare stems in mid to late spring. It is multi-caned, deciduous and grows to 1.2 m (4 ft).

DEUTZIA nikko has similar flowers but a low prostrate spreading habit of growth, making it ideal for rockeries or

as a front row subject. In winter the foliage turns deep purple before dropping. 0.3 m (1 ft) × 1 m (3 ft).

EURYOPS pectinatus is a yellow daisy bush with grey ferny foliage which flowers from mid autumn to mid spring and is an extremely hardy sub-shrub for a hot dry position. *E. athanasiae*, with fine green foliage, is frequently mislabelled as *E. pectinatus*.

HEBE species Some of the smaller growing hebes can be most useful if

LEFT: Heliotropium arborescens *'Lord Roberts'* *and rose 'The Fairy' are happy companions in* *full sun, where their cherry pie perfume is at* *its best.*

dead-headed or lightly pruned. *H. pimelioides* has small-leafed foliage which turns purple in winter. It opens spikes of soft mauve blue flowers above a neat bun shape in spring, summer and autumn. 0.5 m (1.5 ft). Taller is *H. speciosa*, a pretty pink often sold as 'Bouquet of Flowers', opening in mid summer and repeating to mid autumn. *H. speciosa* 'Blue Gem', an English cultivar, is widely grown and almost always in flower. It is improved by removing the spent flowers. *H. hulkeana*, native to New Zealand, is a delightfully pretty hebe when in flower and is either pale lilac or lavender blue. It reaches 1 m (3 ft) or less, and is said to be more prolific if regularly but lightly pruned.

HELIOTROPIUM (cherry pie) takes its common name from its very sweet fragrance. *H. arborescens* has green foliage and a light mauve flower. *H. arborescens* 'Aurea' has lime green foliage and the same mauve flower and is best in dappled shade. *H. arborescens* 'Lord Roberts' has deep green foliage, shaded to purple at times, with deep violet flowers. All have a spreading habit. Grow in micro climates sheltered from frost in a warm aspect.

INDOGOGERA decora is called pink wisteria because it resembles, in miniature, a raceme of wisteria. It is a spreading deciduous shrub opening its rich pink 15 cm (6 in) long pendulous flowers in late spring and then

continuing spasmodically until late autumn. Valuable for erosion control as it has a suckering habit.

LAVANDULA **species** Like Marguerite daisies, lavenders are top favourites in cottage gardens, with *L. dentata* often heading the list because it flowers from mid autumn to late spring. It must have full sun in a well drained position with good air circulation. 1 m (3 ft). As it finishes, the English lavenders take over, with *L. angustifolia* (syn. *L. officinalis, L. vera*) opening their lavender blue spikes. *L. x intermedia* is responsible for the cultivars 'Alba', 'Rosea', 'Dwarf Hidcote' and 'Dwarf Munstead', which are at their best in cooler regions.

LAVANDULA × ***allardii*** (Mitcham lavender) is a hybrid cross between *L. dentata* and *L. angustifolia*. The flowers are purple, on very long spikes, and only occur in summer. I find its size—1.5 m (5 ft) × 1.5 m (5 ft)—can be too demanding of space in small gardens when considered against its short flowering period.

LAVANDULA ***pinnata*** **'Sidonee'**, new to the scene, is almost perpetually in flower, opening a triple head of deep lavender blue flowers on very long stems high above its ferny grey foliage. It is a sport which occurred in the garden of a friend of mine called Sidonee. There is also a town called Sidonee in Spain, though the origin of *L. pinnata* is thought to be the Canary Islands.

***LAVANDULA* stoechis** (Spanish lavender), common throughout Europe and particularly Spain, has purple flowers with a distinguishing pair of rabbit-ear petals at the tip of the perfumed flowers. It has two main flushes: the first in winter and the second in early summer, with spasmodic blooming in between. There is a dwarf form called *L. pedunculata*, with the same big rabbit-ear flowers and the same flowering period.

***PARAHEBE* catarractae 'Alba'** The botanists have divided the genera *Hebe* and separated these softer foliaged little gems. 'Alba' covers itself in spring, summer and late autumn with small white flowers which have tiny bird's-eye dots of mauve in the centre. *Parahebe fraseri* flowers similarly, but is lavender blue. Both are great with old roses and prefer just a little shade in summer.

***SALVIA* leucanthe** (Mexican sage) is a soft-wooded sub-shrub which flowers from mid summer to late winter, producing long spikes of magenta flowers which have a white lip hanging in a pendulous fashion along the underside of the spikes. It needs hard pruning in late winter, cutting it back to 15 cm (6 in) above ground level. As Mexican sage spreads by suckering, some root pruning with a sharp spade is also advantageous.

ABOVE: *Daisies, poppies (yet to open), dianthus and iris were selected by Pat Taylor of Sydney for her full sun garden.*

***SPIRAEA* 'Anthony Waterer'** (pink may) is a low spreading cultivar which occasionally throws up cream leaves among its green foliage, which is deciduous. The cerise pink flowers are carried throughout summer. 0.6 m (2 ft) × 0.8 m (2.6 ft).

CHAPTER 8

Old-fashioned Roses and Their New Companions

In the past decade the number of books written about old-fashioned roses has increased to the point where many gardeners, new and old, are discovering for themselves how beautiful and rewarding the old roses can be when correctly chosen, placed and grown. Heritage rose society members in many countries have busied themselves collecting old roses from neglected gardens or cemeteries in order to identify and make available many which have long since vanished from nursery catalogues. Some of these are only suited

❦

LEFT: *David Austin's rose 'Moth' is aptly named. As it opens, its fluted petals are reminiscent of pretty moths.*

to exchanging amongst the membership.

Rose breeders have been very active during the past two centuries, working with the species and varieties already known and then crossing them with new material brought to the Western world, particularly from China. It was four *Rosa chinensis* varieties introduced in 1752 that gave us remontant or repeat flowering roses. Until then, the rose breeders had had to work with Gallicas, Damasks, Albas, Centifolias and Moss Roses. The four roses from China that proved to be so valuable were 'Slater's Crimson', 'Parson's Pink' (correctly called 'Old Blush'), 'Hume's Blush' and 'Park's Yellow', and without them the rose would not be as revered as it is today.

There followed Portland, Boursalt, Bourbon and Hybrid Perpetuals which, as further crosses took place, gave us Noisettes, Tea Roses, early Hybrid Teas and Hybrid Musks. Breeders in rose growing countries such as France, England, Germany, Ireland, the United States and New Zealand have poured the modern Hybrid Tea onto the market, encouraged by the success of Meilland's beautiful rose 'Peace', released in 1945 to mark the end of the war.

In 1903 in the town of Sangerhausen, in East Germany, a rosarium was established. Today it covers 12.5 hectares (31 acres) with a further 2.5 hectares (6 acres) to be opened in 1993. The rosarium lists 6500 kinds, including species, Noisettes, Hybrid Teas, old Tea Roses and Ramblers, as well as Floribunda and modern Hybrid Teas. It is from this garden that the National Trust in England was supplied with some missing varieties for its old-fashioned rose garden at Mottisfont Abbey in Hampshire.

The rose buyer is faced with a bewildering choice but if some parameters are applied to the task—such as colour and growth habit—it may become easier. One has only to turn the pages of *Roses* by Roger Phillips and Martyn Rix to realise there must be parameters, for only gardeners on large acreages can indulge themselves as collectors.

There is a valid argument that once-flowering or spring-only roses should

FAR LEFT: *Climber 'Meg' at Sissinghurst, skilfully trained around windows.*

LEFT: *'Carabella', an Australian rose, is very like apple blossom. It is used here as a Pillar Rose.*

not be as maligned as they often are, because many shrubs such as the *Philadelphus, Deutzia,* and *Spiraea* species are also once-flowering. For those of us who have restricted space, sprawling or large Shrub Roses like 'Complicata', 'Fantin Latour' or 'Fritz Nobis', lovely though they are, must be passed over for repeat-flowering beauties. Nor do I ignore roses introduced in the past 30 years which look old-fashioned or mix well with the tried and true old roses.

It is not possible in one chapter to write about every old rose ever named. My preference is for roses which are repeat flowering, with two notable exceptions: 'Meg' and 'Albertine'. The latter was released in 1921 and is a

vigorous Climber, bearing salmon pink double blooms. 'Meg' has large salmon apricot semi-single blooms with deep amber stamens. Removal of the hips is said to induce autumn rebloom. 'Meg' was introduced in 1954 and is also a vigorous Climber of great beauty.

BUSH ROSES

Because roses need full sun positions and because many gardeners have few of these, it becomes even more important to think about the size of the desired rose and its place in the overall scheme, which is why some of the little Bush Roses are so popular.

'CECILE BRUNNER' 1881, whose buds are so prized by florists, only grows to 1 m (3 ft). Often I have heard someone say, 'But my "Cecil Brunner" [dropping the 'e'] is ten feet tall [3 m]' and have patiently explained that what they have or had was in fact 'Bloomfield's Abundance'. There is a white form of 'Cecile Brunner' with a buff tone to the bud. There is also the ever popular 'Perle d'or', with apricot buds which open to loose-petalled pink flowers. It is the buds which make it so appealing. All three flower from mid spring to early winter and can be grown in tubs.

'THE FAIRY', 'LITTLE WHITE PET' and 'GREEN ICE' are also able to be grown in tubs but look great in the ground as the front row or foreground to taller roses. 'The Fairy', a dwarf Polyantha, introduced in 1932, grows to 0.5 m (1.5 ft) × 1 m (3 ft), and because of its generous flowering and soft pink colour has remained in steady demand.

'HEIDISOMMER', also from Kordes, is a companion to 'Roseromantic'. It grows to 1 m (3 ft) × 1.5 m (5 ft) and flowers

'LITTLE WHITE PET' 1970 is a good companion rose for 'The Fairy', having pink buds opening to double white in long sprays and repeating for nine to ten months. Both look equally lovely as weeping standards.

'ROSEROMANTIC' Sometimes, a comparatively young rose fits the bill so well that it demands attention and 'Roseromantic' from Kordes is a good example. It opens its soft pink single blooms in multi-headed sprays six times between mid spring and early winter if dead-headed. Being a single, every hip starts to develop into a seed pod and, if

left, it will concentrate its energy in ripening to the detriment of flowering. Why I like it so well is for its growth habit of 1 m (3 ft) × 2 m (6.6 ft), which makes it ideal on an embankment or as a foreground shrub.

Old-Fashioned Bush Roses

Little Bush Roses are very sought after by gardeners with courtyards or small villa gardens, who have known and loved such buxom beauties as 'Duchesse

ABOVE: 'Heidisommer' from Kordes has a low spreading habit and is a great performer.

RIGHT: 'Dame Prudence', seen here with Oxypetalum caerulea, is a small bush for tub or foreground.

equally well, with a lemon bud opening to semi-double cream blooms which quickly fade to white.

'GREEN ICE' 1971 is a low compact growing Miniature and well named. The double blooms turn green with age and in late autumn it develops pink edges to the flowers which continue right through winter.

de Brabant' and hanker for the form and perfume without the bulk. Their prayers have been answered by David Austin, an English rose breeder, but before listing these delightful newcomers we will look at some of the old roses that qualify.

'**Autumn Delight**' 1933 is classified as a Hybrid Musk but is reminiscent in growth habit of a Floribunda. It is well named because, although perpetual, its most welcome display comes in late autumn when the yellow buds open to display cream semi-single blooms borne in clusters on top of the summer water shoots. Fragrant. Height: 1 m (3 ft).

'**Dainty Bess**' is a Hybrid Tea introduced by Archer in 1925. It has charmed rose lovers ever since. Its single clear rose pink blooms are characterised by wavy petals and a central boss (or prominence) of bright red stamens. They are borne in clusters with good repeat flowering. Fragrant. Height: 1 m (3 ft).

'**Devoniensis**' 1858 (magnolia rose) is always admired for its fully double, sometimes quartered, cream blooms of Tea Rose bud shape which develop a

RIGHT: *'Mrs R.M. Finch' repeats from early spring to mid winter in our garden.*

soft pink centre in cool or overcast weather. It will often produce a bouquet of blooms on top of a water shoot and is very fragrant. Height: 1 m (3 ft). There is also a climbing form.

'**Francis Dubreuil**' 1894, named for a tailor who became an expert rose grower, is an old Tea Rose with the most powerful true old rose fragrance. The deep black-red velvety blooms are superb in spring and repeat until winter, but it will burn at the edges of the petals in heat waves.

'**Gruss An Aachin**', a Hybrid Tea raised by Geduldig in 1909, is a rose of variable colour but is always a delight,

appreciated for its ability to harmonise with its neighbours. It has cupped creamy white blooms that can tone pearl pink or apricot at the centre according to the weather. Scented. Height: 1 m (3 ft).

'**Lady Brisbane**' (also known as 'Cramoise Superieur') was introduced in 1832 and is a little China Rose which rarely exceeds 75 cm (30 in) but is valued for its continuous display of cupped deep crimson globular blooms.

'**Mrs R. M. Finch**', popular in New Zealand and due for revival in Australia, was introduced by Mr Finch of Victoria, Australia, in 1923. It is a soft pink

Floribunda whose repeat flowering performances has it on display from mid spring through to late winter when it has to be pruned. Height: 1 m (3 ft).

'OLD BLUSH' 1752 ('Parsons's Pink China' or 'Common Monthly') grows to 1 m (3 ft) and opens its lavender to rose pink blooms almost continuously from mid spring to late winter when it, too, has to be pruned. Height 1 m (3 ft).

'SOUVENIR de la MALMAISON' 1843, qualifies as a good garden choice in every respect except one. It grows to 1 m (3 ft) and continuously opens its pale pink double cupped blooms, which are regularly quartered and deliciously fragrant. However, it is notorious for balling in showery weather and is subject to powdery mildew. In a dry climate it can put on a magnificent display right into winter. There is also a climbing form.

'SOUVENIR de ST ANNE'S' is a sport of 'Souvenir de la Malmaison', which occurred in Ireland. It has the same delicate pink colouring, but the flower is a charming semi-double which fades to white in hot weather. It has more vigour than its parent and can reach 2 m (6.6 ft). Again, the foliage can be prone to mildew. A rose that I saw in New Zealand gardens would be a good substitute for 'Souvenir de St Anne's', although it is not yet available in some countries.

'Pearl Drift', introduced by Le Grice in 1980, is a *Rosa bracteata* Hybrid Shrub Rose with very healthy foliage and the same wonderful, soft pink flower form. Watch for its introduction.

SMALL FLORIBUNDA ROSES

Some small and relatively modern Floribunda Roses are offered for consideration.

'AMBER QUEEN' from Harkness 1984, which won Rose of the Year 1984, is a deep yellow that does not fade in strong sunlight. Fragrant. Height: 1 m (3 ft).

'EDELWEISS', a Floribunda raised by Poulsen 1970, has fragrant semi-double cream blooms and could be used as a companion to 'Amber Queen'.

'SHADY LADY' is a very recent introduction from Meisecaso and cannot be omitted because of its ability to

❦

BELOW: *'Shady Lady' is popular with gardeners who have semi-shaded gardens.*

flower well in partial shade. The cherry red semi-single flowers with pale centres are borne in clusters in typical Floribunda style. With removal of the spent blooms it will continue to flower right into winter.

SHRUB ROSES

Moving on to roses which reach 1.5 m (5 ft), we find a wealth of shrub roses—those below this height are termed Bush Roses. In 1962, a tutor in horticulture whose knowledge I greatly respected described the rose as a magnificent cut flower but a lousy shrub. Thinking back and remembering the flood of lanky modern Hybrid Tea Roses then described as Grandifloras, I tended to agree, but not today.

'DUCHESSE de BRABANT' 1857, another weak-necked Tea Rose, is a firm favourite nevertheless because of its soft shell pink cupped fully double blooms, which are richly fragrant and produced non-stop from spring to early winter when it must be pruned. Because it is still covered with flowers at that time, I and others have fallen into the trap of leaving it unpruned, but it is a mistake not to be repeated as its growth is too vigorous. 1.5 m (5 ft) x 1.5 m (5 ft) is the optimum to aim for.

'ICEBERG', raised by Kordes in 1958 and classified as a Floribunda, is the most popular of roses. It mixes beautifully with the true old-fashioneds and the more recently introduced English Shrub Roses bred by David Austin. The pure white blooms carry a touch of pale pink in autumn and winter and its repeat performance is tremendous.

'MRS B. R. CANT' 1901, is another very fragrant Tea Rose with large cupped blooms with an informal centre, the colour being deep rose pink to bronzy red, paler on the reverse, with a very long flowering period.

'MME ABEL CHATENAY' 1895 is an old favourite with a modern look. The pointed bud opens to display reflexing petals that are pale pink inside and deeper pink on the outside. It has a tall spreading habit and is fragrant.

'WHITE DUCHESSE de BRABANT', only recently introduced in Australia, is similar in all respects, the white flower with a flush of pearl pink in the centre petals.

Small Shrub Roses

Four that I grow, and which do not exceed 1.2 m (4 ft), include:

'HONEYFLOW', raised by Reitmuller and released in Australia around 1960, is a multi-caned shrub rose bearing large trusses of white single blooms edged with pale pink. The latter colour is more evident in autumn and on overcast days.

'JEAN DUCHER', introduced prior to 1889, is a winter delight, but also generous in other seasons. The soft apricot peach Tea Rose blooms are very fragrant. In good soils it can exceed 1.2 m (4 ft) but is controllable.

'LADY HILLINGDON' 1910 is a Tea Rose of rich old gold colouring which, like 'Iceberg' and 'Jean Ducher', blooms from early spring to mid winter. It has dark red new growth, turning bronze green, and distinctive red bark. The flower has a weak neck which is not a disadvantage when growing the climbing version as you look up into the flowers. It looks fantastic on a grey stone wall.

HYBRID MUSK ROSES

Many of the Hybrid Musks were raised by the Reverend Pemberton of East Anglia and released by him in the 1920s. They are of loose spreading habit and require space either vertically or horizontally. Some lend themselves to being trained as weeping standards.

'BALLERINA' 1937 grows like a fountain, sending up arching canes which radiate out from the centre to form a shrub of 1.8 m (6 ft) × 2.4 m (8 ft). It is later to flower, covering itself in late spring with soft cherry pink small single blooms, each with a white centre along each cane. It repeats in autumn to a lesser extent. Some fragrance.

'BUFF BEAUTY' Bentall 1939 is well named. The multi-headed sprays of semi-double blooms, which open buff yellow and fade to lemon and cream with age, are displayed on arching canes. It can be trained as a broad spreading shrub, a weeping standard, or espaliered as a moderate climber on a fence. This richly fragrant rose repeats freely.

'CORNELIA' Pemberton 1925 is similar to 'Buff Beauty' in growth habit, but its coppery pink buds open to soft lavender pink semi-double fragrant blooms in long sprays.

'ERFURT', named for a city in Germany, is a Hybrid Musk raised by Kordes in 1939. The white rippling petals are edged carmine pink and the semi-double fragrant blooms are borne in clusters on a compact bush of 1.5 m (5 ft) in height. It repeats from spring to autumn.

'FELECIA' Pemberton 1928 can develop into a tall bushy shrub of 2 m (6.5 ft) × 2 m (6.5 ft) if space permits. The salmon pink semi-double blooms have a touch of creamy buff in the centres. Very fragrant and repeat flowering.

'PENELOPE' Pemberton 1924, parentage 'Ophelia' × 'Trier', is a delight in all seasons but particularly in late autumn, when cool nights bring a flush of soft pink into the semi-double creamy white fragrant blooms which are produced in huge trusses along the arching canes. It has a spreading habit that responds to being used against a fence.

'SADLER'S WELLS' is a very recent introduction in this class and has Floribunda-like clusters of strawberry red single blooms, each with an ivory centre and decidedly wavy petals. It has long canes produced in an upright fashion and it repeats well. 'Erfurt' could well be a suitable companion for 'Sadler's Wells'.

❧

LEFT: *'Penelope' has blooms that come in clusters and are always a delight.*

FOLLOWING PAGES: *Mottisfont Abbey Heritage Rose Garden in Hampshire, England, was designed by Graham Thomas for the National Trust. Standardised 'Little White Pet' roses are centred in each arch.*

Rugosa Roses

It is important to also include the species *R. rugosa*, which originated in Japan, for its value both as a rose for salt-exposed coastal gardens and its acceptance of partial shade. The range of colours available is restricted to white, pink, red, lavender and one hybrid lemon yellow called 'Agnes'. The bushes are characterised by their unusually coarse foliage and numerous prickles. The majority carry large crimson hips in autumn.

'Blanc Double de Coubert' is one of the most popular hybrids flowering pure white, very fragrant and recurrent. Introduced in 1892, it has the climber 'Sombreuil' as one of its parents. The wayward canes need early pruning to encourage a compact shape up to 2 m (6.6 ft). *R. rugosa* 'Alba' is the other parent and it has a single white bloom with petals that curl inwards to hide its true beauty.

'Fimbriata' Morlet 1891, with fringed white petals, is a tall grower, having the climber 'Mme Alfred Carrière' as one of its parents.

'Frau Dagmar Hastrup' 1914, a soft pink single, is undoubtedly everyone's first choice, growing to 1.2 m (4 ft) × 1.5 m (5 ft) with pruning to control its

dimensions. It carries its main flush in spring with repeat spasmodic blooming in summer.

'Martin Frobisher' 1968, raised at the Canadian Department of Agriculture, is a hybrid Rugosa × *R. pimpinellifolia* that flowers double soft pink, is scented, repeats freely and has red bark on the new growth, which is thornless in infancy.

ABOVE: *'Frau Dagmar Hastrup' is not difficult to place and will grow in coastal areas.*

Climbers

Again, because few of us can place as many Climbing Roses as we fancy, it is important to look at the growth habits and select those types best suited to the area. For courtyard gardens where wall space is at a premium, Climbing Miniature Roses worth considering are 'Jeanne Lajoie' and 'Softie'.

'ABRAHAM DARBY' Austin 1985 has a Climber, 'Aloha', as one of its parents and so I have not even attempted to grow it as a shrub. Planted to clothe an arch, it has very large apricot gold fully double cupped blooms which age to deep pink, with an irresistible myrrh fragrance. Flowers mid spring to mid winter.

ABOVE: *'Charles Austin' as a Pillar Rose in the garden of Joanna and Peter Masfen of Auckland.*

✿

'CHARLES AUSTIN' Austin 1973 and **'YELLOW CHARLES AUSTIN' Austin** 1981 are in the same category as 'Leander' Austin and to obtain repeat flowering they must be 'firmly pruned', according to Austin's own advice.

'CRESSIDA' Austin 1983 is a moderate Climber which lends itself to being displayed in a trainer. The soft lax canes are too wayward to control as a shrub. It has a creamy apricot fully double flower of myrrh fragrance and a decidedly pink flush in autumn. Repeats freely.

✿

ABOVE: *'Abraham Darby' has a very strong myrhh fragrance; it is seen here tubbed by Suzanne Turley.*

'CYMBELINE' Austin 1982 is much better displayed as a Climber than struggling to control its wayward growth as a Shrub. It has the most divine myrrh fragrance and soft pink fully double blooms, with a greyish influence as it ages. It repeats from mid spring to winter.

'GAY VISTA' Reitmuller 1960 is a moderate Climber suited to espaliering on a fence panel where it will repeat from mid spring to mid winter. It has cerise pink single flowers, each with a white eye, and they are produced in large trusses at the ends of arching canes. Lightly fragrant. It is sometimes listed as a Shrub Rose.

'JEANNE LAJOIE' was given to me by Mary Glasson, in whose garden I first saw its beauty and potential. It has perfectly formed small pointed buds in clusters opening to a soft carmine pink bloom. Mary's plant was growing in an elegant metal trainer, which she had had the local blacksmith make especially to her design, but it can also be trained on a tripod or against a small lattice panel.

'LEANDER' Austin 1982 Some Climbers lend themselves to use as Pillar Roses and 'Leander' has such upright canes as to qualify, although eventually the canes do arch. The clusters of fruity fragranced double flowers open apricot but soon fade to pink. Spring to winter repeat.

ABOVE: *'Gay Vista' puts on a great repeat show for all who drive in our gate.*

🌿

'LUCETTA' Austin 1983 (re-released 1992) has similar arching growth and is well suited to be espaliered or trained as a Climber. Soft blush pink fading to white, the blooms can be as large as 15 cm (6 in) across when produced singly, but they also occur in clusters.

'MOTH' Austin is one of the most unusually coloured and simply delightful moderate Climbers one could wish for, and yet Austin himself does not hold it in high regard. Some roses perform better in another country and 'Moth' is a good illustration of this, being well suited to Australian conditions. I describe the colour on opening as a beige milk coffee, ageing to dusky pink, and the flower is well named. As the flowers sit on horizontally trained canes, the fluted petals remind one of moth wings. Sometimes listed as a Shrub Rose.

ABOVE: *'Windrush' is loved for its simplicity and lemon yellow buds.*

🌿

'SOFTIE', a very recent introduction similar to 'Jeanne Lajoie', in every respect except that it has soft apricot buff buds which, as they open, fade to pale lemon. Both are definitely little Climbers.

Climbers to Use as Pillar Roses

Three moderate Climbers that lend themselves to being used as Pillar Roses are 'Champney's Pink Cluster', 'Golden Wings' and 'Pierre de Ronsard'.

'CHAMPNEY'S PINK CLUSTER' was the first Noisette 1811 and has large sprays of cupped blush pink tinged lilac blooms, which are fragrant. Repeats.

'GOLDEN WINGS' Shepherd 1956 is a hybrid of *Rosa pimpinellifolia* with single deep butter yellow blooms and honey red stamens, which are very attractive. Although described as a tall Shrub, mine has gone into a trainer to control its long canes.

'PIERRE de RONSARD' Meilland 1986 is one of the few very new old-fashioned looking Pillar Roses to be included for it has undeniable charm. The very large cupped blooms have ivory cream outer petals with a centre packed full of rich pink inner petals, a slight musk fragrance, and the blooms ball in prolonged wet weather.

Vigorous Climbers

A few of the roses already described elsewhere are also offered as Climbers, including 'Cecile Brunner', 'Dainty Bess', 'Devoniensis', 'Iceberg', 'Mme Abel Chatenay' and 'Souvenir de la Malmaison'.

'ALTISSIMO' raised by Delbard-Chabert in 1966, is a brilliant large scarlet red single climbing Floribunda with a very upright habit, making it a popular choice, particularly on a white wall.

ABOVE : *A tunnel of climbing 'Iceberg' at Ohinetiti garden, Christchurch, New Zealand.*

❧

'BLACK BOY' Alister Clark 1919 has a richly perfumed black red bloom opening from a pointed bud. The blooms fade in spring but hold their colour well with its second flowering in late autumn.

'CARABELLA' Reitmuller 1960 is the most popular Climber sold in our nursery because it covers itself with great trusses of apple blossom single white blooms edged pale pink, as does its sister 'Honeyflow'. Light fragrance and vigorous growth. We have used it as a Pillar Rose supported by a broad half hoop, but it could also cover a pergola.

ABOVE : *'Clair Matin' putting on a great display for Sally and Bay Allison.*

❧

'CLAIR MATIN' 1960, a Shrub–Climber, produces soft salmon pink blooms very freely, is fragrant, and perpetually in flower.

'CREPUSCULE' 1904, a Noisette, is popular for its old gold pointed buds which open with more than a hint of salmon in cooler climates. Described as a Shrub–Climber, it is probably much happier as the latter where it will cover a small pergola and put on a great display from early spring to mid winter.

'CRIMSON GLORY' 1938 The Bush form was introduced in 1935. It is a deep red

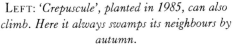

LEFT: *'Crepuscule', planted in 1985, can also climb. Here it always swamps its neighbours by autumn.*

Hybrid Tea which, from a large pointed bud, opens to velvety crimson and is very fragrant. Repeat flowering.

'LAMARQUE', a Noisette raised by Marechal in 1830, has a tea scent. Its parentage, 'Blush Noisette' × 'Park's Yellow' from China, has given us a white rose with lemon towards the centre which is sometimes quilled in this fully double flower. The nodding blooms are an advantage as a Climber.

'LORRAINE LEE' Alister Clark 1930. The Bush form was introduced in 1924. It is a Tea Rose with very fragrant deep pink blooms, described by Heather Rumsey as shrimp pink. It is grown and loved for its winter flowering habit and is better for being pruned in early autumn.

'MME ALFRED CARRIERE' is extremely vigorous in growth. The very fragrant white blooms are touched with pale pink at the centre. Raised by J. Schwartz in 1879, it has remained very popular.

'NEW DAWN', raised in 1930 by Dreer Somerset, is a soft silvery pink Climber with three definite flushes—in spring, summer and autumn. Described as a large rambler up to 6 m (20 ft), it certainly requires hard pruning in winter unless you are sending it up a tall tree.

'OPHELIA', the Bush form Hybrid Tea, was introduced in 1912 and the Climber followed in 1920. The large pointed buds open soft apricot, quickly fading to near white in strong spring sunshine. It is fragrant and repeats.

'SEAFOAM' is too useful to omit. Released in 1965, it can be employed as a moderate screening Climber, as a sprawling groundcover on an embankment, or as a weeping Standard, the latter being the most beautiful amongst weepers. The small semi-double pure white fragrant blooms are produced in clusters in spring, summer and autumn when the flowers are flushed pale pink.

'SOUVENIR de MME BOULLET' 1930 opens from a very large pointed bud, the old gold blooms shade to lemon at the centre. It is sometimes mistaken for Lady Hillingdon, but the growth is much more vigorous and it is very floriferous when the arching canes are horizontalised.

'SPARRIESHOOP' Kordes 1955 is a very vigorous Climber which produces medium single blush to a light salmon pink blooms with very pale centres and buff stamens. The multi-cluster heads of single blooms are displayed terminally on stiff canes. There is a climbing white form available in New Zealand and a Shrub form as well.

DAVID AUSTIN'S ENGLISH ROSES

As a child I always looked forward to dessert at the end of dinner and I have saved the most tempting until last— David Austin's English roses. Again, these shall be divided into groups according to their growth habit commencing with the small Bush types. David Austin's first breakthrough came in 1961 with the once-flowering 'Constance Spry', which also has a myrrh fragrance. 'Chianti' followed in 1965, with large *gallica*-like deep crimson blooms ageing to purple, although because of its colour and one-season blooming, it has not been really popular. The only other once-flowering rose released by him was 'Shropshire Lass', which has white single poppy-like blooms edged pink.

His aim throughout the breeding program was to produce old-fashioned looking, repeat flowering, fragrant roses in which he has been eminently successful. Some are of delicate tones while others are either deep or very unusual colours.

Many of the Austin roses already released have proved to be much more vigorous than the dimensions published in his catalogue, and it is interesting to note that in the 18th edition of the catalogue (released 1990), there is a much greater emphasis on small Bush Roses.

Small Bush Roses

'CANTERBURY' was an early release in 1969 and is an unusual rose: the soft warm pink single blooms have slightly wavy petals which resemble a semi-double camellia. Fragrant and compact but very floriferous from mid spring to early winter. 1 m (3 ft) × 1 m (3 ft).

'CHARMAIN' 1982 is a very full petalled cupped flower of deep pink with an old rose fragrance. 1 m (3 ft) × 1 m (3 ft) and repeats freely.

'DAME PRUDENCE', another early release, has been dropped by Austin.

Infinitely charming, it grows into a moderate little bush producing pink and white bicolour blooms from spring to winter. It is an ideal companion for 'Wife of Bath'.

'DOVE' 1894 (released in 1992) has smallish dainty blush pink Tea Rose buds opening to a blush white, making it a useful harmoniser. Height: 1 m (3 ft).

'FAIR BIANCA' 1982 is a white rose with a button eye reminiscent of 'Madam Hardy'. It has good fragrance, the outer cup of petals being filled with flattened and reflex petals. It repeat flowers and is compact at 1 m (3 ft) × 0.8 m (2.5 ft).

'PRETTY JESSICA' 1983 is perfect for the small garden and very old-fashioned in appearance, with warm rich pink globular blooms of strong fragrance. It is ideal in a tub. 0.8 m (2.5 ft) × 0.6 m (2 ft).

'PROSPERO' 1982 performs well in our garden and is admired for its unusual *gallica*-like blooms, which remind people of a small dahlia bloom. The deep crimson flower ages to purple. Fragrant, repeats spring to winter. Height: 1 m (3 ft).

'TAMORA' 1983, a little gem of salmon apricot fading to buff yellow, it is not likely to be dropped from catalogues for it is outstanding both in the deeply

cupped blooms of myrrh fragrance and its compact growth to 1 m (3 ft).

'WIFE OF BATH' 1969 has globular or peony-like soft lavender pink blooms, which fade to paler pink at the outer edges. They are abundantly produced and have a strong myrrh fragrance. Spring to winter. 1 m (3 ft) × 1 m (3 ft).

'THE YEOMAN', wrongly released in Australia as 'Lilian Austin', and totally dissimilar in every way, is a little gem. Already dropped by Austin and some of his agents because it is said to be difficult to propagate, it is ideal as a tub or front row subject. Growth is less than 1 m (3 ft), usually between 0.7 m (2.3 ft) and 0.8 m (2.6 ft) on a stiff little bush, but the flowers are a rich mix of apricot salmon ageing to pink, with that unforgettable myrrh fragrance. Do not hard prune, and dead-head for continuous blooming.

Large Bush Roses

All the small Bush Roses previously listed repeat from spring to winter and so, too, do those larger growers about to be listed.

'BELLE STORY' opens as a cupped in-curved full semi-double bloom of rich warm pink fading to silvery pink,

opening wide to display attractive golden stamens. 1.2 m (4 ft) × 1.2 m (4 ft).

'CLAIRE ROSE' 1986 has large soft pink flowers very much in the manner of the quartered 'Souvenir de la Malmaison', but it fades with age to almost white. Fragrant. 1.2 m (4 ft) × 1.2 m (4 ft).

'DAPPLE DAWN' is a soft but warm pink single bloom, paler at the edges. It is vigorous and very floriferous, but can be hard-pruned if space is at a premium. 1.5 m (5 ft) × 1.2 m (4 ft).

ABOVE: *'The Friar' can look much pinker in early spring and late autumn.*

'ELLEN' 1984, is a Shrub with a flower similar to that of 'Abraham Darby' and a strong fragrance. 1.2 m (4 ft) × 1.2 m (4 ft).

'THE FRIAR', probably superseded by 'Perdita', has proven itself to be a reliable two-tone apricot rose of great appeal. 1.2 m (4 ft) × 1 m (3 ft).

'GERTRUDE JEKYLL' 1986, seen in New Zealand with robust arching growth, has typical old rose formation blooms of rich pink and a delicious old rose fragrance. 1.5 m (5 ft) × 1.2 m (4 ft).

ABOVE LEFT: *'Heritage' has great appeal.*

ABOVE RIGHT: *'Hero' blooms generously over nine months.*

LEFT: *'Ellen' opens a rich apricot with paler outer petals.*

'HERITAGE' 1984 is destined to be a top favourite because of its beautiful cupped, full petalled, clear shell pink, the kind of bloom painted by the Dutch masters. It has an old rose fragrance, and a robust bushy habit. 1.2 m (4 ft) × 1.2 m (4 ft).

'HERO' 1982 has large double satiny deep pink blooms, abundantly produced on an open arching caned shrub which can also be trained as a Pillar Rose. 1.2 m (4 ft) × 1.5 m (5 ft).

'IMMORTAL JUNO' 1983 is a cupped pink double with more than a hint of blue, making it a deep lavender pink with mauve overtones. An old rose fragrance. 1.5 m (5 ft) × 1.2 m (4 ft).

'JACQUENETTA' 1983, only released in 1992, is a single flowered rose of unusual colouring. A warm apricot pink with a suggestion of beige, it ages to blush pink. The wavy petals are part of its charm. As one of its parents is 'Charles Austin', the growth is composed of arching canes, making it useful against a fence.

'LILIAN AUSTIN' 1973, is a semi-double to double of deep salmon pink tinted orange and apricot. As it opens fully it displays a yellow base to each petal. Arching cane growth. 1.2 m (4 ft) × 1.2 m (4 ft).

'MOONBEAM' 1983 For those who love soft colours, this large semi-single does sometimes produce more than five petals, and opens to a pale blush apricot fading to creamy white. Prune hard for a compact bush of 1.2 m (4 ft) × 1.2 m (4 ft).

'OTHELLO' 1986 has a rich dark crimson full petalled and cupped formation of blooms with a strong old rose fragrance. Upright to 1.2 m (4 ft) × 1 m (3 ft).

'PERDITA' 1983, can open perfect quartered flowers from a pointed bud of

softest apricot blush with a pronounced apricot centre turning pink in cooler weather. Fragrant. 1.2 m (4 ft) × 1 m (3 ft).

'REDCOAT' 1973 is yet to be appreciated for its abundantly produced single cyclamen red blooms. The growth habit is loose and mine has improved by being contained within a circular trainer.

'THE REEVE' 1979 has deep lavender pink globular flowers, sometimes in-curving and freely produced, which make it a rose of very great appeal. 1.5 m (5 ft) × 1.2 m (4 ft).

'SWAN' 1987 is a strongly growing Shrub Rose producing clusters of white rosette-shaped flowers with soft lemon buff centres. Arching canes capable of more than 1.2 m (4 ft) × 1.2 m (4 ft).

'SYMPHONY' 1986 is a soft lemon yellow fading at the outer edges with a tight rosette of petals. Not yet trialled for dimensions, but listed at 1.2 m (4 ft) × 1 m (3 ft).

'THE SQUIRE' 1977 has large deep, sometimes quartered, blooms of rich dark crimson which can burn in hot weather, but until we see 'William Shakespeare' (due for release in 1992), it will remain the best red to come our way. 1.2 m (4 ft) × 1 m (3 ft) and ours is tubbed.

ABOVE: *'The Squire' is popular with male gardeners.*

'TROILUS' 1983 has a deep cupped flower of soft honey buff to apricot cream with a sweet honey fragrance to match. The colour is best appreciated in cooler weather. Sturdy, upright growth. 1 m (3 ft) × 1.2 m (4 ft).

'WENLOCK' 1984 has a medium to large fully petalled fragrant flower of crimson, freely produced on a robust shrub of 1.2 m (4 ft) × 1.2 m (4 ft).

'WILLIAM SHAKESPEARE' 1987 is the result of crossing two beauties: 'Mary

Rose' and 'The Squire'. The deeply cupped full petalled dark crimson blooms have a strong old rose fragrance. 1.2 m (4 ft) × 1.2 m (4 ft).

'WINDRUSH' 1984 is still in short supply but worth having for its lovely simple single blooms, sometimes with extra small petals, opening lemon yellow buds which quickly fade to white. Two generations removed from 'Golden Wings', one of its grandparents, its flowers are larger and it makes a good companion for 'Graham Thomas'.

Vigorous Shrub Roses

Why haven't I listed 'Mary Rose' or 'Graham Thomas' yet? Together with 'The Prioress', I class them as really vigorous Shrubs.

'GRAHAM THOMAS' 1983, named for the famous rosarian Graham Stuart Thomas, has a deep canary yellow cupped fully petalled double bloom which is generously produced on fast growing canes. At Roseneath, a nursery north of Auckland, New Zealand, I saw

it trained as a climber up to 3 m (10 ft) with its canes skilfully pruned to produce a wonderful display. 'Windrush' was planted in front of it. Ours is kept as a shrub of 1.5 m (5 ft) × 1.5 m (5 ft).

'THE PRIORESS' 1969 has delicate blush pink fragrant cupped blooms, which fade quickly to white but it is capable of reaching 2.2 m (7.2 ft) × 1.5 m (3 ft) by late autumn and requires heavy pruning to control its dimensions.

'MARY ROSE' 1983, named after Henry VIII's wooden flagship which was raised from The Solent, is a deservedly popular lavender pink many petalled rose. It has a damask fragrance and grows to 1.6 m (5.2 ft) by autumn in a bushy upright manner. Always a joy. It has a pure white sport called 'Winchester Cathedral'.

The excitement of every rose grower is rewarded with the opening of the first buds of new plants which were acquired and planted during the winter season or later from containers. The time spent poring over catalogues and books can, in due course, result in the pleasure of seeing new flowers in your garden.

The Austin roses for which I wait

LEFT: *'Windrush' in front of 'Graham Thomas' trained as a Climber at Roseneath Nursery, New Zealand.*

LEFT: *The delicate blush pink bud of 'The Prioress' retains its colour on overcast days.*

BELOW: *'Desprez à Fleur Jaune' is expertly trained over the entry arch to the garden of Joan and Keith Innes.*

impatiently are 'Winchester Cathedral', 'Potter and Moore' (which looks similar to 'Wife of Bath', though one can never really be sure until it is trialled). Others are 'Francine Austin' (a low growing white), 'Jayne Austin' (a lemon version of 'Graham Thomas'), 'Sharifa Asma' (which could be a substitute for 'Dame Prudence'), 'Bibi Maizoon' (which might replace 'Charmain') and 'Brother Cadfel' (a soft pink that grows to 0.8 m (2.6 ft). Little Bush Roses of great beauty are sure of a place in our gardens.

PROBLEMS WITH ROSES

I am constantly asked for the old-fashioned roses that are resistant to pests and diseases, and I answer that all roses are attacked by aphids and in showery weather no rose is resistant to black spot. Some are better than others.

Some are more susceptible to powdery mildew than others and nothing will stop rose louse scale from multiplying

on roses in part shade if the grower will not use his or her spray equipment. Hosing aphids off buds is not really successful as they crawl or fly back, or are carried back by ants, very quickly. Flowers of sulphur will help control powdery mildew but usually when it is rampant the weather is too showery for the powder or dust to stay on the leaves. As a rose lover, you have to face up to keeping your loved bushes, shrubs and climbers in a healthy state or close your eyes to their condition and not complain about poor foliage and poor flowers. For those who wish to pick lovely blooms, rose culture is included in the chapter on maintenance.

Rose Sickness

Rose sickness is a term applied to a deteriorating bush that is seemingly surrounded by healthy plants all having received the same amount of moisture and fertiliser. The answer may lie in the preparation of the site.

The preparation of a site for roses is, generally speaking, the same as for any other tree or shrub, as discussed in Chapter 2. With normal care it can be expected to support roses for upwards of 30 years. However, many of us do not stay at one address for so long, or we wish to place some new and beautiful variety that we cannot live without, and in small gardens with limited sunny positions, we may want to plant a new rose where one is already established.

The soil that the old rose bush occupies must be completely removed, because it is suggested by some rose authorities that the rotting roots of an old rose left in the soil will adversely affect the new plant, and it will not thrive. It is an important point to remember if you buy a property with an established rose garden and you find the

ABOVE: *'Mary Rose' develops into a great shrub and repeat blooms generously.*

roses unappealing, either in flower form or growth habit.

CHAPTER 9

Perennials, Groundcovers and Free-Seeding Annuals

I never cease to be amazed at the expectations of some beginners who want the perfect plant; that is, one that flowers all year round, does not become untidy, requires no water, no food, no pruning or trimming and no staking. I calmly answer that the Lord has not yet invented the plant they are asking for. If he had, it would be in every garden and then it would quickly lose its appeal.

If you give the same basic ingredients to six chefs they will create six different dishes using various additions, be they

🌿

LEFT: *Shasta 'Chiffon' blooms in mid summer. In hot areas dappled shade is desirable.*

herbs, spices, extra vegetables, noodles, some special wine or whatever. Gardeners will do the same thing with perennials, for if shrubs are the fabric of the garden, then perennials are the accessories, the fillers and sometimes the lace on the cuff.

For the new gardener, the term 'perennial' needs explanation. A perennial is a soft-wooded plant which persists for more than two years and is either evergreen or herbaceous, meaning it dies down for the winter, regrowing from its crown in the spring. A biennial is a plant that flowers twice and then dies or needs to be removed, such as the foxglove, but foxgloves drop so much

seed that they ensure their own survival. Annuals flower only once, and there are some annuals which, because they seed so generously, are synonymous with cottage gardens.

Earlier I mentioned that nature had divided her plants into one-third shade lovers and two-thirds which must have sun. This also applies to perennials and to help those with shady gardens I have categorised them according to height, beginning with groundcovers.

PLANTS FOR SEMI-SHADE

Groundcovers

CAMPANULA istriaca looks very similar to *C. poscharskyana*: they both have sky blue star-shaped bell flowers and identical growth habits, but the latter flowers only in spring whereas *C. istriaca* will continue spasmodically flowering for six months given adequate water.

CAMPANULA portenschlagiana syn. **Muralis** has much smaller foliage and fat little mauve blue bells. All four enjoy light dappled shade.

CAMPANULA poscharskyana 'E. H. Frost' is identical in growth, producing white star-shaped bells on long prostrate stems in mid to late spring.

CAMPANULA poscharskyana 'Lisduggan' has soft lavender pink star-shaped bells, also in mid to late spring.

CERATOSTIGMA plumbaginoides has deep gentian blue small flowers from mid summer to mid autumn. The habit is low—23 cm (9 in)—and it spreads by suckering growth which is controllable. It is deciduous, colouring well in cool climates.

LAMIUM maculatum 'Roseum' is a recent introduction with silver leaves margined green, and soft pink flowers that are produced over a long period in spring and late summer.

LAMIUM maculatum 'White Nancy' has foliage which is almost silver white and a pure white flower. Like 'Roseum' it is long-flowering and a very attractive addition to the shady garden.

LAMIUM maculatam 'Silver Beacon' is similar to 'Roseum' but the flower is deep pink. All three can benefit from trimming as necessary.

LYSIMACHIA nummularia 'Aurea' (creeping jenny) has golden foliage in high light situations but turns green in deeper shade. It has a spillover habit and a yellow flower in early summer.

SCHIZOCENTRON elegans is still sometimes called by its old name of

Heeria or, commonly, Spanish shawl. The fine-leafed trailing stems take root in moist soil and in late spring it produces abundant cerise red flowers, which are not unlike a miniature lasiandra bloom. It will grow in sun but performs better in semi-shade in warm climates.

SCUTELLARIA indica var. japonica is a plant that sends up flower stems to 15 cm (6 in) in autumn and spring, which carry lipped small flowers of blue mauve in a loose spike. The foliage is small and it will spread in dappled shade.

STELLARIA holstea has soft grass-like narrow leaves and a cushiony mat habit of growth. It displays pure white open bell flowers in late winter, and finishes in mid spring according to the weather.

VIOLA cornuta 'Blue Moon' is not a long-lived perennial, but is easily struck from cuttings and has the most charming small pansy face of half sky blue and half cream. Ideal for tucking under the shady side of a large rose bush.

VIOLA hederacea (native violet) has become very popular, for its white flowers with mauve purple centres are produced the whole year round. It has one vice as a groundcover in that it will climb into the centres of other plants, like azaleas, and ultimately cause their deterioration.

VIOLA labradorica is a tough little gem which seeds freely, sometimes into open sunny positions where it will develop bronzy purple foliage which is quite attractive. The flowers are abundantly produced above the foliage, are violet blue and it blooms in spring and autumn.

VIOLA odorata and cultivars (English violet) *V. odorata* flowers are blue violet and very fragrant. They will increase very rapidly and free-seed in both semi-shade and full sun positions. Many gardeners become so addicted to violets that it becomes a challenge to collect the various colours and cultivars, beginning with the single white 'Alba'. *V. odorata* var. 'Rosea' is also sold as 'Rosina' and is a pink violet with a very strong sweet fragrance. It has a better depth of colour than 'Lavender Lady' or 'Lilac Glow'. 'Royal Robe' has the largest purple flower but only a slight fragrance. The commercial violet used for the bunches sold by florists is called 'Princess of Wales'. 'John Raddenbury' is sky blue with a white eye and the yellow violet *V. sulfurea* opens to display an apricot centre. The hardiest double is called 'King of the Doubles' and has both large leaves and large double flowers of lavender purple striped white at the centres.

Viola—no collection would be complete without the double parma violets (*V. odorata*). The pure white is 'Compte

Brazza', 'Marie Louise' is lavender mauve and 'Neapolitan' is pale lavender. All three are extremely fragrant.

VIOLA seiboldiana 'Dissecta' This violet looks so different that at first there is disbelief that it really is a violet. It has a cut leaf and grows as a neat bun shape without runnering. It opens its white fragrant flowers from late autumn to late winter. The seed pods pop open very readily, so there are always bonus seedlings to be relocated.

VIOLA sylvestris (wood violet), in either blue or pink, behaves like *V. labradorica*, flowering in summer as well as winter, but with plain green foliage.

VINCA minor is a small-leafed periwinkle which can be useful between paved car tracks in shade or sun. It works well in dry shade also, but needs controlling if the soil is rich. Apart from sky blue there is a single white, a double plum and a variegated blue form.

Low Perennials

ALCHEMILLA mollis (lady's mantle) needs semi-shade in warm areas. It is loved for its delightfully shaped

scalloped leaves, which trap droplets of water in between the tiny hairs on the leaf's surface. The flowers are lime green and are useful in decorative arrangements.

AQUILEGIA vulgaris and hybrids (granny's bonnets) have long been popular with gardeners for their quaint nodding blooms, which are freely produced throughout spring with a smaller flush in mid summer. *A. alpina*, a deep sky blue single, will grow and free-seed in full sun, but *A. vulgaris*, which comes in many shades of pink, blue and purple to almost black, needs semi-shade. The 'McKana' and

'Dragonfly' hybrids both have very long spurs and larger flowers, rarely pure, but almost always bicolour in some tempting colour combinations. *A. clematiflora* is spurless and very charming, with rows of pointed petals sometimes tipped cream. Other special strains are *A. hybrida* 'Mrs Scott Elliott' with long spurs and 'Nora Barlow', opening from tight little button buds and looking for all the world like grandma's frilly bonnet. *Aquilegia* varieties develop a crown which has a lifespan of about three years, but they scatter so much seed that they can be treated as weeds if they come up in the wrong place.

❦

RIGHT: *A farm garden, just two years old, featuring cottage garden plants that are the choice of Hilda and Neal Rahn, Berry, Australia.*

ASTILBE species in cool climates are grown beside streams, ponds or lakes, but in warm climates, these herbaceous perennials do very well in semi-shade with adequate water. Most frequently seen are the *A.* x *arendsii* varieties: 'Bremen' is lilac pink, 'Hyacinth' is soft pink, 'Fanal' crimson and 'Rhineland' deep rose pink. The feathery flower heads are on stems up to 0.6 m (2 ft) and should be cut as flowering finishes. The foliage is attractive and in cold areas straw over the crown is advised.

ASTRANTIA major 'Rosea' is loved by flower arrangers for its 'posy on a stem' flowers of soft carmine pink suffused with smoky grey in summer. It likes a moist position in part shade. The palmate foliage below the 0.5 m (1.6 ft) long flower stems is also attractive.

BERGENIA species were formerly called *Saxifraga* and are commonly known as London pride. They are broad-leafed evergreen perennials which flower in mid to late winter, in light pink, deep pink and now white. *B. cordifolia* 'Red' has a carmine pink flower and *B. purpurascens* has leaves which turn blood purple in winter. Once popular as an edging plant. Increase by division.

DICENTRA formosa 'Rosea' and 'Alba'
We would all love to grow *Dicentra spectabilis*, or bleeding heart, but if the climate is too warm it is a waste of money and time. Not so with pink lockets or white lockets. Very long flowering from mid spring to mid autumn, the little locket flowers dangle from 0.4 m (1.3 ft) stems held above furry grey green leaves. Herbaceous in cool climates.

EPIMEDIUM × versicolor 'Sulphureum'
is semi-evergreen, the leaves being pink tinged when young. In cool areas it colours well in late autumn. In spring the soft lemon blooms are produced amongst the foliage. Beth Chatto recommends clipping the foliage to get good flowering, but care would be needed in the timing, otherwise you might cut your budding flower stems as well. Tolerates dry shade but does appreciate moisture. Height: 0.3 m (1 ft).

HEUCHERA sanguinea (coral bells) has always been a very reliable performer, provided the shade is only light. Tall flower stems arise from a neat tuft of round green leaves and the flower colour can vary from pale to deep coral pink.

RIGHT: Astilbe plumila *flowers later and longer than other astilbes.*

HEUCHERA sanguinea 'Palace Purple'
has greenish white flowers in summer and the handsome leaves are deep purple in semi-shade. Flower stems reach 0.6 m (2 ft).

HEUCHERELLA tiarelloides 'Bridget Bloom' is a dainty cross with *Tiarella*, having soft pink flowers to 0.45 m (1.5 ft) in spring, summer and autumn. It prefers light soil as well as light shade.

IMPATIENS Plant the double forms only, as the singles behave like weeds. The doubles look like little roses at first glance, and magically bring colour into

the shady garden. Pure white, pale pink, salmon, deep rose pink and scarlet, with minor variations, cover the colour range. They do not like frosty weather. In cold districts lift, pot up and move to a warm sheltered spot for the winter to keep the desired colour. They are easily propagated by cuttings in spring. Height: 0.5 m (1.6 ft).

IRIS unguicularis is evergreen with narrow leaves to 0.4 m (1.3 ft) and in mid winter opens the loveliest soft blue or white flowers amongst the foliage. The blue form is a good companion for white jonquils.

LIROPE muscari 'variegata' The attractive gold and green striped leaves form a clump which is useful as an accent or edging plant in the shady garden. Its jacaranda blue spike flowers are produced in early summer. Suited to all but tropical areas. Height: 30 cm (12 in).

OMPHELOIDES verna (blue-eyed Mary) has bright blue forget-me-not like flowers in spring. It spreads rapidly in the woodland garden tolerating dry shade but flowering more abundantly with adequate moisture. Height: 23 cm (9 in).

POLEMONIUM pulcherrimum 'Blue Dove' is a miniature Jacob's ladder which grows as a low tuft of ferny foliage and in late winter and early spring opens sprays of sky blue flowers. It does not self-sow, but can be divided and looks best in group plantings. Height: 0.3 m (1 ft).

PULMONARIA saccharata (spotted lungwort) is much prettier than its common name implies. They like a damp, shaded location, but not poor drainage. In late winter the flowers open pink and turn blue as they age. The foliage, which is marbled silver and grey green, is very attractive.

PRIMULA species A genus of over 500 species, it includes *P. vulgaris*, the woodland primrose found in England

and Europe. Flowering in spring, its soft lemon yellow blooms are produced singly above broad deep green leaves. Increase is by division.

PRIMULA × juliana is a hybrid strain of soft pale pink to salmon with flowers of similar size to those of *P. vulgaris*.

ABOVE: Polemonium pulcherrimum *'Blue Dove'* and Primula obconica *complement each other.*

PRIMULA obconica has been improved from the original pale lilac found in China in 1880 and is marketed in flower in shades of apricot, white, rose pink and royal blue from early winter to mid spring. If planted in moist semi-shade—after serving as a house plant in good light—they will continue to spot flower, but always handle with gloves on as they can cause skin irritations.

PRIMULA veris (cowslip) has multi-flower stems, a little smaller in size of flower than the primrose and a deeper yellow.

Medium Height Perennials

ACANTHUS mollis (oyster plant or bear's breeches) is not for the tiny courtyard for it will clump to cover 1.5 m (5 ft). The handsome, deeply divided leaves were the inspiration for the tops of the Corinthian columns. The tall flower stem is produced in early summer, after which the plant looks a bit tatty while having a late summer rest, but by autumn it is back to looking fresh again.

ANEMONE* × *hybrida syn. *A. japonica* or *A. hupehensis* (Japanese wind flower) is essential to all shady gardens for the beauty and simplicity of its flowers, which are carried high above attractive foliage in early autumn. Wind anemones are evergreen and spread freely and widely so it is necessary to remove the

ABOVE: *Single pink and white wind anemones* (A. hupehensis) *peep out below a* Mahonia.

spent flower stems before they disperse their fluffy seeds. At the same time use hedge clippers to remove all the old foliage and, using a sharp spade, reduce the clump back to the size you desire, or they tend to swamp other plants. The colour range is 'Alba' (single white), 'Elegantissima' (double satiny pink), 'Kriemhild' (a semi-double rose pink) and 'Whirlwind' (a semi-double large white). There is also a single silver pink called 'September Charm'. They do not like summer drought or exposed windy sites. Foliage to 0.6 m (2 ft) and flower stems to 1 m (3 ft).

CAMPANULA alliarifolia is a summer flowering white belled perennial which reaches 0.6 m (2 ft) liking morning sun or dappled shade, and light moist soil.

CAMPANULA latiloba and *C. latiloba* **'Alba'.** Lavender blue or white, the cup-shaped flowers are thickly set on stiffly erect stems to 0.8 m (2.6 ft) and in warm areas light shade is essential for a good summer display.

CAMPANULA persicifolia and C. persicifolia 'Alba' have cupped bells in deep blue or white on stems reaching up to 0.8 m (2.6 ft). Happier in cool climates and with slightly alkaline soil.

CAMPANULA takesimana from Korea produces tall stems of large tubular creamy white bells, spotted pink within. A very reliable performer in light shade or full sun in cooler regions.

CAMPANULA trachelium 'Bernice' is like a miniature double purple Canterbury bell and is hardy flowering over a very long spring/summer period. Height: 0.6 m (2 ft).

HELLEBORUS orientalis (lenten rose) is every bit as essential as the wind anemone as a mainstay of winter in our garden. Flowering from early winter to spring, it comes in white, pale and deep pink, burgundy and plum, and the flowers are often spotted or finely veined. The deep green glossy serrated leaves are multi-lobed, palmate and always an attribute. Increase is by division as seedlings take at least three years to flower.

HOSTA species The range of *Hosta* species is at last increasing for those who admire the foliage effects that can be achieved when they are correctly placed and well grown. *H. sieboldiana* has very large blue rippled leaves and

ABOVE: *Helleborus flowers for three months in my garden. For decorative work split the cut stems for 5 cm (2 in).*

looks great with the rippled dark green heart-shaped leaves of *H. elata*. Others may prefer it with *H. fortunei* 'Aurea'. There is also a green edged with butter yellow, *H. fortunei* 'Albopicta'; and, of course, the green and white variegated *H. undulata* 'Albo-marginata' has always been great to light up a shady spot. Newer and popular for their fragrance is *H. plantaginea* 'Grandiflora', with heads of long white trumpet bells above large light green leaves. The smaller leafed

cultivar 'Honeybells' is also fragrant. They are herbaceous and snail bait must be used in spring as they are emerging.

PLATYCODON grandiflorus (balloon flower) gets its common name from the way in which the flower bud swells and pops like a balloon. It has roots like small carrots and is late to emerge from the soil in spring, flowering in late spring and early summer in white, pale pink and violet blue on stems to 0.8 m (2.6 ft). It can be divided when the clumps have built up and can also be raised from seed. Cutting of the first flowers will promote a second flowering in mid autumn. Balloon flowers will not

ABOVE: *The annual form of yellow* Calceolaria *has sprung up next to delphinium and the repeat flowering* Campanula rapunculoides.

tolerate poor drainage and will grow in full sun in cooler climates.

POLMONIUM caeruleum (Jacob's ladder) is a ferny foliaged perennial that flowers either sky blue or white to 0.6 m (2 ft) in mid summer and is easily divided in winter. The foliage will burn in full sun.

POLYGONATUM × hybridum (Solomon's seal) is like the balloon flower, in that it is both herbaceous and has a rhizome type root. The dainty white tipped green bell flowers hang from the underside of the arching stems of green foliage in spring. It loves a cool, moist position where it will readily increase to make a good clump.

TRADESCANTIA × andersoniana has a three-petalled flower produced almost all year round in moist, light shade. The long stems are multi-budded and the

plants need to be cut back when they become untidy. The most popular colours are 'Snowflake' (pure white), 'J. C. Weguelin' (pale blue) and 'Carmine Glow' (magenta pink). There is also a dark blue and a deep violet.

Tall Perennials

ACONITUM species (monkshood) do best in cooler regions, but that does not stop those in warmer parts trying it in light shade. The soil needs to be well drained for *A. arendsii*, which has hooded lavender blue flowers in autumn. Height: 1 m (3 ft). *A. napellus* is a deep violet blue summer-flowering monkshood to 1.2 m (4 ft). Both are herbaceous.

ARUNCUS dioicus (goat's beard) can easily reach 1.5 m (5 ft) in a moist rich soil and a semi-shaded position, where its plumes of cream flowers will open in mid summer.

CAMPANULA lactiflora has open bell flowers abundantly produced on tall stems to 1.2 m (4 ft) in lavender blue, white and pink, the latter having the cultivar name of *C. lactiflora* 'Pouffe'. It likes light shade and adequate moisture for good early summer flowering.

DIGITALIS species *D. purpurea* is biennial not perennial, and comes in

ABOVE: *Stately cream foxgloves in Elizabeth and Warren Scott's garden.*

white (sold as 'Alba'), cream and apricot pink. When grown from seedlings, *D. purpurea* will flower lavender pink, mauve and purple. They flower in November on very tall stems and will, if cut just below the finished flower, send up side branches to flower also.

DIGITALIS mertonensis flowers strawberry pink and is quite long-lived, sometimes missing the first spring to establish itself properly for the next.

NICOTIANA affinis Sadly, in Australia importation of the seed of these popular semi-perennial delights has been banned, so now we must all save the seed of what we have to prevent extinction. It is banned because it is related to and might affect the production of tobacco—how ridiculous. To walk in the garden early or late and pass by the fragrant pure white, pink, mauve or cerise flowering, tall plants up to 1.5 m (5 ft)—which close their flowers in the heat of the day—is a joy. To sniff the sweetness of *N. sylvestris*, which has long white tubular bell flowers, is also a joy, and to grow the lime green flowering *N. alata* is a proud achievement. *N. sylvestris* needs to have seed pods snipped off or it can be so free-seeding as to necessitate lots of undesired weeding. *N. affinis* will free-seed and, if cut back when untidy, will grow again from the base, but they are not long-lived and are treated as annuals in cold climates.

THALICTRUM dipterocarpum 'Lavender Shower' I quote my friend David Glen, one of the finest perennial nurserymen in Australia, for this one: 'One of the glories of summer, growing up to 2 m (6.5 ft), with a gypsophila-like cloud of daintily dangling, soft lavender flowers over a base of beautiful bluish, maidenhair leaves'. Sun for cooler regions and light shade for warm to hot districts. There is also a white form of 'Lavender Shower'.

THALICTRUM aquilegifolium The foliage is similar to that of *T. dipterocarpum* but the flower is totally dissimilar. It is a dusty pink pompom of stamens, quite pretty in its own way and worth growing.

PLANTS FOR SUNNY POSITIONS

Perennials

The tremendous range of perennials and groundcovers for sunny positions requires the discerning buyer to think about the colour, height, flowering period and micro climate that they are choosing plants for. There is a vast difference between the hot aspect against a wall compared to an open island bed with good air circulation, and there are many plants which are better performers in one macro climate than another. As an example, the grey foliaged plants (often described as silver foliaged) detest the humidity of February in Sydney, and in a wet summer will be lost through fungal attack, particularly in heavy soils. In cooler regions and lighter soils, they are tremendous—so let's look at these first.

Silver Grey Foliage Plants

ABOVE: *Jill Maunsell has planted lamb's ears, artemesias and santolina (cotton lavender) along this pathway.*

ACHILLEA clypeolata has grey green foliage and flat heads of yellow flowers throughout summer. Height: 1 m (3 ft).

ACHILLEA 'Moonshine' is a hybrid from Alan Bloom, with silver grey leaves and bright lemon yellow flat flower heads produced through spring and summer. Height 0.6 m (2 ft).

ANDROSACE lanuginosa is a pretty little groundcover that seems not to mind humidity and is a good performer in both cool and warm regions. It has clusters of small flowers on short stems above its small silver leaves from spring to autumn in white with a pink eye, and pale pink and lavender mauve with a darker eye.

ANTHEMIS punctata syn. *A. cupaniana*, with grey ferny foliage and white long stemmed daisy flowers, is a groundcover that is happier at elevation or where the nights are cool. Low and spreading habit to 23 cm (9 in).

ARTEMESIA abscinth is one of the ingredients of vermouth. It is a sprawling grey green plant best suited to the herb garden and reaches 0.6 m (2 ft) × 1.2 m (4 ft) if allowed. Three English *Artemesia* cultivars due to be released in Australia soon are 'Lambrook Silver', raised by the late Margery Fish, *Artemesia* 'Powis Castle' and *Artemesia* 'Valerie Furness'. All will need trialling in a warmer climate. They will be fine for cooler districts.

ARTEMESIA arborescens (silver wormwood) is tough, reliable and puts up with dry soil in half-day shade, asking only for regular light trimming to keep it a neat bun shape of 1.2 m (4 ft) × 1.2 m (4 ft).

CENTAUREA gymnocarpa is sometimes sold as dusty miller but this common name is also used for *Senecio cineraria*. The ferny silver grey leaves of this plant are enough to make it worth growing, but added to this is the spring display of tall branching stems carrying mauve pink cornflower type blooms in profusion. Foliage height: 0.6 m (2 ft); flower stems to 1 m (3 ft).

CERASTIUM tomentosum (snow in summer) is actually a spring flowering groundcover with, as you would expect, white flowers covering the grey hairy leaves described as tomentose. In humid weather it can collapse in the centre, but as autumn begins, it can be refurbished by taking rooted pieces from the extremities to start a new carpet effect. It also works well as a spillover.

ABOVE LEFT: *Clove pinks edge a gravel path backed by 'Iceberg' roses in the garden of Paddy and Sam Maling, Christchurch, New Zealand.*

ABOVE RIGHT: *A silver pear, artemesias and centaureas blended by Maryan Bishop, The Roseaire, Auckland.*

DIANTHUS species (clove pinks) are amongst the most fragrant of groundcovers, but their nomenclature is in a hopeless muddle in the trade. One of the all-time favourites is *D. plumaris* 'Mrs Sinkins', a double white with a beautifully strong clove scent, which is spring flowering. In fact all bloom then but some go on to flower over a very long period, for example, *Dianthus* 'Mars', a small bright red, and 'Norgate's White', which has just a touch of pale pink in the centre. *Dianthus* 'Pike's Pink', a spring only double lavender pink, has a very strong perfume, as does the double mauve pink called 'Old English'. There is an apricot salmon called 'Arthur', which has a fine red line running through each petal in a circle. Margery Fish listed 47 in her book *Cottage Garden Flowers*. All revel in gritty, free-draining, slightly alkaline soil and full sun.

DIGITALIS heywoodii has grey foliage and a spike of foxglove bells tinged pink in the bud but opening to cream. It flowers for months in summer and autumn in a sunny location. Height: 0.7 m (2.3 ft).

EURYOPS pectinatus see page 103.

GAZANIA 'Buccaneer' is very long flowering, displaying its deep golden yellow daisies above grey foliage. It is an excellent groundcover with the same advantages as *Euryops*.

HELICHRYSUM petiolatum is a groundcover which can spread rapidly, climb, or drape down an embankment, so long as you are in charge of the secateurs. If kept trimmed, it will build upon itself to ultimately reach 1 m (3 ft) × 1 m (3 ft), by which time, in my garden, it is time to start another one, as too much cutting back displays a poor interior.

ABOVE: Anthemis tinctoria *provides a sunny yellow splash against the grey* Helichrysum petiolatum.

LAVANDULA The lavender species have already been listed with sun loving shrubs on pages 104 and 105.

LYCHNIS coronaria x flos-jovis (campion) has grey foliage and a single cerise flower displayed on multi-branched stems of 0.6 m (2 ft). There is a pure white form and also one called *L. coronaria* var. 'Oculata', or the rose-eyed campion. All three will free-seed very generously and just as well because a wet summer often sees them rotting off. However, they do provide an attractive display in late spring and early summer.

NEPETA faassenii (catmint) is a favourite groundcover for use amongst roses. Its soft mauve flowers are carried on 23 cm (9 in) stems above the soft grey green, finely serrated leaves. It spreads to cover 0.5 m (1.6 ft) and drapes over a wall very nicely. In frosty areas do not cut it back going into winter, but leave the old foliage to protect the centre, from which new shoots will arise in early spring. Then it is time to cut away the old leaves.

PLECTRANTHUS argentatus appears on page 101 and is not affected by humidity.

POTENTILLA argyrophylla has typical strawberry-like leaves of light silver and a lemon single flower. It is a tufted plant and looks very attractive when the hairy silver leaves are used, in contrast to *P.*

atrosanguinea, which is more grey green and has a blood red flower.

SANTOLINA chamaecyparissus (cotton lavender) can be used as a low clipped edging to herb gardens in cooler regions but not in humid climates where it will suddenly develop a foliage collapse, usually on one side. Height 0.5 m (1.6 ft).

SENECIO maritima (dusty miller) has silvery grey ferny leaves and a head of small bright yellow daisies in late spring. It is used as a bedding plant in cooler climates but dislikes hot wet summers.

STACHYS byzantina syn. *S. lanata* (lamb's ears) is a very popular border edging subject. Its very felted leaves of light silver grey ensure its popularity. Like *Lychnis*, it can collapse, although usually you are left with enough good pieces to start again. Division tends to reduce the production of 0.3 m (1 ft) flower stems which carry a purple pink flower spike.

TANACETUM haradjanii (silver feathers) is a delightful little groundcover for a rockery pocket. It is easily propagated by division or cuttings and should be renewed regularly.

TANACETUM ptarmiciflorum (Canary Island tansy or silver feathers) until recently was listed as *Chrysanthemum* *ptarmiciflorum*. It has very fine silvery grey ferny foliage up to 1 m (3 ft) × 1 m (3 ft) and in late spring will carry heads of small single white daisies. It must have perfect drainage and hates too much moisture at its feet.

TEUCRIUM fruticans (shrub germander) is not affected by humidity.

Groundcovers

ANTHEMIS tinctoria (Dyer's camomile) has very bright golden yellow daisies held above ferny green foliage from mid spring to mid autumn. One plant easily spreads to cover 1 m (3 ft).

ANTHEMIS tinctoria 'E. C. Buxton' is similar, with a soft lemon yellow daisy; *A. tinctoria* 'Wargrave's Variety' has a cream daisy. All three respond to being trimmed for neatness; it is vital at the end of autumn, or when persistent rain or humidity send the foliage black towards the centre. They soon recover.

ARENARIA montana covers itself with pure white flowers which open wide and contrast beautifully with the grass green foliage in spring. It has a creeping habit, tolerates light shade and works well as a spillover.

BRACHYCOME multifida (cut leaf native daisy) needs no introduction; its small

mauve daisies, which are continuously produced above the very fine foliage, make it a great standby in full sun or light shade. 'Break O' Day' has purple daisies and a bronze cast to the foliage.

CONVOLVULUS mauritanicus is loved for its deep mauve blue salver flowers of 3 cm (1 in) diameter, which are profuse along its trailing stems from late spring to mid autumn. One plant will spread to cover 1 m (3 ft) or spill over a retaining wall most delightfully.

ABOVE: *Sun loving* Anthemis tinctoria *'Wargrave's Variety' is a great harmonising groundcover.*

COREOPSIS 'Mini Gold' is a very low growing, winter flowering species with a single deep yellow bloom on short stems of 15 cm (6 in). Increase is by division.

ERIGERON karvinskianus syn. *E. mucronatus* is still sold under its former name. Commonly called seaside daisy

and, wrongly, baby's tears, it is a tough, versatile little charmer. It free-seeds to pop up in paving cracks or wall crevices and will spill over delightfully. It has small white daisies opening with a pink reverse, which are magnificent in spring. Flowering continues for ten months, resting only in late winter. Known as Edna Walling's signature plant and used by her on broad step risers, it stands hard cutting back.

❧

LEFT: *Little mauve* Brachycome *daisies below a low growing Reitmuller rose we have called 'Chip's Apple Blossom'.*

BELOW: *Rose 'Raubritter', a spring only beauty, seen here with* Convolvulus mauritanicus *at Parnell Rose Garden, Auckland.*

EVOLVULUS pilularis is very similar to *Convolvulus mauretanicus*, flowering with deep sky blue salver shaped flowers all through summer, but it is frost sensitive.

GAZANIA hybrida and species (treasure flowers) have long been touted as drought and salt resistant. The colour range has been greatly extended from the old common orange into cream, pink, gold and a red with narrow foliage called Firechief. *G. splendens* 'Alba' has cream daisies, with each petal finishing yellow against a black eyeliner inner circle, hence the over-used common name of black-eyed Susan.

GERANIUM cinereum var. *subcaulescens* is a neat tufted cranesbill which slowly expands in a rockery or foreground position. Its chief attraction, apart from the scalloped dark green leaves, lies in its magenta flower, which has a black eye. Divide in winter with care.

GERANIUM incarnum is fast in expanding to cover an area of 0.5 m (1.6 ft) or to spill over a wall, and has fine grassy green foliage. The flowers are magenta pink and are profusely produced from late winter to mid spring with spot flowering continuing through summer. It free-seeds generously.

GERANIUM renardii has green grey foliage which is tomentose, scalloped,

and broadly lobed. The flowers are white with mauve veining and they are carried in clusters on stems of 15 cm (6 in) above the foliage over the winter/spring period. In a well-drained sunny position, it will spread to cover 0.6 m (2 ft).

GERANIUM sanguinium (bloody cranesbill) has magenta flowers in spring carried above a mound of cut leaf foliage but *G. sanguinium* 'Alba' seems to enjoy a more sprawling habit and repeats in mid summer. The most desirable *G. sanguinium* var. *striatum* is truly lovely, with soft pink open flowers, finely veined light cherry red. It will spread slowly and puts on a great show in late winter to early spring, repeating in mid summer.

ABOVE: *The pink evening primrose* Oenothera speciosa rosea *blooms from spring to early autumn.*

LYSIMACHIA 'Gold Clusters' has larger leaves than creeping jenny (*Lysimachia nummularia*). It has plain green and clusters of golden yellow flowers that appear in spring and summer.

OENOTHERA glaber is a low growing, deep butter yellow evening primrose which is very eye-catching in late spring and summer. The foliage is green bronze and can reach 45 cm (1.5 ft), but is usually lower. Trim after flowering.

OENOTHERA speciosa rosea (pink evening primrose) does not close its flowers during the day as does *O. bienis*, and remains as a green groundcover in

winter. It will send up flowering stems in mid spring and continue to early autumn. If cut to within 10 cm (4 in) of the ground with the hedge clippers and immediately fertilised, in mid summer it will quickly send up another neat mound of flowers. It can be invasive; I control ours with a mild herbicide that does not affect the worm population.

OENOTHERA texensis has smaller, deeper pink flowers and a prostrate habit. It is also long summer flowering.

ORIGANUM vulgare 'Aureum' is a tremendous groundcover for the herb or yellow garden, covering 1 m (3 ft)

easily, without being as invasive as oregano. By mid summer its leaves are butter yellow and may burn in heat waves, but these are easily snipped off.

PHLOX divaricata is a spring flowering deep blue phlox with narrow green leaves of 5 cm (2 in) in length that is wrongly sold as 'Chattahoochee' in Australia. It has a creeping habit until ready to throw up its flowering stems. The colour makes it a good harmoniser. Height: 0.5 m (1.6 ft) in flower.

PHLOX stolonifera 'Blue Ridge', 'Pink Ridge' and 'Ariane' The latter is the fragrant white form. All are prostrate with a creeping habit and in flower in late winter and early spring. They are easily divided.

PHLOX subulata Gardeners in cool climates use many cultivars effectively, but they do not like humidity.

POTENTILLA species are interesting plants. Some species have strawberry-like foliage, while others have deeply divided leaves.

POTENTILLA nepalensis 'Miss Willmott' is probably the best known and most widely grown for its deep carmine strawberry-like flowers in summer and spreading habit.

POTENTILLA nepalensis minor has very neat small foliage and sprays of little apricot gold flowers in spring. The validity of the name is in some doubt.

SILENE maritima (witch's thimble) is a lovely groundcover in full sun or light shade, provided it is in well-drained soil. The white petals extend beyond a fat little balloon bladder and are produced abundantly from spring to winter. Humidity will cause foliage loss at the centre, but the outer perimeter will have enough roots to restart the mat of spreading stems.

THYMUS species *Thymus serpyllum* cultivars have long been popular in sunny situations, for their aromatic matting foliage and their flowers, which are attractive to bees. *T. serpyllum* 'Coccineus' is bright purplish crimson, while 'Pink Chintz' had deep rose red flowers. *Thymus × citriodorus*, the lemon scented thyme, flowers soft pink, spreads in a mat and has culinary uses. *Thymus nitidum* and *T. nitidum* 'Albus' both have white flowers above bright green foliage.

VERBENA erinoides is a fine-leafed species flowering white, purple or bright pink, the latter being dubbed 'Lipstick' by the trade. It spreads rapidly and loosely, but both the white and the pink are useful for their six months of flowering, which ends as winter begins.

BELOW: *Yellow* Potentilla recta *and* P. warrenii *are planted in this garden. Note rose 'Golden Wings' in a rose trainer.*

VERBENA × hybrida has much larger leaves and each flower head is like a miniature bunch of flowers on a stem. The colour range is amazing, ranging from pure white, pale and deep two tone pink ('Pink Baby'), deep rose pink, coral, 'Candystripe' (which is pink with white spokes down each petal), deep red, mauve and purple to a lighter purple known as 'Blue Queen'. Our plant of 'Candystripe' has sported a white that is very softly suffused with pale pink, which we called 'Candy Ice', and a rose pink spoked white which we named 'Candy Carnival'.

VERONICA species *Veronica incarnum*, with soft grey green foliage and a sky blue spike flower, is better in cooler climates with adequate moisture. *V. spicata* 'Nana' will spread in a mat and produces 15 cm (6 in) stems topped with purple spikes, while *V. spicata* 'Barcarolle' has a mat of green leaves with pink flower spikes to 0.4 m (1.3 ft), though it frequently shows a black fungal leaf spot in humid areas.

Low Perennials

ACHILLEA ptarmica 'The Pearl' spreads by suckering growth sending up stems of deep green narrow leaves topped with heads of double white daisy-like button blooms, not unlike feverfew, in summer and autumn. Great in posies. Height: 0.3 m (1 ft).

AGAPANTHUS 'Dwarf Blue' and 'Dwarf White' There is such confusion over the naming of these gems, with the trade having labels made for *A.* 'Nana' (dwarf blue), 'Queen Anne' (dwarf white), 'Baby Blue', 'Peter Pan' and 'Tom Thumb' (all dwarf blue), and 'Snow Drops' (dwarf white). One thing I do know is that they are great for planting with daylilies or similar, and after three years will have formed a very neat clump of 0.5 m (1.6 ft) which can be divided. Good cut flowers.

ARMERIA maritima (thrift) comes from the rocky coastline of the Mediterranean, so it likes a gravelly, free-draining soil and not too much water. The foliage is presented as a tuft of grass-like leaves with pink or white pompom flowers like miniature drumsticks held aloft. Cultivar 'Isobel Burdett' is deep pink. They begin blooming in early spring and will continue into autumn.

ASTER dumosus (dwarf asters) in pink are 'Lady Henry Maddocks' and 'Marjorie' and in blue 'Dwarf Nancy' and 'Victor'. They grow as a green groundcover until flowering time in summer, when they send up flower stems to 23 cm (9 in). Cut back after the first flowering for a second crop.

CHRYSANTHEMUM morifolium 'Little Bob' is a double pink cultivar which, if cut back between flowerings, will cover itself with bloom in early and late summer and late autumn. It is another useful posy flower and can be divided in winter.

CHRYSANTHEMUM rubellum 'Clara Curtis' and 'Mary Stoker' These two are low growing—0.35 m (1 ft)—and very long flowering single daisy types. 'Clara Curtis' is soft lavender pink and 'Mary Stoker' is a soft lemon to apricot gold. They repeat from late spring well into autumn, which makes them worth including.

DIASCIA ambigua, dubbed pink cherub by one wholesaler, is a long flowering, low growing perennial with very deep salmon pink blooms that are almost continuously produced provided it is given a light cutting back as each flush finishes. Good drainage and reasonable moisture are essential and it can take light shade.

DIASCIA virgilis is similar, with a soft shell pink flower. It appreciates a little light shade or a morning sun aspect.

FELICIA amelloides 'San Anita', 'Royal Blue' and 'Variegata' were formerly called *Agathaea* or kingfisher daisies. These compact little gems are wonderful harmonisers. The small 6 cm (2.4 in) sky blue to deep blue daisies are produced almost perpetually if the plant is dead-headed. They are easily propagated from cuttings, which need to be renewed every two to three years.

HELIPTERUM anthenoides (alpine paper daisy) is an Australian native that is irresistible to gardeners and, while likely to be perennial in cooler regions, I find needs perfect drainage and a little shade in warmer climates to give repeat performances each spring. The wine red buds open to display pure white paper daisies of 2 cm (1 in) diameter in late winter and early spring.

PENSTEMON heterophyllus performs better in climates free of high humidity, but its unusual pink blue tubular bell flowers are so appealing as to make us all try anyway. The flowers open in spring and repeat in early autumn, and it likes morning sun or dappled shade positions where the drainage is perfect and it is not overwatered. Height: 0.3 m (1 ft).

PHYSOSTEGIA virginica 'Nana Albas' is a dwarf version of the hardy tall obedient plant that is summer flowering, the pure white flowers taking full sun or part shade. Easily divided in winter. Height: 0.3 m (1 ft).

SALVIA coccinia 'Rosea' is for warm areas only. Reaching 0.5 m (1.6 ft), it has a bicolour flower of salmon apricot on the lower lip and white above. Long

spring to autumn performance, then cut back to encourage new spring growth.

SCABIOSA anthemifolia 'Pink Lace' and 'Mauve Lace' What a delight this pincushion is. The habit is low with light grey green ferny foliage, spreading to cover 0.8 m (2.6 ft). It produces its pretty pink or mauve lacy flowers on long stems suited to picking from spring to winter if dead-headed. Full sun is best.

SEDUM 'Vera Jameson' There are many in this genus worth growing but this one is particularly desirable, with its arching purple blue leaves and attractive dusty pink flowers which open in autumn. *Sedum* species do not like to be overwatered and prefer a hot, well-drained spot. Cut back in winter for new spring growth. Height: 25 cm (10 in).

VERONICA spicata 'Blue Spire' does not have the same leaf as other *V. spicata* cultivars. It is broader and glossier. The flower is a fat spike of blue purple hue which is abundantly displayed in mid summer. Height: 0.4 m (1.3 ft).

Medium Height Perennials

There is a wealth of beautiful perennial plants which flower in heights varying from 0.6 m (2 ft) to 1 m (3 ft) and,

once again, it is the habit, colour and timing of the flowering which must influence choices. The *Achilleas* lead the field.

ACHILLEA millefolium 'Cerise Queen' has been around for such a long time that it has fallen from favour, but suddenly the field has opened up with the 'Galaxy' hybrids. In the main they were a bit of a disappointment, however, except for 'Appleblossom', and they all flowered below 0.6 m (2 ft). I have a pale pink, name unknown, which is a delight in the garden or vase where it has a life of ten days. Others on offer are 'Salmon Beauty' which is an apricot salmon, and 'Lilac Queen', both growing to 0.7 m (2.3 ft).

ACHILLEA × taygetea, one of the parents of *A.* 'Moonshine', has soft lemon flowers and grey green foliage similar to *A.* 'Cloth of Gold'. The latter has flat heads of golden yellow blooms and both reach 1 m (3.3 ft).

AGAPANTHUS campanulatus subspecies *patens* has fine foliage and tall flower stems that carry a small round head of sky blue bells which are more reflexed than other *Agapanthus* species. It is frost hardy. Height: foliage, 0.5 m (1.6 ft); flower stems, to 1 m (3 ft).

ANGELONIA angustifolia loves warmth and does not mind humidity but hates frost. The pretty little snapdragon-like flowers come in white, pink, purple and white marbled purple. They are summer/autumn flowers, liking a rich, well drained soil, and adequate moisture. They are native to Brazil and Mexico. Height: 0.7 m (2.3 ft).

ASTER alevis has bluish leaves and pale violet flowers early and late in summer. All can be divided in winter. Height: 1 m (3 ft).

ASTER frikarti from Switzerland is my favourite perennial, for it has jacaranda blue 5 cm (2 in) daisies from late spring to mid winter on a compact bush that is cut right back in late winter. It is herbaceous but will regrow to reach 0.8 m (2.6 ft).

ASTER novae-angliae is a North American species, of which the cultivars 'Barr's Pink' and 'Harrington's Pink' are so dissimilar in foliage as to make one begin to wonder. The soft blue 'Plenty' and 'Perry's White', in foliage and flower type, resemble 'Harrington's Pink'. All can reach 1 m (3 ft).

ASTER novi-belgii (Michaelmas daisy) contributes to the summer–autumn display, throwing up tall stems covered with small daisy flowers of about 4 cm (1.5 in) diameter. Some, like the garnet red 'Winston Churchill', will flower in summer and again in autumn.

'Eventide', with purple blue flowers, can reach 1 m (3 ft) and 'Coombe Rosemary', a deep violet, 0.9 m (2.9 ft).

ASTER vimineus (Easter daisy) is distinguished from other species by its finer foliage and 2–3 cm (0.8–1.2 in) pink or white daisies. Flowering period: early to mid autumn. Height: 1 m (3 ft).

CAMPANULA rapunculoides can spread widely but is able to be controlled with herbicide and I would not be without it, for it is the most reliable of campanulas in a warm climate, sending up its tall spires of lavender blue pendulous bells in mid winter, mid summer and at least several times in between. It will also flower in semi-shade but not so frequently. Height 0.8 m (2.5 ft).

CATANANCHE caerulea (cupid's dart) likes cooler regions better (but not severe winters), perfect drainage and less rather than more when it comes to watering. It has pretty violet blue flowers, which are toothed as if cut with pinking shears, 3 cm (1.2 in) in diameter.

CATHARANTHUS roseus (Madagascar periwinkle), like *Angelonia angustifolia*, loves warmth and humidity and detests frost, but is a very useful colour spot accent plant in shades of white, rose pink with a deeper eye, cyclamen purple

or white with a red eye (called 'Peppermint Cooler' in the trade). Height: 0.6 m (2 ft).

CENTAUREA dealbata flowers with lavender mauve thistle type blooms from late spring to autumn above ferny foliage and requires full sun and good drainage. Height: 0.7 m (2.3 ft).

CHEIRANTHUS mutabilis (winter joy) is a perennial wallflower which can be a bun-shaped sub-shrub to 1 m (3 ft), flowering mauve purple from mid winter to early summer. It is evergreen, hardy and needs reasonably good drainage.

CHRYSANTHEMUM parthenium (feverfew) is another medicinal herb of yesteryear. It is not truly perennial but more frequently biennial. *Matricaria* is the most used name for these pretty little daisies. We grow three forms in our garden, only one of which has a cultivar name. 'White Bonnet' has double pure white daisies similar to *Achillea* 'The Pearl' but with a tiny green eye. The domed cream form I call 'Pincushion' because it has a central raised dome surrounded by a single row of tiny cream petals. The third, for which I have no name, is again pure

❧

RIGHT: Lavandula pinnata *'Sidonee', seen here with white feverfew daisies, becomes a deeper blue colour in winter.*

white with a double row of petals around a golden yellow centre. The latter variety generously free-seeds and I allow this to happen after the second flowering. They are cut back to within 15 cm (6 in) of ground level after the first flowering.

COREOPSIS *grandiflora* 'Sunburst' is the double yellow flowered form. The single form is called the railway flower in some areas of Australia, because it grows along railway tracks in many regions, such is its hardiness. The double gives a very bright show in both spring and summer and harmonises with daylilies or dark blue flowers very nicely. Dead-heading promotes freer flowering. Height: 0.6 m (2 ft).

COREOPSIS *verticillata* 'Moonbeam' is much more refined, with finely divided grass-like foliage of bright green. It sends up single pale lemon eight-petalled daisies of 3 cm (1 in) diameter over a long mid summer/autumn period. It is herbaceous and looks super with soft blue flowers. Height 0.6 m (2 ft).

ECHINACEA *purpurea* and *E. purpurea* 'Alba' Formerly classified as a *Rudbeckia* and commonly known as the cone flower, its chief characteristic is that, as the pink or cream petals age, they angle themselves downwards below a prominent cone of future seed. The multi-headed flower stems reach 1 m

(3 ft) and are produced from late spring to winter. It is herbaceous.

ERIGERON *speciosus* has been hybridised to give some really lovely daisy flowering perennials with names like 'Charity' (light pink), 'Dignity' (violet mauve), 'Festivity' (lilac pink) and 'Sincerity' (a mauve blue). The individual daisies can be 5 cm (2 in) across and reach 0.6 m (2 ft) in profusion in spring.

ABOVE: *Pink cone flowers (*Echinacea purpurea*) are popular, as is the cream form.*

ERYNGIUM species To many, the sea hollies look like exalted thistles, but in the hands of flower arrangers they are transformed into very special flowers. *E. anethystinum* has a metallic blue cone flower surrounded by a blue ruff on stems reaching 0.7 m (2.3 ft) in summer and autumn.

ERYNGIUM varifolium 'Variegatum' begins with a rosette of deep green leaves marbled white. It will send up stiff branching stems of mauve pompom flowers surrounded by fierce silvery spines. Height: 0.7 m (2.3 ft).

Eryngium × zabelii 'Blue Hills' The spiny silvery flowers mature to an intense metallic blue and it has a long flowering period from late spring to mid autumn. Care is needed when weeding nearby. Height: 0.8 m (2.6 ft).

GERANIUM 'Criss Canning', a hybrid named for the well-known Victorian flower painter, is a cross between *G. pratense* and *G. himalayense*, which gives us large geranium flowers of the most intense violet blue with red veining.

GERANIUM ibericum has violet blue flowers of 2 cm (0.8 in) diameter in panicles on stems 0.6 m (2 ft) long and immediately above leaves which, like *G. renardii*, are roundish, deeply cleft and woolly, except they are green, not grey. Summer flowering.

GERNAIUM pratense (hedgerow cranesbill) has similarly sized deep sky blue flowers and deeply divided foliage with flowering stems to 0.8 m (2.6 ft). It is herbaceous. *G. p.* 'Alba' is the white form and there are now some very interesting cultivars and hybrid crosses.

GERANIUM pratense 'Silver Queen' is a pale silvery violet. *G. pratense* 'Striatum' is palest silver grey marbled with soft blue.

GEUM chiloense 'Lady Stratheden' flowers double lemon yellow on tall stems above broad hairy green foliage in mid spring. 'Mrs Bradshaw' is an ideal companion, having scarlet red flowers. Both grow in great profusion to 0.8 m (2.6 ft).

GYPSOPHILA paniculata 'Bristol Fairy', used extensively in floristry, is only perennial in cooler regions, where it will send up its long flowering stems with a cloud of small double white flowers in early summer. There is also a double pink form of *G. paniculata* called 'Flamingo'. Grows to 0.7 m (2.3 ft).

HEMEROCALLIS (hybrids)—the modern hybrid daylilies are without parallel as reliable perennials. Some are evergreen and some herbaceous, and it is important to consult a specialist catalogue and, if possible, visit the nursery at flowering time. The complexity of flower colour

BELOW: Hemerocallis *'Green Dragon' is a much admired repeat flowering day lily.*

combinations is such that they almost defy catalogue descriptions. Mine commence flowering in late spring for 8–10 weeks, and then repeat generously in autumn. Flower stems can reach 0.9 m (2.9 ft) and they will flower in full sun or part shade.

KENTRANTHUS ruber (valerian) is a tough perennial that is tolerant of drought and alkaline soils. I have seen it growing out of stone walls in English villages, but in gardens it really romps. It comes in white, pink and light red, free-seeds, and flowers almost perpetually to a height of 0.6 m (2 ft). Cut back to keep it tidy. Evergreen.

KNIPHOFIA **dwarf hybrids**—the old red and yellow red hot poker is still a valued plant in dry area farm gardens, but nowadays there are some really attractive hybrids of less stature. *Kniphofia* 'Little Treasure', with soft coral buds, opens to soft yellow. Height: 0.75 m (2.5 ft) *K.* 'Maid of Orleans' has green buds opening to ivory white. Height: 1 m (3 ft).

LEUCANTHEMUM × superbum (shasta daisy)—we've come a long way since the only type seen was the common single white. Now there are a number of cultivars on offer, commencing with 'Esther Read'. It has a cushion of fine petals at the centre of the white daisy flower which opens in three seasons:

ABOVE: *Red* Centranthus, *deep blue* Cynaglossom *and white* Lychnis *used at Ayrlies, garden of Beverly and Malcolm McConnell, of Auckland.*

RIGHT: *Here the Pillar Rose 'Titian' is enhanced by foxgloves.*

spring, mid summer and late autumn. 'Chiffon' has a double row of narrow petals, frilled and divided at the ends like an elk horn, of pure white radiating from a yellow centre, and flowers in mid to late summer. 'The Swan' has many rows of thin petals in a ruffle around its central yellow disc and can measure 10 cm (4 in) across. It commences flowering in late spring and early

LOBELIA fulgens (cardinal flower) opens brilliant scarlet flowers in summer, repeating in autumn after being dead-headed. Recently introduced were white and sky blue forms and a cultivar called 'Cinnabar', which has deep lipstick pink blooms on 0.8 m (2.6 ft) stems.

LYTHRUM salicaria (purple loosestrife), a native of Europe, now has numerous cultivars of softer colours, the deep rose pink being named 'Brightness'. Once used as a medicinal herb, it likes rich soil and will flower in sun or part shade in summer. Height: 0.7 m (2.3 ft).

MONARDA didyma (bergamot or bee balm) is another herbal plant, and the

summer. I suspect that it is also sold under the name 'Shaggy'. 'Cobham's Gold' is double white with a yellow centre in the manner of 'Esther Read', and 'Wirral Supreme' is a very tall version of 'Esther Read'. In our garden we have a double form with stiffly radiating petals which, until we can trace its valid name, we have dubbed 'Florist's Double' as it is an excellent cut flower. The very early flowering single white, called *Chrysanthemum minima* or *C. minima* 'Polaris', I have eliminated as it was too free-seeding and has become a pest in my area. All the cultivars can be divided in winter.

ABOVE: *The flowers of shasta 'The Swan' can measure 10 cm (4 in) across. It flowers in early summer.*

RIGHT: Lobelia fulgens *'Cinnabar' is a great middle height border plant.*

LINARIA purpurea (purple toadflax) sends up a slender erect spike of bluish purple little flowers on branching stems above blue green foliage to 0.9 m (2.9 ft). There is also a pink form and a cultivar called 'Canon Went', which does not like humidity. The first two flower from late spring to autumn and are very free-seeding.

OSTEOSPERMUM 'Starry Eyes' Once called *Dimorphotheca* or black-eyed Susan, these African daisies have long been popular for hot dry banks, but the new cultivars with a spoon twist to the end of each petal, called 'Pink Whirls' or 'Whirlybird', fascinate gardeners. Unfortunately, they can revert in part or whole to the plain form. 0.5 m (1.6 ft) × 1 m (3 ft).

LEFT: *The soft mauve bergamot 'Enfield Gem' is most appealing and easy to place.*

BELOW: *Nepeta is a favourite edging plant for lovers of old roses. Sally Allison uses it to outline soft curves.*

bees certainly do love it. Bergamot is one of the ingredients of the distinctive Earl Grey tea. 'Cambridge Scarlet', a vivid scarlet colour, flowers on 1 m (3 ft) stems. 'Enfield Gem' is deep lavender mauve and 'Croftway Pink' is a soft pink. The flower petals make an interesting addition to salads. All flower in mid summer on stems of 1 m (3 ft). The lemon scented bergamot has a light mauve purple bloom.

NEPETA 'Six Hills' is the taller catmint, reaching 0.6 m (2 ft) and flowering with mauve spikes over the spring to autumn period. It is delightful when used amongst old-fashioned roses; it needs full sun and good drainage.

OXYPETALUM caeraleum (tweedia) is a half-hardy plant which is best described as a loose scrambler. With careful removal of ripening seed pods, it can be kept low and in flower from mid spring to mid autumn. It has the most unusual electric blue flowers, the colour of which is irresistible to most gardeners. The trick is to let the last seed pods ripen for harvesting as it can be lost in a wet winter.

PENSTEMON species originated in North America and there seems to be considerable disagreement in classification between American and English reference texts.

PENSTEMON barbatus syn. *Chelone barbata* 'Evelyn' seems to be the only cultivar available. It has reddish pink tubular bells 2 cm (0.8 in) in length produced on stems which can reach 0.7 m (2.3 ft) and is very free flowering from spring onwards. It is most valuable for its late autumn/early winter colour. The foliage is very narrow.

PENSTEMON x gloxinioides are large hybrids with longer, fatter bells measuring 5 cm (2 in) × 4 cm (1.6 in). Seed companies market them as 'Sensation' or 'Hyacinth' strains because their bells are carried in closely packed pendulous heads. Apart from the white 'Swan Lake' and a mauve and white called 'Susan', there is a scarlet which is white inside called 'Red Ensign', a deep burgundy and many other combinations with the inside of the bell being white striped pink, red or mauve. They are easy to grow and flower from mid spring to late autumn, asking only for normal care and dead-heading. The clumps expand by putting roots down where they touch the soil, so it is easy to replenish the stock. They have the broadest leaves and flower stems reach 1 m (3 ft).

BELOW: Phlox maculata *'Alpha' and the white form 'Omega' are great in borders.*

ABOVE: Penstemon *'Swan Lake' is a very useful harmoniser that flowers for eight months.*

PENSTEMON hartwegii 'Firebird' has bright red bells 4 cm (1.6 in) in length, with slightly wider foliage. Height: 0.8 m (2.6 ft). *P. hartwegii* 'Garnet' has similarly sized cyclamen red bells which are a great colour accent to pink roses.

PHLOX maculata 'Omega' and 'Alpha' are recent introductions which are more suited to warm, humid districts. They have narrow glossy deep green foliage and carry heads of fragrant *Phlox* flowers from late spring through summer if dead-headed. 'Omega' is white with a tiny pink eye and 'Alpha' is bright lavender pink. Height: 0.6 m (2 ft).

PHYSOSTEGIA virginiana grows to 1 m (3 ft) and comes in white, pink and soft mauve. It is known as the obedient plant, not because it is well behaved but because you can move the flowers to face a certain direction and they will stay in that position in the vase. It can be grown in part shade also, and is very wide-spreading.

POTENTILLA recta and P. warrenii both have deeply palmate leaves that are serrated. The branching flower stems carry numerous heads of single pale lemon for *P. recta* and deep buttercup yellow for *P. warrenii*. Height: 0.6 m (2 ft).

SALVIA species The *Salvia* represents a very large genus numerically but there are a few that are invaluable to all gardens.

SALVIA farinacea and S. farinacea 'Alba' can be bought in punnets in early spring or raised from seed but they are perennial and will come again where winters are not severe. Popularly called

LEFT: Salvia farinacea *'Blue Bedder' is deservedly popular in massed plantings.*

'Blue Bedder', they can reach 0.8 m (2 ft) in a neat habit of bushy growth which makes them useful harmonisers, the blue sometimes bordering on deep violet.

SALVIA nemerosa 'Rosea' has deep dusty pink flowers in summer reaching 0.8 m (2.6 ft) and is a useful cut flower.

SALVIA patens is loved by gardeners for its gentian blue flowers which, while not abundantly produced in summer, can be stunning in autumn. It is happier in light shade in warm areas. Herbaceous. Height: 0.6 m (2 ft).

SALVIA sclarea (clary sage) is popular as a herb garden plant. It is biennial and easily raised from seed, having large heart-shaped leaves, with branching flower stems of bluish white flowers to 1 m (3 ft). Var. *turkestanica* has white flowers tinged pink.

SCABIOSA caucasica (grandma's pincushion) never fails to delight with its blue, white or lavender lilac flowers

❦

BELOW: Scabiosa anthemifolia *'Pink Lace' is one of the old-fashioned flowers gardeners love.*

which have a central cushion surrounded by ruffled petals. It likes a well-drained soil, near neutral pH, and a cool rather than humid climate. Deadheading promotes flowering. Stems reach 0.7 m (2.3 ft).

SIDALCEA monarch 'Party Girl' The watermelon pink flowers are produced on 0.8 m (2.6 ft) stems in tall spikes which open over a very long summer period. Adequate moisture and deadheading are essential, as is good drainage.

x SOLIDASTER hybridus is a cross between a dwarf aster and a *Solidago*, or golden rod. The result is a dwarf form resembling golden rod but with tiny soft lemon daisy flowers in autumn. A good cut flower.

STOKESIA laevis (Stokes' aster) is one of the best performing perennials and the most reliable in warm, humid climates. The jacaranda blue flowers are 6 cm (2.3 in) across and abundantly borne on branching stems to 0.6 m (2 ft) in early and late summer. There is also a white form.

VERONICA spicata (speedwell) is another indispensable perennial with sky blue or white spikes of bloom in late spring and summer. Height: 0.6 m (2 ft).

LEFT: *Both mauve lace and pink lace* Scabiosas *are long flowering groundcovers for picking.*

❧

than 1 m (3 ft) if you take the trouble to stake it or support it unobtrusively. The flowers are continuously opened from mid spring to late autumn, at which time it should be cut to near ground level. It free-seeds very readily.

HELIOPSIS helianthoides (light of Lodden or false sunflower) has a bright golden yellow bloom 9 cm (3.5 in)

❧

ABOVE: Agapanthus inapertus *and* Rudbeckia laciniata *'Golden Glow' are strong accents in any scene.*

Tall Background Perennials for Full Sun

AGAPANTHUS inapertus is not so common but is very desirable, with stems to 1.2 m (4 ft) and heads of deep royal blue pendulous bells which open in mid summer.

AGAPANTHUS orientalis—in summer we are well accustomed to seeing great displays of blue and white *A. orientalis,* the lily of the Nile, which does so well in hot, dry locations, sending up mop heads of deep sky blue or pure white pendulous bells to 1.2 m (4 ft).

GAURA lindheimira (white butterfly bush) is also capable of reaching more

across and is completely double, having a central cushion of small petals surrounded by a single row of longer petals. The flowers are produced on branching stems to 1.2 m (4 ft) in mid summer, and it would be a good companion for *Agapanthus inapertus*, given adequate water, as all *Agapanthus* are gross feeders.

HESPERIS matronalis (sweet rocket or dame's violet) is popular for its evening scented white or mauve summer flowers which resemble heads of single stock. When well grown they can reach 1.2 m (4 ft) and will self-sow. In warm climates they can be biennial.

HYPOESTES aristata is a background subject that will flower in sun or part shade to 1.5 m (5 ft), a soft lavender mauve in late autumn. Frost sensitive.

LATHYRUS latifolius (perennial sweet pea) is not self-supporting but looks fabulous when allowed to climb through a winter flowering deciduous shrub such as *Viburnum* x *burkwoodii*. 'The Pearl' is pure white and the lavender pink is called 'Pink Pearl'. There is also a soft bicolour form. They are herbaceous and I remove the straw of the sweet pea growth in late autumn.

LOBELIA cardinalis 'Victoria' has the same deep red flower as *L. fulgens* but the foliage is burgundy purple, which

makes it very distinctive at the back of the border. Dead-heading prolongs flowering from summer to autumn and unobtrusive staking is advisable. Height: 1.5 m (5 ft).

REHMANIA angulata (Chinese foxglove) is a very versatile wide-spreading perennial. From a basal rosette of leaves it will send up tall flower stems of pendulous foxglove-like bells to 1.2 m (4 ft) in sheltered positions, with shorter spikes on exposed sites. The flowers in mild climates will start in late winter and continue through spring and summer but in cold areas it will become herbaceous.

RUDBECKIA laciniata 'Golden Glow' Many of the *Rudbeckia* species have yellow daisy flowers with a dark brown eye and carry the over-used name of black-eyed susan. *R. laciniata* 'Golden Glow', however, has deep golden double flowers with no colour change at the centre and handsome dissected or laciniate leaves, hence the species name. It grows to 2 m (6.6 ft) and flowers in autumn.

SALVIA dorisiana has wonderfully scented foliage, some say like ripe pineapples. It bears rose pink flowers from early winter to mid spring. The leaves are broad and hairy and in very warm climates part shade is advisable. Frost hardy to –4°C (25°F), it needs

pruning after flowering to control its dimensions. 1.2 m (4 ft) × 1.2 m (4 ft).

SALVIA grandiflora 'Azurea' is a herbaceous perennial reaching 1.2–1.5 m (4–5 ft). The foliage is very narrow and the heavenly deep sky blue flowers begin to open in mid summer finishing around mid autumn. Unobtrusive support is necessary.

SALVIA regia flowers royal blue to purple, producing very long spikes up to 0.5 m (1.6 ft) in length for ten months of the year, resting in late winter. It is frost hardy to –4°C (25°F) and grows in a bun shape to 1.2 m (4 ft) × 1.2 m (4 ft). Regular trimming is advisable to keep a neat appearance.

SALVIA uliginosa (bog sage) is another sky blue tall growing perennial which brings a soft appearance to the garden, but it is very invasive, though easily controlled with a herbicide. Height 1.5 m (5 ft) and the flowering takes place from mid spring to late autumn, at which time it is cut down to 23 cm (9 in).

VERBASCUM olympicum for those in cool climates is a most magnificent grey foliaged plant with golden yellow flowers in summer. Height: 1.8 m (6 ft).

VERBASCUM phoenicemum is commonly called Aaron's rod when

ABOVE: *This border planned by Beth Chatto contains* Verbascum olympicum *and the white flowering* Crambe cordifolia.

flowering yellow in pastures, but there are strains which will open pale pastel as well as bright colours including apricot, carmine salmon and violet to 1.2 m (4 ft). It free-seeds and is a useful vertical accent biennial.

ANNUALS

Many gardeners new to cottage garden plants express the view that they want to cease planting annuals in favour of perennials, not realising that some of the free-seeding annuals, such as heart's-ease and forget-me-nots, can and do carry the garden in late winter when the herbaceous perennials are dormant.

Some clever gardeners choose to mix certain annuals with perennials and roses when the colour, height and flowering period suits a particular colour scheme. As an example, in a garden in Auckland, New Zealand, I saw a gentle blend of lemon yellow snapdragons, antirrhinum, and cream foxgloves, together with a tall cream mignonette. An annual with almost navy blue flowers called *Cerinthe major*, native to

Switzerland, was used as accent. I have not seen either the mignonette, which may be *Reseda alba*, or *Cerinthe major* used in Australia as yet.

The annuals listed here have been included because they have a long association with cottage gardens, are loved, extremely pretty or very useful and therefore valued.

ALTHAEA (hollyhocks) were grown widely a hundred years ago and are still

ABOVE: *Felicia daisies and white alyssum are useful spillovers for raised beds.*

ABOVE: *The navy blue flowers of* Cerinthe major *contrast against white valerian.*

popular today, even though the foliage is attacked by rust. Growing up to 2 m (6.6 ft) tall, they look marvellous against cottage walls which afford some wind protection. The singles of yesteryear are still popular, but now seed merchants are offering 'Summer Carnival' mixed, which will bloom for 3–4 years, and 'Chater's Double' mixed, which form camellia-like blooms in lovely pastel colours.

ALYSSUM (sweet Alice) has persisted in our garden without ever having been planted by us. It is, as I write, forming the lace on the cuff of the oak tree garden on the north-east side and is spilling out over the mower edge strip to soften the edge most beautifully. I treat it as a weed if it germinates too close to something newly planted, for it can smother a smaller plant while your back is turned. It will germinate in gravel but performs wonderfully in rich moist situations, and flowers almost perpetually. Height: 23 cm (9 in).

AMMI majus is not Queen Anne's lace, though its flower is so similar that the nursery industry has mistakenly had

LEFT: *White sweet Alice,* Mysotis *and lime green* Euphorbia *combine well under old-fashioned roses like 'Jean Ducher'.*

ABOVE: *A medley of delphiniums, campanulas and Queen Anne's lace backed by the Climbing Rose 'Cecile Brunner'.*

labels made calling it just that. The foliage of the true Queen Anne's lace (*Daucus carota*) is very like the foliage of the carrot, whereas *Ammi majus* has trifoliolate bright green leaves, and does not grow as tall or become a pest. Great cut flower. Height: 1 m (3 ft).

BELLIS perennis (lawn daisy) is not perennial, but when grown in cooler climates it never fails to delight visitors from warmer regions. Hybridisers have worked to offer such temptations as the 'Pomponette' series which are great colour spot fillers in late winter and early spring.

CLEOME spinosum (spider flower) is a tall growing, strongly scented annual for filling background gaps or, in the case of the pure white, to soften a brightly coloured rose. Other colours are mauve, deep rose pink and a paler two tone pink. Very free-seeding, it flowers spring to autumn.

COSMOS is another tall background annual which can be very useful if working on a pink and white scheme. A couple of new varieties which are worth trying are the 'Chantilly' cottage garden series, with rose and white picotee flowers, or the 'Sea Shells Mixed', with unusual fluted petals. Height: 0.9 m (2.9 ft).

CYNOGLOSSOM nervosum (Chinese forget-me-not) comes in deep sky blue, pure white or pink. Once you have introduced it into the garden, it is so generous with self-seeding that it is possible to have the blue, in particular, in flower all year round. To some it is a weed with pestiferous seeds, but as the colour intensifies with colder nights, I would not be without it for its contribution to the winter garden. I keep the white and the pink well away from the blue and each other. Dead-heading prolongs flowering but usually there are a multitude of seedlings to replace the parent.

DELPHINIUM 'Blue Butterfly' is a dwarf variety of the most intense blue and very hardy in late winter/early spring as a colour harmoniser. Height to 0.3 m (1 ft).

❧

LEFT: *The free seeding Californian poppy* (Eschscholtzia) *is here combined with silver* Artemisia *'Powis Castle' on the left.*

ABOVE: *Pink, white and mauve spider flowers* (Cleome *species) are grand fillers at the back of borders.*

ESCHSCHOLTZIA californica
(California poppy) in bright orange is
not everyone's cup of tea, but the cream
is delightful in my yellow garden.
It drops seed generously, which
commences germinating in early winter.
A great show is displayed by early spring
and carries on until mid summer. A new
series called Mission Bells gives some
pink shades.

LUNARIA biennis (honesty) is grown
for its silver disc seed pods which are
used in decorative work. It has large
heart-shaped leaves and pink, white or
mauve flowers in spring. The form *L.
biennis* 'Variegata' has white flowers and
lovely variegated leaves, best in part
shade. It free-seeds readily.

MYSOTIS alpestris is the low growing,
spring flowering forget-me-not that can
spread widely to form a carpet under
everything taller than 0.3 m (1 ft). The
blue and white forms seem
constitutionally stronger than the pink.
They commence flowering in late
winter, reaching a crescendo by early
spring and are best removed by mid
spring. They drop enough seed to repeat
the following spring. They will also
germinate in favourable weather in mid
summer but in this case need to be
controlled. They need to be kept back
from rose stems and iris rhizomes—in
fact, from anything that they are likely
to smother—but they are so pretty

when viewed as a sea of blue. In Europe
they are often used effectively with red
tulips.

NIGELLA damascena (love-in-a-mist)
is a must for the softness that it adds to
the garden in late spring. Colours are
soft sky blue, white, pink and deep blue,
and there is a new strain called 'Persian
Jewels'. The sky blue comes back year
after year amongst the roses and in late
spring looks so lovely.

**PAPAVER somniferum subspecies
paeoniflorum** is a very large peony-like
poppy, usually with fringed petals. In
New Zealand it comes in many colours,
from pure white, through pinks, scarlet

and plum. The opium poppy has similar
foliage but with a single mauve flower
with a purple base to each petal. It is
banned and one can be heavily fined if
found growing it.

PAPAVER rhosis (Flanders poppy) gets
its common name from the blood spilt
on Flanders' fields during many battles.
It is a delight in mid to late spring when
planted amongst white feverfew daisies
and will drop enough seed to ensure
survival and a good showing next
spring.

BELOW: *Heather Cant's much admired roadside
garden combines shrubs, roses, perennials and
annuals.*

Tropaeolum **'Alaska'** (nasturtium) in the herb garden or a hanging basket in light shade is a very rewarding annual. The variegated leaves and flowers can be used in salads and sandwiches. The abundant seed lies on the top of the soil under the foliage and is easily germinated. The colours are strong but can be selected out if you want only lemon, yellow, deep red or deep rose pink. Full sun or part shade suits them in the garden but they burn in heat waves or at –4°C (25°F).

Viola **tricolor** (heart's-ease or johnny jump-ups). The commercial variety of these miniature pansies is purple and golden yellow, but there are others which flower lemon, cream and mauve on one flower, or blue and purple in combination. They drop so much seed as to come up very thickly in late winter or in summer, as does *Mysotis alpestris* but they are at their best by mid winter through to late spring. Train yourself to recognise the tiny seedlings which have scalloped leaves and do not weed them out for they put on a great winter/ spring display.

I may not have mentioned your favourite annual for colour harmonising—perhaps *Nemophila* species or white *Primula malacoides*, both valuable amongst strongly coloured azaleas. More than half the fun of gardening lies in experimentation so if

ABOVE: *Once you are inside the Cants' garden the close plantings of annuals and perennials under 'Crepuscule' takes your eye.*

you want pink pansies under a favourite white rose or to try a new double pink snapdragon, go right ahead and try.

CHAPTER 10

Bulbs

For avid gardeners there is always a fascination in collecting and placing a few bulbous plants to enrich their lives and gardens. It is not my intention to cover the very well-known species like daffodils, tulips for cooler climates, hyacinths or jonquils, though in my own garden clumps of fragrant jonquils are one of winter's delights. I would prefer to extol the virtues of some of the lesser known treasures which deserve consideration.

ALSTROEMERIA The Butterfly Hybrids available to florists are starting to be offered by bulb companies. The Ligtu Hybrids are popular in England and offer interesting colours, such as salmon pink, cherry pink, lemon and soft gold. All have fleshy roots and many are herbaceous, dying down after the spring flowering. Ligtus grow to more than 1 m (3 ft).

LEFT: Salmon pink Alstroemeria, Ligtu hybrids (left foreground) used at Cobham Court add a strong accent to this superb border.

AMARYLLIS belladonna (naked lady lilies) derive their common name from the fact that the flower stem appears before the foliage arises in late summer. They are fragrant, extremely hardy and come in various shades of pink and light cyclamen. The white is called 'Hathor'. They ask only to be planted with their necks above ground level and are grand in a hot, dry corner, though they will flower in semi shade. Height: 0.8 m (2.6 ft).

ARUM see *Zantedeschia*.

BABIANA stricta, like *A. belladonna*, is a South African bulb which likes a sunny position. Although its colours can be vibrant, the white and two tone lavender blue varieites are well worth having.

BLETILLA striatum is a herbaceous ground orchid that flowers in spring, sending up stems of cyclamen purple flowers to 0.3 m (1 ft). It likes leaf mould incorporated into the planting soil in semi shade and to be mulched with leaf mould when dormant.

CALLA These lilies have received attention recently, with dwarf pink and dwarf cream being offered. The spotted leafed yellow flowering variety is called *C. elliotiana*. These are deciduous. See *Zantedeschia* for an evergreen dwarf white.

CLIVEA miniata We are all familiar with the evergreen orange spring flowering variety, but there are new hybrids being offered in combinations of gold, deep orange red and primrose yellow.

CYCLAMEN I refer here not to the large flowered house plants but to the species with tiny rabbit-ear flowers, which are highly regarded for their ability to grow and flower in dryish root-infested semi-shade. *C. hederifolium* has lovely green grey leaves, marbled and variegated in paler shades. The flowers, either white or pink, appear on naked stems before the foliage, but as they continue from late summer the later flowers are held above the foliage. They wind their seed pod in a tight spring-like coil back to ground level for germination.

DIERAMA pulcherrimum (fairy's fishing rod) has tall narrow foliage to 0.8 m (2.6 ft) in a clump and in late spring will give rise to ascending long arching flower stems which carry pendulous bells in pink, mauve or the rarer white. It is a favourite for placement beside ponds, but will also grow in dry situations, and free-seeds even in the roadside verges at elevation.

EUCHARIS grandiflora (Amazon lily) has fragrant orchid-like flowers with small daffodil cup centres, several per stem. In cold climates it is a conservatory plant, but in any area it is best potted in a peaty orchid compost and managed by dryish rest periods between flowerings. The Amazon lily appreciates adequate food and water prior to flowering and in warm areas will flower in spring, summer and autumn.

FREESIA refracta The old-fashioned fragrant freesias that free-seed along the roadsides in some regions are part of the joy of spring, but now there is also a very large, pure white fragrant species called *F. refracta* 'Alba' that is very desirable. Height: 0.4 m (1.3 ft).

***GLADIOLUS* species** I refer here not to the florist's types, but to those with small blooms. The miniature *G. nanus*, which are white with a pink diamond in the base of each petal, and the pure white 'The Bride' are both worthy of placement. There is also a miniature red called 'Herald Comet' and a creamy green with thin lime stripes inside the petals called 'Tristis'.

GLORIOSA rothschildiana* and *G. superba are fragrant climbing lilies of

unusual orchid-like flower form, scarlet edged golden yellow on each wavy petal. They are a delight on a summer's evening and will climb through the branches of a shrub. Lovely with *Solanum jasminoides*, providing the main root of the potato vine is not robbing them of moisture. They regrow each year if taken up in winter and appreciate a mulch of compost.

ABOVE: Babiana, *grown here with cyclamen* Ixia, *comes in soft or bright colours to suit all tastes.*

❧

HABRANTHUS robustus flowers in early to mid summer and has small crocus-like pink open bell flowers. It is a South African bulb that likes a warm position. Height: 23 cm (9 in).

RIGHT: *The orchid-like climbing lily* Gloriosa *has a strong fragrance on summer evenings.*

IRIS Tall Bearded and Louisiana. The beauty of these plants which grow from rhizomes (a swollen root stock) cannot be denied. The range is so extensive that it is advisable to consult a specialist's catalogue and try to visit the grower in the season of blooming for better colour harmony in your garden. They prefer full sun and must have good drainage.

LEUCOJUM species Many gardeners looking at *L. aestivum*, frequently sold as *L. vernum*, will call them snowdrops, but they are not—their common name is snowflakes. The petals of each little white bell are marked with a green spot and they are great for planting with hydrangeas because they flower when the hydrangeas have to be cut back.

LEUCOJUM autumnalis flowers in mid autumn with tiny white bell flowers held above thin cylindrical grass-like foliage.

LILIUM species Most of us are familiar with the November or Christmas lily, *L. longiflorum*, for its pure white fragrant trumpet flowers are always lovely in the garden or vase and they are not difficult to grow. Height: 1 m (3 ft). They like full sun, a rich compost at planting time, adequate moisture and

LILIUM speciosum is better known as the tiger lily and the pink form is like a smaller version of *L. excelsior*. I have seen the orange form used in full sun in an effective display with blue and white *Agapanthus*.

MORAEA neopavonia (peacock iris) has the three-petalled white flower typical of the wild iris, but each petal base is spotted with a large spot of iridescent peacock blue. It has thin grassy foliage and flowers in spring. Height: 0.6 m (2 ft).

NERINE (spider lily) is native to South Africa. The naked stems shoot up in early autumn to flower in full sun in shades of pale and deep pink, rosy red and white. It prefers a well-drained soil.

can be left undisturbed for several years if well mulched and fertilised. New varieties of Asiatic lilies are on offer in catalogues and they flower from late spring onwards, but prefer light-dappled shade in warm districts. Height: 1 m (3 ft). *L. auratum*, known as the Japanese gold-ray lily, is white with a gold stripe in the centre of each petal and red spots down each side of the stripe. A stem can carry 30 blooms. It will not tolerate alkaline soils. Height: 1.8 m (6 ft).

LILIUM excelsior is an Asiatic hybrid which is also very tall, 2 m (6.6 ft),

with huge 15 cm (6 in) diameter pink flowers striped burgundy down the centre and spotted burgundy stopping short of the tips and white margins. It is highly fragrant, flowering from early to mid summer.

LILIUM regale is a late flowering white lily with a gold throat and pink reverse to the petals. It free-seeds along roadside verges in some regions and sends down a root to develop the bulb at a level in the subsoil to suit its moisture needs, so they are impossible to dig up and better left for everyone's enjoyment. A fragrant species reaching 1.2 m (4 ft).

POLIANTHUS tuberosa is widely used in bridal bouquets, its waxy white flowers giving off a strong sweet fragrance. The tubers bloom only once and should then be discarded, by which time there will be lots of offsets to replant in an enriched, lime-free, well-drained soil. They flower in summer and autumn and appreciate

ABOVE: Habranthus *deserves to be more popular, with its pretty pink flowers opening in summer.*

RIGHT: *The tall bearded iris 'Avalon Bay' has intense deep blue blooms in spring and reblooms in autumn.*

fragrant lavender pink flowers in mid winter and again in summer. Not for the coldest areas as its foliage looks poor at –4°C (25°F).

WATSONIA species are not to everybody's taste, but in New Zealand one hybridiser showed me large belled forms in colours not previously available. For those working in drought affected areas, and for large farm gardens, these will be very welcome.

LEFT: Lilium excelsor *has tremendous perfume and very handsome flowers of 15 cm (6 in) diameter.*

BELOW: Cyclamen hederifolium, *with its tiny rabbit-ear petals, performs well under trees over several months.*

plenty of water until the foliage begins to yellow, when they should be lifted and separated. Do not water while dormant.

SCHIZOSTYLIS coccinea is an evergreen bulb which deserves greater popularity for it has a long flowering period commencing in mid summer through to late autumn. *S. coccinea* is tomato red, but there is a lovely white form and a cultivar called 'Mrs Hegarty' which is soft salmon pink. Their rhizome roots are easily divided in late winter and they are not suited to frosty districts but will stand –4°C (25°F).

TULBAGHIA fragrans This is not the society garlic, with onion scented foliage and violet flowers, but a species with a broader strap leaf, like an *Agapanthus* only lighter green. It produces heads of

ZANTEDESCHIA aetheopica (arum lily) is not loved by everyone and yet it is so valuable beside water or in the garden in either sun or shade, and it is very long flowering. A new dwarf white cultivar called 'Kiwi Calla', with foliage to 0.4 m (1.3 ft) and flowering stems to 0.6 m (2 ft), will bloom from late autumn to mid spring.

ZANTEDESCHIA aetheopica 'Green Goddess' prefers shade, though I have seen it effectively used in full sun beside a dam. The spathe flower is white in the throat and green in the upper half. As a cut flower it has a vase life of three weeks with regular water changes.

ZEPHYRANTHES candida (storm lily) has a white crocus-like bell flower, for about eight weeks in late summer to early autumn, which it produces above evergreen shiny grass-like deep green foliage. It is a very useful edging plant and increases readily. Divide in late winter.

ZEPHYRANTHES rosea has flatter leaves like *Habranthus robustus*, is a deeper shade of pink and readily multiplies in hot climates.

RIGHT: Zantedeschia aethiopica *'Green Goddess'* *flowers over many months and combines well in* *a vase with* Euphorbia palustris.

CHAPTER 11

Maintaining the Garden

Sometimes you can read a gardening book and miss what the reviewer had to say on the dust jacket because you are so keen to absorb the author's knowledge and experience. This happened to me with a book Margery Fish wrote called *A Flower For Every Day*, which was first published in 1965 by David and Charles. Only recently did I read the words 'Gardening for her was a daily excitement', and so it is for really keen creative gardeners worldwide.

When lecturing to groups I have often said about maintenance, 'Gardening is like housework—if you cease all activity, it very quickly shows', and as with any kind of repetitive work, it is the attitude of mind which governs whether it is enjoyable or boring.

Your gardening activities obviously

🌱

have to be fitted in with family life and/or career responsibilities, but the best method of ensuring success and pleasure is to do a little as often and as regularly as possible. This avoids the muscle injury and fatigue that inevitably result from having to clean up a garden that is overgrown with weeds and crying out for attention.

If you buy a property with an overgrown garden, it is better to work in one area at a time and then, as the third or fourth section is reached, go back and weed the first section again, for it is easier to remove newly germinated weeds than those which have deep and extensive roots. Some weed seeds remain viable for very long periods—after eight years I have almost eliminated a small species of morning glory vine, but still the odd one appears now and then.

Take some before and after photographs and keep a diary of your activities and progress, for it is very easy to forget what you used when the citrus

or roses were last sprayed, or the exact time and place where those special bulbs were planted, unless you have marked the spot. By all means follow the advice of a gardening yearbook to begin with, but as time goes by your own diary will be referred to more and more. Whether it is early morning or later in the day, do not attempt the heaviest job with back muscles which are not fully relaxed, for that is tempting fate. Ask for assistance with heavy lifting jobs.

We all have favourite gardening tools and amongst mine are a kneeling pad for use when weeding and a very sharp drainer's spade for cutting planting holes in root-infested ground. It has a long narrow blade and is popular with New Zealand gardeners but not frequently seen elsewhere. Gradually I have established a routine when setting off from the toolshed, with the wheelbarrow serving to transport the spade, a light fork, kneeler, secateurs, weeding knife, sticks and tie string (green plastic-coated tape), a plastic bag for the odd oxalis bulb that goes into the garbage bin, hat, gloves, and a bin of compost for mulching or soil improvement if planting; then I am ready to start. My weeding knife is a stainless steel fish boning knife which is deliberately kept blunt to avoid accidents, and it is a wonderful tool, used properly.

The more gardening you do the more you train yourself to be observant of the needs of your plants, whether it is

LEFT: *Watsonias in the dry garden of Jacqui Sutherland, Pirinoa, New Zealand.*

recognising stress from lack of water (wilting foliage), insect attack, or nutritional deficiencies. You also learn to snip, dead-head, cut back, trim or prune to control over-vigorous growth, and to stake and tie before a strong wind flattens the flower stems of something you have been expectantly nurturing.

How much time does it take? Well, how much time have you got to spare for your hobby? I can remember a neighbour, many years ago, who boasted he could construct a garden for me that would only need four hours a week, including cutting the grass, but his plant choices were not mine. When the hobby is shared, as it is in our garden, so the chores are shared, but if you are a lone gardener, try to find a short period each day, particularly in summer, in which to garden, perhaps in the late afternoon when the heat of the day is waning. Others prefer the early morning—and remember, it is easier to weed after soaking rain.

The greatest excitement comes, after having prepared a section, with the actual placement and planting of the plants, but it is the maintenance of those plants which brings the gratification of creative achievement.

WATER

Plants are like children in that they need food and water in order to grow, but how much water and how often? Irrigation systems have revolutionised gardening for busy people, but they are not foolproof. Ants can and do make nests in the risers of microjets. Plants grow up in front of outlets, thus blocking the even distribution. It is advisable to check regularly that the system is working properly, for the plants that are being starved of water will not thrive.

Fully automatic systems mean that some grey foliage plants can receive too much water for their needs and will be lost. Gardening is full of compromises. One compromise might be that you have a manually controlled system which can be operated according to the needs of the plants. Where large trees are sucking the moisture heavily, the system will need to be operated more frequently for the benefit of the smaller underplantings.

Gardens without irrigation systems may need to be watered only once a week in winter, unless there are drying winds for several days (wind blowing across leaf surfaces dehydrates by removing moisture, even in winter), but twice a week in autumn and early spring, and three times a week in summer.

Heat waves will cause burnt foliage and stress to some tender foliaged plants even when they are watered every second day. Late afternoon or early evening watering in summer is most

lavenders, red-hot pokers (*Kniphofia* species) and as many drought resistant types of garden plants as she could find that were pleasing in her compositions. Her meagre summer rainfall cannot be augmented as the tank water is needed for household use and emergency firefighting. Few true gardeners can bear to look upon parched plants.

❧

LEFT: *Abutilons flower almost perpetually and must be pruned even when in full flower to achieve a good shape.*

BELOW: *Hybrid* Kniphofia, *seen here harmonising with roses 'Sunny Honey', are very drought tolerant.*

beneficial. Adequate and deep watering is far better than surface splashings, which do not encourage the roots to forage deep in search of moisture. Disturb the crust to see if the soil is dry before deciding to turn on a sprinkler.

In areas where frosts are common it is advisable to water in the morning in winter so that the soil drains and rewarms before nightfall. Afternoon watering can result in greater frost burn because plant cells filled with moisture can freeze, thus causing plant death.

Recently I met a woman who gardens without the benefit of artificial watering in summer. Her dry garden was inspirational with masses of daffodils which are dormant in summer,

MULCH

One effective way of conserving moisture and assisting in the suppression of weeds is to mulch the surface of the soil. This can be done with homemade compost, spent mushroom compost, eucalyptus leaf litter mulch or with the various other mulch materials on offer.

Spent mushroom compost, unless it is aged, cannot be used near azaleas, camellias, daphnes or rhododendrons because it is frequently very alkaline.

Eucalyptus leaf litter mulch should contain equal parts of chopped leaf, twig and branch wood. The leaf content will decompose first and it needs to be renewed or topped up as it becomes thin on the ground, which can happen in fewer than three years.

Pine chip or pine flake needs to be supplemented with regular fertilising because, as the wood begins to rot, it will rob the plants of nitrogen.

Fine-rooted groundcovers will not spread out over mulch materials like

PREVIOUS PAGES: *(Left) Perennial border at Ivy Cottage, Dorset. (Right) Pretty perennials planted by Alan Izzard, New Zealand.*

RIGHT: *Clematis hybrid 'Nelly Moser' loves rich feeding, mulch, adequate water and a little dolomite occasionally.*

coarse pine bark because it prevents them from putting down roots into moist soil. Weeds with airborne seeds, such as thistles, will germinate in the mulch but are easily extracted, as indeed are all other types of weeds which appear on a mulched surface.

FEEDING THE GARDEN

Homemade compost, properly made, will, if renewed in spring and late summer, be sufficient to nourish perennials unless your soil is a poor sandy loam, in which case you will need to supplement the compost. There are many types of organic and inorganic plant foods on offer. Animal manures, blood and bone, seaweed and cottonseed meal are organic fertilisers. Pelleted poultry manure is organic, but the very small ball-bearing type pelleted products popular for feeding potted plants are inorganic chemical fertilisers useful for boosting or supplementing other food forms.

Cottonseed meal is the ground-up seed of the cotton plant. It is so nutritious that produce merchants sell it as poultry food. It is excellent for fertilising camellias, azaleas, rhododendrons, daphnes, citrus and dwarf conifers because it does not burn

the foliage or stress the plant as some inorganic products can do if applied to dry ground and not thoroughly watered in. Any unused cottonseed meal needs to be stored in a lidded bin.

Blood and bone is one of the safest plant foods, because its nutrients are released slowly, but it is not as high in nitrogen as cottonseed meal. The latter can be used every three months, commencing in spring, for azaleas in tubs or other containers.

Pelletised poultry manure has become very popular with gardeners in the last decade for it, too, does not burn plants.

For poor soil areas it is effective for about two months, by which time plants like citrus and roses will need another handful or two, depending on their size.

There are many forms of inorganic fertilisers marketed for special purposes, such as lawn food and rose and citrus food, which are specially formulated to stimulate growth, particularly in spring,

❧

BELOW: *The claret ash (centre back) has doubled in size in seven years and sucks moisture from my yellow garden.*

and there are general-purpose inorganic products as well.

For the lawn feeding program at Colonial Cottage, we begin in late winter or early spring with lawn food, which is high in nitrogen to stimulate growth after winter. The grass is again fed in late spring and late summer either with a finely pelletised form of poultry manure, or ammonium nitrate, which looks like brown sago. It must be very evenly applied over the dampened lawn and immediately watered until the chemical is all dissolved, for it is easy to burn the grass with this form of plant food. Store ammonium nitrate in a lidded bin. Regular use of ammonium sulphate will result in very poor grass as the soil pH drops to a dangerously acidic level.

Roses should be fed with rose food in late winter, immediately after pruning, mulched with compost and fed pelletised poultry manure in late spring and late summer with the mulch being renewed in summer. Abundant blooms only come with adequate food and water and the control of aphids, caterpillar and fungal diseases such as black spot, which can cause defoliation.

SPRAYING

People who don't want to use chemical sprays because they consider it is bad for the environment must either give up

trying to grow roses or azaleas—which are the two highest maintenance plants I know—or find control methods which satisfy their peace of mind. The majority of gardeners accept that unless a fungicide spray is used against black spot attacking roses, the plant is going to suffer and be debilitated—and most customers are very critical if offered a rose with just one leaf exhibiting black spot.

Overhead watering late in the day will encourage black spot because the foliage

stays wet for longer. We use a systemic fungicide but when rain prevents spraying we, too, have outbreaks of black spot. Garlic sprays for aphid control are popular with people concerned about the environment, but those gardeners with stone fruit trees wanting to control fruit fly maggots

❦

BELOW: *Standardised wisterias need regular trimming to control summer growth.*

know that only a systemic insecticide will ensure a harvestable crop.

The most important advice is to treat all poisonous chemicals with great respect. Wear protective clothing when spraying, keep chemicals out of reach of children, preferably in a locked storage area, and keep spray equipment clean at all times. Always keep two separate sprayers, one for herbicides and one for insecticides, clearly labelled, for you cannot completely wash out herbicide and it can cause plant death if accidentally sprayed onto wanted plants.

Herbicides are available that leave no residue in the soil, but they still have to be handled with care. Such herbicides can be sprayed on to bark which is more than four years old, tree bases for example, without adverse effect but are death to green foliage. Use only on windless mornings, so that drift is not carried onto desired plants by the wind.

PRUNING

Pruning skills are acquired, like most gardening skills, with practice. Early in our marriage we lived opposite an

BELOW: Austin's rose 'The Reeve' blooms most generously with regular fertilising and adequate water.

elderly retired couple who had what I call 'a bits and pieces' garden, because their budget was such that Fanny had had to create her garden with slips and cuttings acquired from friends. It was vastly overcrowded initially, and we all agreed that if everything she planted grew, it would become a jungle. Old Rupert, taking his morning constitutional, always took the secateurs in his hand and could be observed snipping and cutting back to keep the pathways free of intrusive growth. Sometimes he was a bit ruthless, much to Fanny's chagrin.

Sharp tools are essential, and the secateurs, branch cutters and pruning saw all need to be properly maintained and stored, and never left out in the rain to rust. Clean the blades after use and apply a thin film of petroleum jelly to the surface of the pruning saw. How to prune a shrub or a Bush Rose is one of the greatest concerns for beginners. In the preceding chapters advice has been given on how and when to prune. In the case of spring flowering shrubs, remember that if you prune in winter when they are bare of leaves you will be cutting off the flowering wood needed for the spring display.

Rose pruning is not the problem that the novice might think it is. It begins in early winter, with the climbers being done first. Once-flowering roses may be pruned immediately after flowering but in areas of high summer temperatures, it

LEFT: *This 'Carabella' Climber is trained over a metal tiered half hoop to achieve a canopy of bloom. Half the vertical canes are removed in late winter.*

vigour of the plant. There are, however, many old-fashioned roses, such as 'Duchesse de Brabrant', 'Crepuscule' and 'The Prioress', which I treat far more ruthlessly, for they have such vigorous growth habits. 'Honeyflow' is an exception in that it is necessary to leave at least 10 canes of 0.6–0.7 m (2–2.3 ft) in length in order to get a good crown of growth and blossom. It resents ruthless pruning and takes a long time to recover.

Summer water shoots coming from above the bud union, or below the soil surface, if the variety is on its own roots, are the future branch structure of the bush or climber. In varieties like 'Devoniensis' and the true Dwarf 'Cecile Brunner', these water shoots will carry a bouquet of flowers at about 1 m (3 ft) height. When the flowering is finished, cut them back to an outward pointing eye—although, with a variety such as 'Sadler's Wells', nipping the top of a water shoot at 0.6 m (2 ft) will make it branch instead of shooting up to 2 m (6.6 ft) before flowering.

Some of the Hybrid Musks, such as 'Cornelia' and 'Buff Beauty', want to spread widely and flower along the

is safer to prune in winter and avoid exposing too much bark to the sun. Burnt bark results in poor growth.

The aim is to skeletonise the long canes needed to produce spur growth in early spring, either fanning them out, training them horizontally onto plastic-coated wires stretched taut or, in the case of Pillar Roses such as 'Carabella', cutting out a percentage of the old vertical canes. Often a customer will say, 'But old-fashioned roses are not pruned like modern Hybrid Tea Roses, are they?'. It depends on the rose, but most are pruned exactly the same way. One of the best texts available on pruning roses

appears in *The Ross Guide to Rose Growing*, which is listed in Further Reading, at the back of this book.

Each bush has to be studied and pruned according to its growth habit. Small bushes should not be cut back to near ground level as I once saw a farmer do. Miniatures such as 'Green Ice' should be reduced by 60 per cent and the centre cleaned out by removing dead and very thin, spindly growth. Roses which only grow to 1 m (3 ft) need dead, twiggy, spindly or poor internal growth removed first, after which they should be cut back to an outward pointing eye by 60 per cent or less, depending on the horizontal canes. One gardener I know has achieved a pleasing result by training 'Cornelia' along a dividing fence. Understanding the natural growth habit of the subject is the key to successful pruning of both roses and shrubs. In our garden, rose pruning must be completed by mid August as the sap can begin to rise this early, forcing the dormant growth buds to swell and burst into leaf.

The results of regular maintenance of the garden are threefold: firstly, you will have a better groomed garden with healthier and more attractive plants; secondly, your creativeness will contribute to your own good health, both mentally and physically; thirdly, the environment you create can be a source of pleasure, not only to you but to all those who come into contact with it. Even non-gardeners respond to beautiful surroundings.

Who knows, one day you may open your garden to members of the local

garden club or to the public. Ninety-nine point nine per cent of public visitors respect the fact that they are in a private garden and will appreciate your efforts. Gardeners are, on the whole, kind, friendly and generous with tips, hints, and sometimes seeds or cuttings if the person making the request is polite,

ABOVE: *To share the beauty of the garden and one's hospitality with friends is always a rewarding experience.*

respectful and tactful. I speak as one who visits and is visited. I wish you all happy, creative gardening.

Further Reading

Barrett, Margaret (ed.) 1980, *The Edna Walling Book of Australian Garden Design*, Anne O'Donovan, Melbourne.

Chatto, Beth 1989, *The Green Tapestry*, Collins, London.

Fish, Margery 1980, *Cottage Garden Flowers*, Faber & Faber, London.

Hobhouse, Penelope 1985, *Colour in Your Garden*, Collins, London.

Lees-Milne, Alvide & Verey, Rosemary 1987, *The New Englishwoman's Garden*, Chatto & Windus, London.

Lloyd, Christopher 1984, *The Well Chosen Garden*, Elm Tree Books, London.

Macoboy, Stirling 1986, *What Flower is That*, Weldon Publishers, Sydney.

Phillips, Roger & Rix, Martyn 1991, *Perennials* (Volumes I & II), Pan Books, London.

Ross, Deane 1990, *The Ross Guide to Rose Growing*, Lothian, Melbourne.

Rowell, Raymond 1980, *Ornamental Flowering Shrubs in Australia*, Reed, Sydney.

Rowell, Raymond 1980, *Ornamental Flowering Trees in Australia*, Reed, Sydney.

Stackhouse, Shirley 1993, *Shirley Stackhouse's Gardening Year* (revised edition), CollinsAngus&Robertson Publishers, Sydney.

Verey, Rosemary 1990, *Good Planting*, Frances Lincoln, London.

Walling, Edna 1943, *Gardens in Australia: Their Design and Care*, Oxford University Press, Melbourne.

Walling, Edna 1947, *Cottage and Garden in Australia*, Oxford University Press, Melbourne.

Watts, Peter 1981, *The Gardens of Edna Walling*, The Women's Committee of the National Trust of Australia (Victoria).

Index

Page numbers in italics refer to illustrations.

Aaron's rod (*Verbascum phoenicemum*)
159-60
Abbot, Marylyn *v*
Abelia
  x *grandiflora* 86-7
    'Francis Mason' 87
    'Variegata' 87
Abutilon 63, *179*
  x *hybridum* (Chinese lantern) 87
    'Golden Fleece' *87*
  megapotamicum 'Variegatum' 102
  savitzii 100
Acanthus mollis (oyster plant; bear's
  breeches) 135
Acer
  buergeranum (trident maple) 78
  palmatum (Japanese maple) 75, *78*, 78,
    80-1, 83, 90
    'Atropurpureum' 69, 78
    'Aureum' 78, *79*
    'Nigrum' 78
    'Osakazuki' 23
    'Senkaki' (coral barked maple) 76, 78
Achillea
  'Cloth of Gold' 147
  clypeolata 139
  millefolium 'Cerise Queen' 147
    'Galaxy' hybrids 147
    'Appleblossom' 147
    'Lilac Queen' 147
    'Salmon Beauty' 147
    'Moonshine' 139, 147
  ptarmica 'The Pearl' 146
  x *taygetea* 147
Acmena smithii (lilli-pilli) 24, 31
Aconitum (monkshood) 137
  arendsii 137
  napellus 137
Adam, Dell and Eric *43*, 62
Agapanthus 90
  'Baby Blue' 146
  campanulatus patens 147
  'Dwarf Blue' 146
  'Dwarf White' 146
  inapertus 158, *158*, 159
  'Nana' 146
  orientalis 158
  'Peter Pan' 146
  'Queen Anne' 146

'Snow Drops' 146
'Tom Thumb' 146
Agathaea 146-7
Agryranthemum frutescens (Marguerite
  daisies) 102
Alchemilla mollis (lady's mantle) 131
Allison, Sally and Bay *119*, *154*
Allium christophii 65
Alstroemeria
  Butterfly hybrids 167
  Ligtu hybrids 167, *167*
Althaea (hollyhocks) 161
  'Chater's Double' 161
  'Summer Carnival' 161
alyssum (sweet Alice) 4, 6, 19, *69*, 161-2
Amaryllis belladonna (naked lady lily) 167
  'Hathor' 167
Amazon lily (*Eucharis grandiflora*) 168
Amberley, New Zealand 4, 7
Ammi majus 162
Androsace lanuginosa 139
Anemone (Japanese wind flower) 54, 56,
  135
  x *hybrida*
    'Alba' 135
    'Elegantissima' 135
    'Kriemhild' 135
    'September Charm' 135
    syn. *A. hupehensis* 56, 90, 135, *135*, 136
    syn. *A. japonica* 135
    'Whirlwind' 135
Angelonia angustifolia 147-8
annuals 160-5
Anthemis
  punctata syn. *A. cupaniana* 139
  tinctoria (Dyer's camomile) *141*, 142
    'E.C. Buxton' 142
    'Wargrave's Variety' 142, *142*
antirrhinum 160
aphids 25, 126, 182
Aquilegia (granny's bonnets) 9, *50*, 54, 71,
  131
  alpina 131
  clematiflora 9, 131
  hybrida
    'Dragonfly' 131
    'McKana' 131
    'Mrs Scott Elliott' 131
    'Nora Barlow' 131

longissima 9
vulgaris *50*, 54, 131
Arabian jasmine (*Jasminum sambac*) 92
arabis *73*
Arbutus unedo (strawberry tree) 76, 84
arches, garden *11*, 43
Ardisia crenulata 100
Arenaria montana 142
Armeria maritima (thrift) 146
  'Isobel Burdett' 146
Armytage, Captain and Mrs David 7
Artemesia 139, *140*
  abscinth 139
  arborescens (silver wormwood) 139
  'Lambrook Silver' 139
  'Powis Castle' 139, *163*
  'Valerie Furness' 139
artichoke, globe (*Cynara scolymus*) 58, *58*
arum lily (*Zantedeschia aetheopica*) 63, 173
Aruncus dioicus (goat's beard) 137
ash, claret *181*
ash, golden (*Fraxinus excelsior*) 76, 79
Aster
  alevis 148
  dumosus (dwarf aster) 146
    'Dwarf Nancy' 146
    'Lady Henry Maddocks' 146
    'Marjorie' 146
    'Victor' 146
  frikarti 148
  novae-angliae
    'Barr's Pink' 148
    'Harrington Pink' 148
    'Perry's White' 148
    'Plenty' 148
  novi-belgii (Michaelmas daisy) 148
    'Coome Rosemary' 148
    'Eventide' 148
    'Winston Churchill' 148
  vimineus (Easter daisy) 148
Astilbe 132
  x *arendsii*
    'Bremen' 132
    'Fanal' 132
    'Hyacinth' 132
    'Rhineland' 132
Astrantia major 'Rosea' 132
Aucuba japonica 'Variegata' (gold dust
  shrub) 87-8

Austin, David 53, 55, *109*, 112, 114, 121
Austin roses 62, 69, 71, *109*, 114, 117,
  118, 121-5, *183*
Australian Camellia Research Society 50
Ayrlies, Auckland *152*
Azalea 15, 27, 56, 58, 61, *84*, 90, 100
  'Hexe' 102
  indica hybrids 93-4
    'Alba Magna' 93
    'Alphonse Anderson' 93
    'Exquisite' 93-4
    'Jean Alexander' 94
    'Kalimna Pearl' 93
    'Lady Poltimore' 94
    'Morti' 53, 94
    'James Belton' 6
    'Pink Lace' 102
    'Red Wing' 102
    'Ruth Kirk' 6
    'White Lace' 102

Babiana stricta 167, *168*
baby's tears 143
Baker, Mary *42*, *43*
balloon flower (*Platycodon grandiflorus*)
  136-7
bamboo 25
Banksia marginata (silver banksia) 76
bear's breeches (*Acanthus mollis*) 135
Bechtel's crabapple (*Malus ioensis* 'Plena')
  80
bee balm (*Monarda didyma*) 153-4
bees 9
begonias 63
belladonna lily 15, 167
Bellis perennis (lawn daisy) 162-3
  'Pomponette' 162-3
Berberis thunbergi
  'Atropurpurea' 94
  'Keller's Surprise' 94
  'Nana' 94
bergamot (*Monarda didyma*) 153-4
  'Cambridge Scarlet' 154
  'Croftway Pink' 154
  'Enfield Gem' 154, *154*
Bergenia (London pride) 132
  cordifolia 'Red' 132
  purpurascens 132

Betula pendula (silver birch) 6, *19*, *23*, 69, 79, *79*, 82, 84
Bickleigh Vale, Victoria 7
birch, silver, *see* silver birch
Bishop, Maryan *140*
blackberry 23
black-eyed Susan
   (*Dimorphotheca*) 154
   (*Gazania splendens* 'Alba') 143
   (*Rudbeckia*) 159
bleeding heart (*Decentra spectabilis*) 133
Bletilla striatum 167
bloody cranesbill (*Geranium sanguinium*) 144
bluebells 6
blueberry ash, native (*Elaeocarpus reticulatus*) 50, 77, 82
blue-eyed Mary (*Ompheloides verna*) 134
bog sage (*Salvia uliginosa*) 159
bottlebrush, scarlet (*Callistemon citrinus*) 88
bottlebrush, weeping scarlet (*Callistemon viminalis*) 76
bougainvillea 55
Bouvardia
   humboldtii 102
   leiantha 'Duchesse of York' 103
box (*Buxus*) *12*, 64
   sempervirens *100*, 100-1
box hedge 68
Brachycome multifida (cut leaf native daisy) 142, *143*
'Break of Day' 142
Buddleia
   davidii (butterfly bush) *1*, 88
      'Lockinch' 88
      'Royal Red' 88
      'White Bouquet' 88
      'White Profusion' 88
   salvifolia 88
bulbs 15, 167–173
Burnley Horticultural College 6
butterfly bush (*Buddleia davidii*) 88
Buxus (box) *12*, 64
   sempervirens *100*, 100-1

Calceolaria 137
calico bush (*Kalmia latifolia*) 92
California poppy (*Eschscholtzia californica*) *163*, *164*
Californian lilac (*Ceanothus*) 91
Calla elliotiana 167
Calliandra haematocephala (powder puff flower) 88
Callicarpa dichotoma (purple bead bush; Chinese beauty berry) 94-5

Callistemon
   citrinus (scarlet bottlebrush) 88
      'Burgundy' 88
      'Candy Pink' 88
      'Endeavour' 88
      'Harkness' 88
      'Mauve Mist' 88
      'Reeves Pink' 88
   viminalis (weeping scarlet bottlebrush) 76
Callitris columellaris (white cypress pine) 75
Calodendrum capense (Cape chestnut) 77
Camellia 15, 27, 88-91
   hybrids
      'Scented Gem' 52, 91
      'Scentuous' 52, 91
      'Tiny Princess' 52
   japonica 25, 26-7, 50, 82, 84, 88, 90
      'Betty Ridley' 88
      'Blushing Beauty' 88
      'Bob Hope' 88
      'Desire' 88
      'Dr Louis Polizzi' 88
      'Ecclefield' 88
      'Great Eastern' 88
      'Julia France' 88
      'Laurie Bray' 88
      'Lovelight' 88
      'Pink Gold' 88
      'Sally Fisher' 88
      'Silver Chalice' 88
      'Wildfire' 88
   lutchuensis 52, 91
      'Margarete Hertrich' 54
      'Nuccio's Gem' 54
   reticulata 88, 90
      'Dr Clifford Parks' 91
      'Howard Asper' 91
      'Lasca Beauty' 91
      'Valentine Day' 91
      'Valley Knudsen Orchid' 91
   sasanqua 21, *24*, 24-5, 36, 50, 52, 84, 88, *88*, 90, 91
      'Edna Butler' 91
      'Hiryu' 91
      'Jane Morgan' 91
      'Jennifer Susan' 91
      'Marie Young' 21
      'Moonlight' 61
      'Plantation Pink' 91
      'Pure Silk' 91
      'Russhay' 91
      'Setsugekka' 91
      'Wynne Rayner' 88
      'Yuletide' 34, 91
   vernalis 'Star Above Star' 52, 91
Campanula 135-6, *162*

   alliarifolia 135
   istriaca 129
   lactiflora 'Pouffe' 137
   latiloba 135
      'Alba' 135
   persicifolia 136
      'Alba' 136
   portenschlagiana syn. *Muralis* 129
   poscharskyana
      'E.H. Frost' 129
      'Lisduggan' 130
   rapunculoides *54*, *137*, 148
   takesimana 136
   trachelium 'Bernice' 136
camphor laurel 73
campion (*Lychnis coronaria* x *flos-jovis*) 141
Canary Island tansy (*Tanacetum ptarmiciflorum*) 141-2
Candelabra primula 86
Cant, Heather and Richard 31, *33*, *164*, *165*
Cape chestnut (*Calodentrum capense*) 77
cardinal flower (*Lobelia fulgens*) 153
cardoon (*Cynara scolymus*) 58
Caryopteris
   incana 103
   x *clandoniensis* 101
Catananche caerulea (cupid's dart) 148
Catharanthus roseus (Madagascar periwinkle) 148
   'Peppermint Cooler' 148
catmint
   (*Nepeta faassenii*) 19, 141
   (*Nepeta* 'Six Hills') 154
Ceanothus (Californian lilac) 91
   'Blue Pacific' 91
   'Trewithin' 91
Cedrus deodara (deodar) 33
Centaurea 140
   dealbata 148
   gymnocarpa (dusty miller) 139
Centranthus 152
Cerastium tomentosum (snow in summer) 139
Ceratopetalum gummiferum (NSW Christmas bush) 77, 84
Ceratostigma
   griffithi 101
   plumbaginoides 130
   willmottianum 103
Cercis siliquastrum (Judas tree) 61
Cerinthe major 160-1, *161*
Chaenomeles
   japonica (flowering quince) 95
   speciosa
      'Falconnet Charlet' 95
      'Moerloosei' 95

   'Nivalis' 95
   'Rosea Pleana' 95
   'Simonii' 95
Chatto, Beth 2, *8*, 133, 160
Cheiranthus mutabilis (winter joy) 148
cherry, Japanese (*Prunus serrulata*) 62, *80*, 81
cherry pie (*Heliotropium*) 104, *104*
China Roses, *see* roses
Chinese beauty berry (*Callicarpa dichotoma*) 94-5
Chinese beauty bush (*Kolkwitzia amabilis*) 97
Chinese elm (*Ulmus parvifolia*) 29
Chinese forget-me-not (*Cynoglossom nervosum*) 163
Chinese foxglove (*Rehmania angulata*) 159
Chinese lantern (*Abutilon* x *hybridum*) 87
Chinese pistachio (*Pistacia chinensis*) 29, 81
Chinese tallow tree (*Sapium sebiferum*) 29, 81
Choisya 84
   ternata (Mexican orange blossom) 91
Christmas bush, NSW (*Ceratopetalum gummiferum*) 47, 77
Christmas lily (*Lilium longiflorum*) 169
Christmas tree, New Zealand (*Metrosideros excelsus*) 77
Chrysanthemum
   minima 'Polaris' 153
   morifolium 'Little Bob' 146
   pallidosum 66
   parthenium (feverfew) *54*, 71, 148-50
      'Pincushion' 148
      'White Bonnet' 148
   ptarmiciflorum 141-2
   rubellum
      'Clara Curtis' 146
      'Mary Stoker' 146
Citharexylum spinosum (fiddlewood) 77
clay 16
clematis 35
   'Marie Boisselot' (syn. 'Mme le Coultre') 62
   'Nelly Moser' *180*
   'William Kennett' *43*
Cleome spinosum (spider flower) 163, *163*
climate, macro/micro 20
climbing plants 34-5, *see also* roses, climbing
Clivea miniata 167
clove pinks (*Dianthus*) 47, 60, *60*, *105*, 140, *140*
Cobham Court, Kent *57*, 167
Coke, Patricia 65, *66*
Collier, Gordon *14*, *56*, 57

Colonial Cottage *1, 47, 49, 49-54, 58*

colour and harmony 12, 55–71

columbine 90

compost 14-15, 39, 71, 180

cone flower (*Echinacea purpurea*) 150, *150*

conifers *73, 75*

Convolvulus mauritanicus 142, *143*

coral bells (*Heuchera sanguinea*) 47, 133

coral tree (*Erythrina* x *sykesii*) (syn *E. indica*) 24

cordyline 3

Coreopsis
    grandiflora 'Sunburst' 150
        'Mini Gold' 142
    verticillata 'Moonbeam' 150

Cosmos 33
    'Chantilly' 163
    'Sea Shells Mixed' 163

Cotinus coggygria 'Purpureus' (purple-leaf smoke bush) 95

Cononeaster 91
    dammeri 103
    glaucophylla 91
    horizontalis 103
    pannosus 36
    parneyi 91

cottage garden, definition 12

cotton lavender (*Santolina chamaecyparissus*) 141

Cottonwood, Auckland 75

cowslip (*Primula veris*) 135

crabapple (*Malus floribunda*) 8, 29

cranesbill, hedgerow (*Geranium pratense*) 151

cranesbill, bloody (*Geranium sanguinium*) 144

Crambe cordifolia 160

creeping fig (*Ficus pumila* 'Minima') 34

creeping jenny (*Lysimachia nummularia* 'Area') 130, 144

crepe myrtle (*Lagerstroemia indica*) 27, *50*, 52, 61, 79-80

crofton weed 23

cupid's dart (*Catananche*) 148

Cupressus
    macrocarpa 21, *74*
    sempervirens 'Swane's Golden' 21

Cyclamen 167
    hederifolium 167, *172*
    Ixia 168

Cynaglossom 33, 69, *152*
    nervosum (Chinese forget-me-not) 163

Cynara scolymus (globe artichoke) 58, *58*

Cypress pine, white (*Callitris columellaris*) 75

daffodils *19*

daisies 12, *25*, 47

daisy, African (*Osteospermum* 'Starry Eyes') 154

daisy, alpine paper (*Helipterum anthenoides*) 147

daisy, cut leaf native (*Brachycome multifida*) 142

daisy, feverfew, *see* feverfew

daisy, kingfisher (*Felicia amelloides*) 31, 146-7, *161*

daisy, lawn 162-3

daisy, seaside (*Erigeron karvinskianus* syn. *E. mucronatus*) 142-3

daisy, shasta (*Leucanthemum* x *superbum*) 47, 152-3

dame's violet (*Hesperis matronalis*) 159

daphne 15, 26, 27, 101

daphne, native (*Pittosporum undulatum*) 23

Daphne odora 101

datura 62

Daucus carota (Queen Anne's lace) 7, *25*, 70, *70*, 162, *162*

daylilies (*Hemerocallis*) 56, 58, 61, 151-2

Decentra spectabilis (bleeding heart) 133

deciduous shrubs 94-9

deciduous trees 78-83

Delphinium 33, 65, 71, *137, 162*
    'Blue Butterfly' 163

deodar (*Cedrus deodara*) 33

design, of cottage gardens 29-45

Deutzia (wedding bells) 95, 110
    gracilis 103
    'Magician' 95
    nikko 103
    'Rosalind' 95
    x *rosea* 95
    scabra 95
        'Pride of Rochester' 95
        'Pink Pom Pom' 95

Dexter, Anne 18

Dianthus (clove pinks) 60, *60, 105*, 140, *140*
    'Arthur' 140
    barbatus (sweet william) 47
    'Mars' 140
    'Norgate's White' 140
    'Old English' 140
    'Pike's Pink' 140
    plumaris 'Mrs Sinkins' 140

Diascia ambigua 146

Diascia virgilis 146

Dicentra
    formosa
        'Alba' 133
        'Rosea' 133
    spectabilis (bleeding heart) 133

Dierama pulcherrimum (fairy's fishing rod) 167-8

Digitalis 137-8
    heywoodii 140
    mertonensis 138
    purpurea 137-8
    'Alba' 137-8

Dimorphotheca 154

diseases, plant 126

dissectum maple 54, *86*

Dodonaea viscosa 'Purpurea' 58

Downderry, Victoria 7

Doyle, Dr and Mrs *32*

drainage 13, 18

drought resistant plants 179

Dural, NSW 47-8

dusty miller (*Centaurea gymnocarpa*; *Senecio cineraria*) 139

dusty miller (*Senecio maritima*) 141

Dutch honeysuckle (*Lonicera periclymenum*) 98

Dyer's camomile (*Anthemis tinctoria*) 142

early spiketail (*Stachyurus praecox*) 99

East Lambrook Manor, Somerset 49, *49*

Easter daisy (*Aster vimineus*) 148

Echinacea purpurea 150
    'Alba' 150

Elaeagnus pungens 'Maculata' 91-2

Elaeocarpus 75
    reticulatus (native blueberry ash) 50, 77, 82

elm, Chinese (*Ulmus parvifolia*) 29

elm, golden (*Ulmus procera* 'Vanhouttei') 76

English oak (*Quercus robur*) 24, *26*, 27

Enkianthus campanulatus 95

Epimedium x *versicolor* 'Sulphureum' 133

Erigeron 60
    karvinskianus syn. *E. mucronatus* 142-3
    speciosus 150

Eryldene, Sydney 4-6, 90, *90*

Eryngium 150
    anethystinum 150
    varifolium 'Variegatum' 151
    x *zabelii* 'Blue Hills' 151

Erythrina x *sykesii*, syn *E. indica* (coral tree) 24

Escallonia rubra var. *macrantha* 21, 92
    'Slieve Donard' 92

Eschscholtzia californica (California poppy) 164
    'Mission Bells' 164

Eucalyptus 73, 74

Eucharis grandiflora (Amazon lily) 168

Euphorbia 162
    palustris 48, 62, 71, *173*

wulfenii 101

Euryops
    athanasiae 103
    pectinatus 103, 140

evening primrose (*Oenothera*) 7, 144

evergreen trees 25, 76-8

Evolvulus pilularis 143

Exochorda racemosa (pearl bush) 97

fairy's fishing rod (*Dierama pulcherrimum*) 167-8

Feijoa sellowiana (fruit salad plant) 92

Felicia amelloides (Felicia daisies) 31, *161*
    'Royal Blue' 146-7
    'San Anita' 146-7
    'Variegata' 146-7

ferns 27, 35

fertilisers 16, 27, 13-14, 84, 181-2

feverfew (*Chrysanthemum parthenium*) *54*, 71, *148*, 148-50

Ficus
    benjamina (weeping fig) 25
    elastica (rubber tree) 26
    pumila 'Minima' (creeping fig) 34

fiddlewood (*Citharexylum spinosum*) 77

Fielden, Lorna 7, 9

Fife, Mike 60-1

firethorn (*Pyracantha*) 93

Fish, Margery 49, 139, 140, 177

Flanders poppy (*Papaver rhosis*) *2*, 164

flowering cherry/Japanese cherry (*Prunus serrulata*) 62, *80*

flowering currant (*Ribes sanguinium*) 98

flowering quince (*Chaenomeles japonica*) 95

forget-me-not (*Mysotis alpestris*) 47, 54, 160, 164, 165

forget-me-not, Chinese 163

Forsythia
    x *intermedia* 97
    'Karl Sax' 97
    'Lynwood' 97
    'Spectabilis' 97

foundation plantings 33-4

Fowell, Pam and Harry *29, 99*

foxgloves 6, *30*, 44, 56, 71, 138, 160

frangipani 47

frangipani, native (*Hymenosporum flavem*) 50

Fraxinus
    excelsior 'Aurea' (golden ash) 76, 79
    raywoodi 79

freesia (*Freesia refracta*) 168

fringe flower (*Loropetalum chinense*) 92

fruit salad plant (*Feijoa sellowiana*) 92

Fuchsia 27, 101

furniture, garden 44

gaillardia 47
garden site, preparing a 13-21
gardens, rear and side 36-42
Gardenia 84
  augusta (syn. *G. florida*) 101
  radicans 101
Garrya elliptica (silk tassel bush) 92
Gaura lindheimira (white butterfly bush)
  33, 158
Gazania (treasure flowers) 143
  'Buccanneer' 140
  hybrida
    'Firechief' 143
  splendens 'Alba' 143
gazebo 45, *45*, 69
Geranium 143-4, 151
  canariensis 50
  cinereum var. *subcaulescens* 143
  'Criss Canning' 151
  himalayense 151
  ibericum 151
  incarnum 143
  pratense (hedgerow cranesbill) 151
    'Alba' 151
    'Silver Queen' 151
    'Striatum' 151
  renardii 143-4
  sanguinium (bloody cranesbill) 144
    'Alba' 144
    var. *striatum* 144
germander (*Teucrium fruticans*) 56, 57,
  142
Geum chiloense
  'Lady Stratheden' 151
  'Mrs Bradshaw' 151
Gladiolus 168
  'Herald Comet' 168
  nanus 168
  'The Bride' 168
  'Tristis' 168
Glasson, Mary 117
Glen, David 138
globe artichoke (*Cynara scolymus*) 58, *58*
Gloriosa 169
  rothschildiana 168
  superba 168
goat's beard (*Aruncus dioicus*) 137
gold dust shrub (*Aucuba japonica*
  'Variegata') 87-8
golden ash (*Fraxinus excelsior*) 76, 79
golden elm (*Ulmus procera* 'Vanhouttei')
  70, 71, *76*
golden rain tree (*Koelreuteria paniculata*)
  79
golden rod (*Solidago*) 157
Gordonia axillaris 24-5, 77, 84
grandma's pincushion (*Scabiosa caucasica*)
  157

granny's bonnets (*Aquilegia*) 9, *50*, 54, 71,
  131
grape, ornamental 34
grass, kikuyu 50
groundcover plants 73, 129-31, 139, 140,
  141, 142-6
guelder rose (*Viburnum opulus*) 99
Gypsophila paniculata
  'Bristol Fairy' 151
  'Flamingo' 151

Habranthus robustus 168, *170*, 173
Hamamelis mollis (witch hazel) 97
Hawaiian hibiscus 55
heart's ease (*Viola tricolor*) *103*, 160,
  165
Hebe 103-4
  hulkeana 104
  pimelioides 104
  speciosa
    'Blue Gem' 104
    'Bouquet of Flowers' 104
hedgerow cranesbill (*Geranium pratense*)
  151
Heeria (*Schizocentron elegans*) 130
Helichrysum petiolatum 66, 140, *141*
Heliopsis helianthoides ('Light of Lodden')
  61, 158-9
Heliotropium (cherry pie) 104
  arborescens 104
    'Aurea' 104
    'Lord Roberts' 104, *104*
Helipterum anthenoides (alpine paper
  daisy) 147
Helleborus 63, 90
  orientalis (lenten rose) 136, *136*
Hemerocallis (daylilies) 56, 58, 61
  hybrids 151-2
    'Green Dragon' *151*
herbaceous border 65, 66
Hesperis matronalis (sweet rocket; dame's
  violet) 159
Heuchera sanguinea (coral bells) 47, 133
  'Palace Purple' 133
Heucherella tiarelloides 'Bridget Bloom'
  133
hibiscus, Hawaiian 55
holly (*Ilex aquifolium*) 92
hollyhocks (*Althaea*) 161
honesty (*Lunaria biennis*) 164
honeysuckle (*Lonicera fragrantissima*) 34,
  97-8
honeysuckle, Dutch (*Lonicera
  periclymenum*) 98
hornbeam *16*
Hosta 63, 69, 71, *86*, 136
  elata 136

fortunei
  'Albopicta' 136
  'Aurea' 136
plantaginea
  'Grandiflora' 136
  'Honeybells' 136
sieboldiana 136
undulata 'Albo-marginata' 136
house, architectural style of 29
humus 13, 16
Hydrangea 71, 97
  'Lacecap' 54, 97
  macrophylla 97
  paniculata 'Grandiflora' 97
  quercifolia (oak leaf hydrangea) 97
  villosa 97
Hymenosporum flavum (native frangipani)
  50
Hypericum
  leschenaultii 92
  x *moserianum* 'Tricolor' 101
Hypoestes aristata 159

Ilex aquifolium (holly) 92
Impatiens 27, 133
Indian hawthorn (*Raphiolepis*) 93
Indogofera decora (pink wisteria) 104
Innes, Joan and Keith *64*, 65, *126*
insect pests 126, 182-3
International Camellia Society 6
Iris v, 86, 105
  bearded *32*, 63, 169
    'Avalon Bay' *170*
    'Flair' *66, 66*
    'Coral Beads' 63, *63*
  florentine (orris root iris) 6
  germanica (purple flag iris) 6
  Louisiana *63*, 169
    'Mary Hunter' *132*
    'Mandolin' *48*
    'Peach Tree' 63
  Moraea neopavonia (peacock iris) 170
  unguicularis 133
iris, wild 170
irrigation systems 27, 178
Isotoma fluviatilis 58, 60
ivy 25, 34
Izzard, Alan *179*

jacaranda 21, 31, 55, 75
  mimosifolia 6, 79, 82, *82*
Jacobs, Kay and Brian 45, *58, 60*, 60-1
Jacob's ladder
  (*Polmonium caeruleum*) 137
  (*Polmonium pulcherrimum* 'Blue Dove')
  134

Japanese cherry (*Prunus serrulata*) 81
Japanese gold-ray lily (*Lilium auratum*)
  170
Japanese maple (*Acer palmatum*) 69, 75,
  78, *78*, 79, 81-2, 83, 90
Japanese wind flower (*Anemone*) 54, 56,
  90, 135, *135*, 136
jasmine (*Jasminum*) 34-5, 36, 92
  orange (*Murraya paniculata*) 21, 93
Jasminum
  azoricum 34
  nitidum 1, 34-5, 92
  officinale (poet's jasmine) 35
  polyanthum 34, 35
  sambac (Arabian jasmine) 34, 92
Jekyll, Gertrude 4
johnny jump-ups (*Viola tricolor*) 165
jonquils 167
Judas tree (*Cercis siliquastrum*) 61
juniper, shore (*Juniperus conferta*) 19
Justicia carnea (syn. *Jacobinia*) 101

Kalmia latifolia (mountain laurel; calico
  bush) 92
kapok vine 23
Kennerton Green, Australia *v*
Kentranthus ruber (valerian) 152
Kerria japonica 'Plena' 97
Kniphofia (red-hot pokers) *179*
  dwarf hybrids 152
    'Little Treasure' 152
    'Maid of Orleans' 152
Koelreuteria
  bipinnata (Pride of China) 79
  paniculata (golden rain tree; varnish
    tree) 79
Kolkwitzia amabilis (Chinese beauty
  bush) 97
Kordes, Wilhelm 110, 111, 114. 115

Laburnum 'vosii' *64*
'Lacecap', *see* hydrangea
lacecap (*Virburnum plicatum* var.
  tomentosum) 99
The Lady of the Woods (*Betula pendula*)
  79
lady's mantle (*Alchemilla mollis*) 71, 131
Lagerstroemia indica (crepe myrtle) 27,
  50, 52, 61, 79-80
  'Eavesii' 80
  indica 'Newmanii' 80
Laity, Judy and Tony 75
lamb's ears (*Stachys byzantina* syn. *S.
  lanata*) *30*, *64*, 69, *139*, 141
Lamium maculatum
  'Silver Beacon' 130

'White Nancy' 130
'Roseum' 130
Lantana camara 23
larkspurs 47
Lathyrus latifolius (perennial sweet pea) 159
'The Pearl' 159
'Pink Pearl' 159
lattice panels *15, 25, 35, 36, 39*
Lavandula 104-5, 141
x *allardii* (Mitcham lavender) 104
angustifolia (syn. *L. officinalis, L. vera*) 104
dentata ix, 7, 70-1, 104
x *intermedia* 104
'Alba' 104
'Rosea' 104
'Dwarf Hidcote' 104
'Dwarf Munstead' 104
pedunculata 105
pinnata 'Sidonee' 104-5, *148*
stoechis (Spanish lavender) 105
lavender *11, 12, 31,* 70-1, 104-5, 141, *148*
lawn 16, 33, 182
lawn daisy (*Bellis perennis*) 162-3
layers, foliage 73, *83, 86*
Le Grice, Edward 113
leadwort (*Plumbago auriculata*) 93
leaf litter 29, 31
Leal, Chris *84*
Lee, Noreen and Ray *86*
lenten rose (*Helleborus orientalis*) 136, *136*
Leptospermum
x *coppersheen 58*
flavescens 'Cardwell' *63*
Leucanthemum x *superbum* (shasta daisy) 47, 152-3
'Chiffon' 152
'Cobham's Gold' 153
'Esther Read' 152, 153
'Shaggy' 153
'The Swan' 152-3, *153*
'Wirral Supreme' 153
Leucojum 169
aestivum 169
autumnalis 169
vernum 169
Leucothoe fortanesiana 92
light of Lodden (*Heliopsis helianthoides*) 158-9
lilies 47, 53, 63, 167, 168, 169-70, 173, *173*
Lilium 169-70
auratum (Japanese gold-ray lily) 170
excelsior 170, *172*
longiflorum (Christmas lily; November lily) 169

regale 170
speciosum (tiger lily) 170
lilli-pilli (*Acmena smithii*) 24, 31
small-leafed (*Syzygium leuhmannii*) 31, 78, 84
Linaria purpurea (purple toadflax)
'Canon Went' 153
Liquidambar 42, 73
styraciflua 84
Lirope muscari 'varietata' 134
Lobelia
cardinalis 'Victoria' 159
fulgens (cardinal flower) 153
'Cinnabar' 153, *153*
Lombardy poplar (*Populus nigra* 'Italica') 75
London pride (*Bergenia*) 132
Lonicera
fragrantissima (honeysuckle) 97-8
periclymenum (Dutch honeysuckle) *95,* 98
Loropetalum chinense (fringe flower) 92
love-in-a-mist (*Nigella damascena*) 47, 164
Lunaria biennis (honesty) 164
'Variegata' 164
Lychnis 152
coronaria var. 'Oculata' 141
coronaria x *flos-jovis* (campion) 141
Lynton Lee, Victoria 7, 9, 53
Lysimachia
'Gold Clusters' 144
nummularia 'Aurea' (creeping jenny) 130
Lythrum salicaria (purpose loosestrife) 153
'Brightness' 153

macadamia nut tree 52
McConnell, Beverly and Malcolm *152*
macro/micro climate 20
Madagascar periwinkle (*Catharanthus roseus*) 148
Maddocks, Cheryl 53
Magnolia 98
campbellii 69
denudata (renamed *M. heptapeta*) 70
grandiflora (Bull bay magnolia) 77, 84
hepterpeta syn. *denudata* (yulan) 80
liliiflora 80
port wine (*Michelia figo*) 93
'Rosea' 98
x *soulangiana 32*
'Brozzonii' 80
'Lennei' *62,* 80
stellata (star magnolia) 78, 98
'Rosea' 98
'Rubra' 98

'Water Lily' 98
magnolia rose ('Devoniensis') 112
Mahonia 135
aquifolium 92-3
beali 92-3
maidenhair fern 35
maintaining a garden 177–185
Maling, Paddy and Sam *140*
Malus 75, 83, 97
floribunda (crabapple) 29, 80, 82, *84*
ioensis 'Plena' (Bechtel's crabapple) 80
'Rosea Plena' 61
spectabilis 80
Mandevilla laxa 36, 47
manure 13-14, 84
maple (*Acer*)
Acer dissectum 54, *86*
Japanese 23, 69, 75, 76, 78, *78,* 80-1, 83, 90
trident (*Acer buergeranum*) 78
marguerite daisies (*Agryranthemum frutescens*) *11,* 102, *103*
Masfen, Joanna and Peter *117*
Matheson, Lesley and Gordon *100*
Matricaria, *see* feverfew
Maunsell, Jill and Bill *73, 139*
may, pink *(Spiraea* 'Anthony Waterer') 105
Melaleuca linariifolia (snow in summer) 77
Melba, Dame Nellie 6
Metasequioa glyptostroboides 62
Metrosideros excelsa (pohutukawa; New Zealand Christmas tree) 77
Mexican orange blossom (*Choisya ternata*) 91
Mexican sage (*Salvia leucanthe*) 105
Michaelmas daisy (*Aster novi-belgii*) 47, *148*
Michelia
doltsopa 69, 78
figo (port wine magnolia) 93
mignonette *ix, 7,* 70, *70,* 160, 161
Mitcham lavender (*Lavandula* x *allardii*) 104
Monarda didyma (bergamot; bee balm) 153-4
'Cambridge Scarlet' 154
'Croftway Pink' 154
'Enfield Gem' 154, *154*
monkshood (*Aconitum*) 137
Moraea neopavonia (peacock iris) 170
Morris, Marion 66, 68, 68-70
Morrow, Elizabeth *38*
Mottisfont Abbey Heritage Rose Garden, Hampshire 109, *109*
Mt Tomah Botanic Gardens *94*
mountain laurel (*Kalmia latifolia*) 92

mulch 14-15, 180-1
Murraya 84
paniculata (orange jasmine) 21, 93
Mussett, Jill and Ted *66, 82*
Mysotis alpestris (forget-me-not) 47, 54, 160, *162,* 164, 165

naked lady lilies (*Amaryllis belladonna*) 167
Nasturtium 47, 61
Tropaeolum 'Alaska' *63,* 165
Neall, Dagmar and Dennis *32*
Neill, Alistair 61-2
Nemophila species 165
Nepeta (catmint)
faassenii 141
'Six Hills' 154
Nerine (spider lily) 170
Nerium (oleander) 93
Ng, Mr and Mrs *31*
Nicotiana 88
affinis 138
alata 138
sylvestris 138
Nigella ix, 71
damascena (love-in-a-mist) 47, 164
'Persian Jewels' 164
November lily (*Lilium longiflorum*) 169
Nyssa sylvatica (tupelo) 75, 80-1

oak, English (*Quercus robur*) 24, *26, 27,* 76
oak leaf hydrangea (*Hydrangea quercifolia*) 97
Ochna serrulata 23
Oenothera
bienis (evening primrose) 7, 144
glaber 144
speciosa rosea (pink evening primrose) 144, *144*
texensis 144
Olea africana (olive) 23
oleander (*Nerium oleander*) 93
olive (*Olea africana*) 23
olive, sweet (*Osmanthus fragrans*) 36, 84, 93
Ompheloides verna (blue-eyed Mary) 134
Origanum vulgare 'Aureum' 144
Osmanthus fragrans (sweet olive) 36, 84, 93
Osteospermum
'Pink Whirls' 154
'Starry Eyes' 154
'Whirlybird' 154
Otacanthus 'Little Boy Blue' 34
ox-eye daisy *2*

Oxypetalum caeraleum (tweedia) 155
oyster plant (*Acanthus mollis*) 135

pansies 47
Papaver
  rhosis (Flanders poppy) 164
  somniferumm (poppy) 164
Parahebe
  catarractae 'Alba' 105
  fraseri 105
Parnell Rose Garden, Auckland *143*
paving 29, 31, 36
peacock iris (*Moraea neopavonia*) 170
pear, silver (*Pyrus salisifolia*) 57
pearl bush (*Exochorda racemosa*) 97
pearl flower (*Pieris japonica*) 93
Pemberton, the Reverend Joseph 114
Penstemon 61, 155
  barbatus syn. *Chelone barbata* 'Evelyn'
    155
  x *gloxinioides* 155
    'Hyacinth' 155
    'Red Ensign' 155
    'Sensation' 155
    'Susan' 155
    'Swan Lake' 34, *155*, 156
  hartwegii
    'Firebird' 156
    'Garnet' 34, 156
  heterophyllus 147
Pentas lanceolata 101, 103
perennials 129-59
pergola 7-8, 12, 16, *31*, 34, 36, 42-3, 63
persimmon tree 68
petrea 36
Philadelphus 71, 98, 110
  x *leomoinee* 'Manteau d'Hermine' 98
  mexicanus 98
  'Natchez' 98
  virginal 98
  x *purpureomaculatus* 98
    'Belle Etoile' 98
    'Etoile Rose' 98
Phlox 144-5, 155, 156
  divaricata 144
  maculata
    'Alpha' *155*, 156
    'Omega' *155*, 156
  stolonifera
    'Ariane' 145
    'Blue Ridge' 145
    'Pink Ridge' 145
  subulata 145
Physostegia
  virginiana 156
  virginica 'Nana Albas' 147
Pieris japonica (pearl flower) 15, 93

pine bark 50
pink may (*Spiraea* 'Anthony Waterer')
  105
pink wisteria (*Indogofera decora*) 104
Pistacia 82
  chinensis 29, 81
Pittosporum
  rhombifolium 78
  undulatum (native daphne) 23
plane tree (*Platanus* x *hybrida*) 73
Platycodon grandiflorus (balloon flower)
  136-7
Plectranthus
  argentatus 56, 101, *102*, 141
  saccatus 102
Plumbago 3, 6, 90
  auriculata (leadwort) 93
poet's jasmine (*Jasminum officinale*) 35
pohutukawa (*Metrosideros excelsa*) 77, 77
Polianthus tuberosa 170
Polmonium (Jacob's ladder)
  caeruleum 137
  pulcherrimum 'Blue Dove' 134, *134*
Polygonatum x *hybridum* (Solomon's seal)
  137
pomegranate, dwarf 6
poplar 26
poplar, Lombardy (*Populus nigra* 'Italica')
  75
poppies 47, 62, *62*, 164
Populus alba 84
Populus nigra 'Italica' (Lombardy poplar)
  75
port wine magnolia (*Michelia figo*) 93
potato vine (*Solanum jasminoides*) 36
Potentilla 145
  argyrophylla 141
  atrosanguinea 141
  nepalensis minor 145
  nepalensis 'Miss Willmott' 145
  recta *145*, 156
  warrenii *145*, 156
powder puff flower (*Calliandra*
  haematocephala) 88
Pratia 60
Primula 47, 134-5
  x *juliana* 134
  malacoides 165
  obconica *134*, 134-5
  veris (cowslip) 135
  vulgaris 134
privacy 20, 21, 84, 86, *see also* screen
  planting
privet 23
pruning 21, 34, 35, 36, 52, 53, 57, 87,
  183-5
Prunus 70, 75, 83, *84*
  campanulata (Taiwan cherry) 81

'Elvins' 81
  serrulata (Japanese cherry) *80*, 81
    'Kwanzan' 81
    'Shimidsu Sakura' 81
    'Shirotae (*syn* 'Mount Fuji') 81
Pulmonaria saccharata (spotted lungwort)
  134
purple bead bush (*Callicarpa dichotoma*)
  94-5
purple toadflax (*Linaria purpurea*) 153
purple-leafed smoke bush (*Cotinus*
  coggygria 'Purpureus') 95
Pyracantha (firethorn) 93
  rogersiana 'Flava' 93
Pyrus salicifolia (silver pear) 57, *140*

Queen Anne's lace (*Daucus carota*) ix, 7,
  25, 70, *70*, 162, *162*
Quercus robur (English oak) 24, *26*, 27

Raphiolepis (Indian hawthorn) 93
  x *delacourii* 21, 93
  indica 93
  umbellata 93
rear and side gardens 36-42
Rehmania angulata (Chinese foxglove)
  159
remodelling 23-7
renovating 23-7
Reseda alba (mignonette) 161
Rhododendron 15, 27, 58, 93-4, 102
  'Alice' 94
  'Beauty of Littlemore' 94
  'Broughtonii' 94
  'Cornubia' 94
  'Countess of Athlone' 94
  'Cynthia' 94
  lochae 'Sweet Wendy' 102
  x *loderi*
    'Mrs E.C. Stirling' 94
    'Pink Pearl' 94
    'Princess Alice' 102
    'Sappho' 94
    'Suave' 102
    'White Pearl' 94
  vireya 102
rhododendron, dwarf 27, 102
Ribes sanguinium (flowering currant) 98
  'Album' 98
  'Carneum' 98
  'King Edward VII' 98
  'Plenum' 98
Robinia pseudoacacia 'Frisia' *1*, 27, 81, 84
Robinson, William 4, 6
Rockleigh, NSW *18, 19, 73, 74*, 97

Rondeletia amoena 94
rose 7, 12, *31, 32, 33*, 47, 109-127
  'Abraham Darby' 71, 117, *117*
  'Agnes' 116
  Alba 109
  'Alberic Barbier' *38*
  'Albertine' 35, 43, 70, *71*, 110
  'Alchemist' 68
  'Aloha' 117
  'Altissimo' 61, 119
  'Amber Queen' 113
  Autumn Delight' 52, 112
  'Ballerina' *26*, 52, 115
  'Balmain Rambler' 69
  'Belle Story' 122
  'Bibi Maizoon' 126
  'Black Boy' 119
  'Blanc Double de Coubert' 116
  'Bloomfield's Abundance' 110
  'Blush Noisette' 120
  'Born Free' *61*
  Bourbon 109
  Boursalt 109
  R. bracteata 113
  'Brother Cadfel' 126
  'Buff Beauty' 68, 115
  'Canterbury' 121
  'Carabella' *110*, 119, 184, *184*
  'Cecile Brunner' 110, 119, *162*
  'Cecile Brunner', dwarf 184
  Centifolia 109
  'Champney's Pink Cluster' 118, 119
  'Charles Austin' 117
  'Charmain' 121
  'Chaucer' 71
  'Chianti' 121
  'Chip's Apple Blossom' *143*
  'Clair Matin' 119, *119*
  'Claire Rose' 122
  'Common Monthly' 113
  'Complicata' 110
  'Constance Spry' 121
  'Cornelia' 115, 184-5
  'Cramoise Superieur' 112
  'Crepuscule' 52, 53, 68, 119, *120, 165*,
    184
  'Cressida' 117
  'Crimson Glory' 119-20
  'Cymbeline' 117
  'Dainty Bess' 112, 119
  Damask 109
  'Dame Prudence' *111*, 121-2
  'Dapple Dawn' 122
  'Desprez a Fleur Jaune' *126*
  'Devoniensis' (magnolia rose) 119, 184
  'Dove' 122
  'Duchesse de Brabant' 52, 111-12,
    114, 184

'Edelweiss' 113
'Ellen' 123, *123*
'Erfurt' 115
'Fair Bianca' 122
'The Fairy' 104, 110, 111
'Fantin Latour' 110
'Felecia' 115
'Fimbriata' Morlet 116
'Francine Austin' 126
'Francis Dubreuil' 112
'Frau Dagmar Hastrup' 116, *116*
'The Friar' *1*, *122*, 123
'Fritz Nobis' 110
Gallica 109
'Gay Vista' 117, *118*
'Gertrude Jekyll' 123
'Golden Wings' 118, 119, 145
'Golden Showers' *68*
'Graham Thomas' 68, 125, *125*
'Green Ice' *1*, 110, 111, 184
'Gruss An Aachin' 112
'Heidisommer' *95*, 110-11, *111*
'Heritage' *34*, 123, *123*
'Hero' 123, *123*
'Honeyflow' 114
'Hume's Blush' 109
'Iceberg' *44*, 56, 114, 119, *119*, *140*
'Immortal Juno' 124
'Jacquenetta' 124
'Jayne Austin' 126
'Jean Ducher' 114, *162*
'Jeanne Lajoie' 117
'Kathleen Harrop' *68*, 69
'The Knight' 53
'Lady Brisbane' ('Cramoise Superieur')
    6, 112
'Lady Hillingdon' 114
'Lamarque' *65*, 120
'Leander' *34*, 117
'Lilian Austin' 122, 124
'Little White Pet' *109*, 110, 111
'Lorraine Lee' 120
'Lucetta' 69, 118
'Martin Frobisher' 116
'Mary Rose' 71, 124, 125, *127*
'Meg' 110, *110*
'Mme Abel Chatenay' 114, 119
'Mme Alfred Carriere' 43, 116, 120
'Mme Gregoire Straechlin' *syn* 'Spanish
    Beauty' *44*
'Monsieur Tillier' 70, *70*
'Moonbeam' 124
Moss 109
'Moth' *109*, 118
Mr Lincoln 61
'Mrs B.R. Cant' 114
'Mrs R.M. Finch' *112*, 112-13
R. mulliganii 12

'Mutabilis' 70
'New Dawn' 34, 43, 120
Noisette 109, 119
'Old Blush' ('Parson's Pink') 52-3, 66,
    66, 109, 113
'Ophelia' 115, 120
'Othello' 124'
Park's Yellow' 109, 120
'Peace' 109
'Pearl Drift' 61, 113
'Penelope' 52, 69, 70, 115, *115*
'Perdita' 124
'Perle d'or' 110
'Pierre de Ronsard' 118, 119
R. pimpinellifolia 116, 119
Portland 109
'Potter and Moore' 126
'Pretty Jessica' 122
'The Prioress' 53, 125, *126*, 184
'Prosperity' 64
'Prospero' 122
Rambler 109
'Raubritter' *143*
'Redcoat' 62, *62*, 124
'The Reeve' *66*, 124, *183*
'Roseromantic' *95*, 110, 111
'Royal Highness' 61
R. rugosa 'Alba' 116
'Sadler's Wells' 115, 184
'Seafoam' 120
'Shady Lady' *113*, 113-14
'Sharifa Asma' 126
'Shropshire Lass' 121
'Slater's Crimson' 109
'Softie' 117, 118
'Sombreuil' 116
'Souvenir de la Malmaison' 113, 119
'Souvenir de Mme Boullet' 120
'Souvenir de St Anne's' 113
'Spanish Beauty' *44*
'Sparrieshoop' *39*, *45*, 69, 120, *121*
'The Squire' 124, *124*, 125
'Sunny Honey' *179*
'Swan' 124
'Symphony' 124
'Tamora' *1*, *63*, *63*, 122
'Tiffany' 61
'Trier' 115
'Troilus' 124
'Veilchenblau' 70
'Wedding Day' *38*, 68
'Wenlock' 124
'White Duchesse de Brabrant' 114
'Wife of Bath' 122, 126
'William Shakespeare' 124-5
'Winchester Cathedral' 125, 126
'Windrush' *118*, 125, *125*
'The Yeoman' *52*, 53, 122

The Roseaire Nursery, Auckland *34*, *98*,
    125, *125*, 140
roses, Austin 62, 69, 71, *109*, 114, 117,
    118, 121-5, *183*
roses, bush *52*, 110-113, 121-5
roses, China 6, 52-3, 66, *66*, 109, 112,
    113, 120
roses, climbing 34, 36, 38, *38*, 39, 43, *44*,
    45, 53, 68, *68*, *69*, 110, *110*, 116-21,
    162, 184, *184*
roses, English 121-5
roses, Floribunda 109, 113-14, 119
roses, hybrid
    musk 109, 112, 114-15, 184-5
    perpetuals 109
    shrub 113
    tea 109, 112, 120, 184
roses, pillar 35, 62, *110*, 117, 118-19, 184
roses, Rugosa 116
roses, shrub 110, 114, 125-6
roses, tea 109, 112, 114, 120
roses, problems with 126-7
roses, pruning 184
rose sickness 127
rubber tree (*Ficus elastica*) 26
Rudbeckia 150, 159
    laciniata 'Golden Glow' *158*, 159
Rumsey, Heather 120
Russell, Helen 7
Ryde School of Horticulture, NSW 48

Sackville-West, Vita 11-12
sage, clary (*Salvia sclarea*) 157
Salix
    babylonica (weeping willow) *82*
    lanata 8
    repens 'Argentea' *8*
Salvia 156-7, 159
    coccinia 'Rosea' 147
    dorisiana 159
    farinacea 156-7
        'Alba' 156-7
        'Blue Bedder' *156*, 157
    grandiflora 'Azurea' 159
    involucrata 'Betheli' 102
    leucanthe (Mexican sage) 105
    nemerosa 'Rosea' 157
    patens 157
    regia 159
    sclarea (clary sage) 157
        var. *turkestanica* 157
    uliginosa (bog sage) 159
Sangerhausen rosarium, Germany 109
Santolina chamaecyparissus (cotton
    lavender) *139*, 141
Sapium sebiferum (Chinese tallow tree) 81
Saxifraga 132

Scabiosa
    anthemifolia
        'Mauve Lace' 147, *158*
        'Pink Lace' 147, *157*, *158*
    caucasica (grandma's pincushion) 157
scale (proportions) 73-74
Schizocentron elegans (*Heeria*; Spanish
    shawl) 130
Schizostylis coccinea 172
    'Mrs Hegarty' 172
Schneideman, Margot and Brett *82*
Schwartz, J. 120
Scott, Elizabeth and Warren *44*, *86*, *138*
screen planting 24-5, 38
Scutellaria indica var. *japonica* 130
sea hollies 150-1
Sedum 'Vera Jameson' 147
Senecio maritima (dusty miller) 141
shade, plants for 56, 129-38
shade, plants for semi- 100-2, 129-38
shasta daisy (*Leucanthemum x superbum*)
    47, 152-3
shore juniper (*Juniperus confera*) 19
shrubs, background 84-105
shrubs, evergreen 84-94
Sidalcea monarch 'Party Girl' 157
side and rear gardens 36-42
Silene maritima (witch's thimble) 145
silk tassel bush (*Garrya elliptica*) 92
silver birch (*Betula pendula*) 6, *19*, *23*, 69,
    79, *79*, *82*, 84
silver feathers (*Tanacetum haradjanii*,
    Tanacetum ptarmiciflorum) 141-2
silver pear (*Pyrus salicifolia*) 57, *140*
Sissinghurst, Kent 11-12, *110*
site, preparing a garden 13-21
snapdragon 69, *71*, 160
snow in summer
    (*Cerastium tomentosum*) 139
    (*Melaleuca linariifolia*) 77
snowball bush (*Viburnum opulus*) 62, *62*,
    99
soils 13-16, 71, 83
Solanum jasminoises (potato vine) 36
Solidago (golden rod) 157
x *Solidaster hybridus* 157
Solomon's seal (*Polygonatum* x *hybridum*)
    137
Somerset, Dreer 120
Sonning I, Mooroolbark, Victoria 7, 9
Sonning II 7, 9
Spanish lavender (*Lavandula stoechis*)
    105
Spanish shawl (*Schizocentron elegans*) 130
speedwell (*Veronica spicata*) 157
spider flower (*Cleome spinosum*) 163, *163*

spider lily (*Nerine*) 170
spillovers *53, 61, 161*
Spiraea 110
 'Anthony Waterer' (pink may) 105
 cantoniensis 'Lanceata' 99
spotted lungwort (*Pulmonaria saccharata*) 134
spraying against insects 25, 182-3
Stachys byzantina syn *S.lanata* (lamb's ears) *30, 64, 69, 139, 141*
Stachyurus praecox (early spiketail) 99
star jasmine (*Trachelospermum jasminoides*) 36
star magnolia (*M. stellata*) 78, 98
Stellaria holstea 130
stephanotis 36
stocks 47
Stokes' aster (*Stokesia laevis*) 157
storm lily (*Zephyranthes candida*) 173
strawberry tree (*Arbutus unedo*) 76
Strobilanthes anisophyllus (syn. *Goldfussia*) 102
Sturtevant, Dallis 58, *58*
sun, plants for full 158-65
sunflower, false (*Heliopsis helianthoides*) *61, 158-9*
sunny position, plants for 102-5, 138-57
'Swan Lake' penstemon 34, *155, 156*
sweet Alice (*Alyssum*) *4, 6, 19, 161-2, 162*
sweet olive (*Osmanthus fragrans*) 34, 93
sweet pea, perennial (*Lathyrus latifoloius*) 159
sweet rocket (*Hesperis matronalis*) 159
sweet william (*Dianthus barbatus*) 47
swimming pool 38-9
sycamore (*Acer pseudoplatanus*) *14*
Sylvester, Toni *38, 100, 121*
Syzygium leuhmannii (small-leafed lilli-pilli) 31, 78, 84

Taihape, New Zealand *14*
Taiwan cherry (*Prunus campanulata*) 81
Tanacetum
 haradjanii (silver feathers) 141
 ptarmiciflorum (Canary Island tansy; silver feathers) 141-2
Taylor, Pat *105*
Teucrium fruticans (shrub germander) *56, 57,* 142
Thalictrum
 aquilegifolium 138
 dipterocarpum 'Lavender Shower' 138

Thomas, Graham *109*
thrift (*Armeria maritima*) 146
thyme 8, 9
Thymus 145
 nitidum 145
 'Alba' 145
 serpyllum
 x *citriodorus* 145
 'Coccineus' 145
 'Pink Chintz' 145
Tibouchina granulosa 94
 'Kathleen' 94
 'Noeline' 94
tiger lily (*Lilium speciosum*) 170
Tintagel, Australia *17*
tobacco bush, wild 23
Toyer, Edith *73*
Trachelospermum jasminoides (star jasmine) 36
Tradescantia x *andersoniana*
 'Carmine Glow' 137
 'J.C. Weguelin' 137
 'Snowflake' 137
treasure flowers (*Gazania*) 143
'tree in a hurry' (*Virgilia oroboides*) 24
trees
 deciduous 75-6
 garden 73-107
 planting 83-4
 removing 23-4, 25-6, 74
 selecting 83-4
 shapes of 75-6
 size of 73-4
Tropaeolum 'Alaska' (nasturtium) 165
tubs, planting in 25, 27, 36
Tulbaghia fragrans 172
tupelo (*Nyssa sylvatica*) 80-1
Turley, Suzanne *ix, 7, 7, 70, 71, 117*
Tweedia caerulea 111
tweedia (*Oxypetalum caeruleum*) 155

Ulmus parvifolia (Chinese elm) 29
Ulmus procera 'Vanhouttei' (golden elm) *76*

valerian (*Kentranthus ruber*) *64, 71,* 152
varnish tree (*Koelreuteria paniculata*) 79
Verbascum olympicum 159, *160*
Verbascum phoenicemum (Aaron's rod) 159-60

Verbena 145-6
 erinoides 145
 'Lipstick' 145
 x *hybrida*
 'Blue Queen' 146
 'Candy Carnival' 146
 'Candy Ice' 146
 'Candystripe' *66,* 146
 'Pink Baby' 146
Veronica 146
 incarnum 146
 spicata (speedwell) 157
 'Barcarolle' 146
 'Blue Spire' 147
 'Nana' 146
Viburnum 99
 x *bodnantense* 'Dawn' 99
 x *burkwoodii* 62, 99
 x *carlcephalum* 99
 carlesii 99
 fragrans (syn. *farreri*) 99
 japonicum 94
 juddii 62, 99
 macrocephalum 62
 opulus (snowball; guelder rose) 99
 'Sterile' *62, 62*
 'Pink Beauty' 99
 plicatum
 'Lanarth' *62,* 99
 var. *tomentosum* 99
views 21, 31-2
Vinca minor 131
Viola 60, *69, 71, 73*
 cornuta 'Blue Moon' *v,* 130
 hederacea (native violet) 130
 labradorica 130
 odorata (English violet) 130
 'Compte Brazza' 130-1
 'John Raddenbury' 130
 'King of the Doubles' 130
 'Lavender Lady' 130
 'Lilac Glow' 130
 'Marie Louise' 131
 'Neapolitan' 131
 'Princess of Wales' 130
 'Rosea' ('Rosina') 130
 'Royal Robe' 130
 seiboldiana 'Dissecta' 131
 sulfurea 130
 sylvestris (wood violet) 131
 tricolor (heart's ease; johnny jump-ups) 165
violet, double 130-1

violet, English (*Viola odorata*) 130-1
violet, native (*Viola hederacea*) 130
violet, parma 130-1
Virgilia oroboides ('tree in a hurry') 24

Walling, Edna 6-9, 53, 143
walls, planting against 34
wandering jew 23
Waterhouse, Professor E.G. 4-6, 90
watering 178-80
Watsonia 172
wedding bells (*Deutzia*) 95, 103, 110
weed growth 15
weeping cherry 'Shimidsu Sakura' 73
weeping fig (*Ficus benjamina*) 25
weeping willow (*Salix babylonica*) *82*
Weigela florida
 'Argenteo marginata' 99
 'Aureo variegata' 99
 'Esperance' *99*
 'Mont Blanc' 99
 'Newport Red' 99
 'Styriaca' 99
white butterfly bush (*Gaura lindheimira*) *33,* 158
white cypress pine (*Callitris columellaris*) 75
Whitehead, Henry and Francis 23
Wigham, Lois 57
willow 26, 76
Wilson, William Hardy 6, 90
wind anemone/wind flower (*Anemone*) 54, 56, 90, 135, *135,* 136
winter joy (*Cheiranthus mutabilis*) 148
wisteria 34, 57, 71, *182*
wisteria, pink 104
witch hazel (*Hamamelis mollis*) 97
witch's thimble (*Silene maritima*) 145
wood violet (*Viola sylvestris*) 131

yucca 3
yulan (*Magnolia hepterpeta* syn. *denudata*) 80

Zantedeschia aetheopica (arum lily) 63, 173
 'Green Goddess' 173, *173*
 'Kiwi Calls' 173
Zephyranthes
 candida (storm lily) 173
 rosea 173